중학교

2-B

학년

한국에서 유일한
중학영문법
알짜 3000제

Iam books

1 ✳ Grammar Points

사진과 대표 예문만 봐도 쉽게 영문법의 개념을 이해할 수 있는 Visual Approach를 도입하여 문법 설명을 시각화하였습니다. 문법 설명은 머리에 쏙쏙!! 예문과 설명은 한 눈에!! 참신한 예문과 원어민들이 실제로 사용하는 표현을 담았습니다.

2 ✳ 서술형 기초다지기

일대일로 대응되는 다양한 문제들을 구성하여 문법 개념을 확실히 이해할 수 있도록 하였습니다. 이를 통해 서술형 문제에 대비할 수 있도록 하였으며 실제 문장 구성 능력을 향상시킬 수 있도록 쓰기 영역을 강화하였습니다. 단순 문법 연습이 아닌 응용·심화 과정을 통해 기초 실력 또한 차곡차곡 쌓을 수 있습니다.

3 ✳ 이것이 시험에 출제되는 영문법이다!

어떤 문제가 주로 출제되는지를 미리 아는 사람과 막연히 공부를 열심히 한 사람의 성적은 하늘과 땅 차이! 12년간의 내신 만점신화를 이루어낸 저자의 비밀노트를 통해 내신문제를 출제하는 선생님들의 의도와 출제유형, 주관식과 서술형의 출제경향을 정확히 꿰뚫어 보는 눈을 키울 수 있을 것입니다.

4 ✳ 기출 응용문제

실제 중학교 내신 시험에서 빈출되는 필수 문법문제와 응용문제를 수록하여 각 chapter에서 배운 문법 사항을 다양한 유형의 문제를 통해 확인하고 연습해 볼 수 있도록 구성하였습니다.

5 ✳ 오답노트 만들기

기출 응용문제 중 틀린 문제를 오답 노트에 정리할 수 있도록 구성하였습니다. 틀린 문제의 문법 개념을 다시 확인하고 해당 문제 유형을 다시는 틀리지 않도록 스스로 공부해 볼 수 있는 코너입니다.

6 ✳ 중간 · 기말고사 100점 100승

학교 시험에서 자주 나오는 빈출유형을 분석하여 출제 가능성이 가장 높은 문제를 중심으로 수록하였습니다. 간단한 객관식 문제를 비롯하여 대화문과 독해문, 주관식 문제 등 다양한 문제를 풀면서 자신의 실력을 정확하게 진단해 볼 수 있습니다.

7 ✳ 평가대비 단답형 주관식

문법 핵심을 파악하고 어법에 맞는 문장을 직접 쓸 수 있도록 구성하여 학교 단답형 주관식 문제에 철저히 대비할 수 있도록 하였습니다.

8 ✳ 실전 서술형 평가문제

교육청 출제경향에 맞춘 서술형 평가대비 문제로, 학생들의 사고력과 창의력을 길러줍니다. 해당 chapter에서 출제될 수 있는 서술형 문항을 개발하여 각 학교의 서술형 평가문제에 철저히 대비할 수 있도록 하였습니다. 단순 암기에서 벗어나 직접 써보고 생각해 볼 수 있는 코너입니다.

chapter 3. 비교급과 최상급
(Comparatives and Superlatives)

chapter 4. 접속사(Conjunctions)

chapter 7. 전치사(Prepositions)

chapter 8. 가정법(Conditionals)

Chapter 1

형용사 (Adjectives)

Unit 01 형용사

1-1 형용사의 역할

She has **beautiful** eyes.
그녀는 아름다운 눈을 가지고 있다.

Her eyes are **beautiful**.
그녀의 눈은 아름답다.

01 형용사는 **명사 앞에서 명사를 꾸며 주거나**, be동사 뒤에서 **주어를 설명하는 보어 역할**을 한다.

It's **cold** weather today. 오늘은 추운 날씨이다. ▶ 명사 수식

The weather is **cold** today. 오늘은 날씨가 춥다. ▶ 주격 보어

We have **serious** problems. 우리는 심각한 문제를 가지고 있다. ▶ 명사 수식

The problems are **serious**. 그 문제는 심각하다. ▶ 주격 보어

02 look, feel, smell, taste, sound, get 등의 감각을 나타내는 동사들은 뒤에 **형용사가 와서 주어의 상태가 어떤지를 표현**한다. 이러한 연결동사 뒤에 형용사 대신 명사를 쓰려면 「like + 명사」로 쓴다.

You **look** happy. 너는 행복해 보인다.

This tea **tastes** good. 이 차는 맛이 좋다.

I **feel** bad about it. 나는 그것에 기분이 나쁘다.

He **looks like** a soldier. 그는 군인처럼 보인다.

03 대부분의 형용사는 명사 앞과 be동사 뒤 모두에 올 수 있지만, **어떤 형용사들은 한 군데에만 쓸 수 있다.**

한정적 용법으로만 쓰는 형용사	서술적 용법으로만 쓰는 형용사
명사 앞에서만 수식	연결동사 뒤에서만 수식
only, drunken, main, elder, inner, outer, live, major, former, upper, lone, right, left	• a-로 시작하는 단어: alive, alone, asleep, afraid, alike, awake, aware, ashamed • 기타: glad, ill, pleased, content, fond, drunk

Please go to the **main** page. 메인 페이지로 가 주세요.

The **drunken** man was lying on the bench. 술 취한 사람이 벤치 위에 누워 있었다.

She is **afraid** of snakes. 그녀는 뱀을 무서워한다.

I was feeling **ill** last night. 나는 지난밤에 아팠다.

서술형 기초다지기

Challenge 1　다음 괄호 안의 형용사를 알맞은 위치에 넣어 문장을 다시 쓰세요.

보기	David watched a movie by himself. (scary) → *David watched a scary movie by himself.*

01. She was a guest on a TV show. (live)

→ _____

02. Nancy is a dentist. (famous)

→ _____

03. Look at the car over there. (small)

→ _____

04. We watched a movie yesterday. (exciting)

→ _____

Challenge 2　다음 괄호 안의 형용사 중 알맞은 것을 고르세요.

01. The children are (asleep / sleep) on the bed.

02. What is the (mainly / main) problem in the Korean economy?

03. A (drunken / drunk) woman was sitting on the corner of the street.

04. The (sleeping / asleep) dog is Kevin's.

05. The twins look (like / alike).

06. He is still (live / alive) somewhere.

07. That (scared / afraid) girl is Tiffany.

1-2 -thing[-one, -body] + 형용사 / the + 형용사

I could see **something white** in the dark.
나는 어둠 속에서 무언가 하얀 것을 볼 수 있었다.

We should protect the rights of **the disabled**.
우리는 장애인들의 권리를 보호해야 한다.

01 -thing, -one, -body로 끝나는 부정대명사는 **형용사가 뒤에서 수식**해야 한다.

People always want something **new**. 사람들은 항상 새로운 것을 원한다.
Do you have anything **better**? 더 좋은 걸 갖고 있니?
Jane had a date with someone **humorous**. Jane은 유머 있는 사람과 데이트를 했다.
I have nothing **particular** to say. 나는 특별히 할 말이 없다.

※ thing, body, one 자체가 한 단어인 경우는 형용사가 앞에서 수식한다.

This fur is not the **real** thing. 이 모피는 진짜가 아니다.
Look at her **beautiful** body. 그녀의 아름다운 몸매를 봐라.
This diamond is not a **real** one. 이 다이아몬드는 진짜가 아니다.

02 「the + 형용사」는 형용사 앞에 the를 붙여 사회적으로 잘 알려진 사람들의 **집단 전체를 나타내는 명사로 쓰이며 항상 복수 취급**한다.

We should donate money for **the poor**. 우리는 가난한 사람들을 위해 돈을 기부해야 한다.
The rich are not always happy. 부자들이 항상 행복한 것은 아니다.
The Government decided to create more jobs for **the unemployed**.
정부는 실직자들을 위해 더 많은 일자리를 만들기로 결정했다.

서술형 기초다지기

정답 p. 2

Challenge 1 다음 괄호 안의 단어를 바르게 배열하세요.

01. I found _____ in the book. (interesting / nothing)

02. Give me _____. (to drink / cold / something)

03. Would you like _____? (something / to drink / hot)

04. I _____ to tell you. (nothing / new / have)

05. He showed me _____. (fun / something)

Challenge 2 다음 두 문장의 의미가 같도록 빈칸을 채우세요.

01. Young people should respect old people.

    = _____ young should respect _____ old.

02. Rich people can afford to travel a lot.

    = _____ rich can afford to travel a lot.

03. You'd better take care of injured people first.

    = You'd better take care of _____ injured first.

Challenge 3 다음 괄호 안의 단어 중에서 알맞은 것을 고르세요.

01. The rich (is / are) not known to spend a lot of their money.

02. The homeless (have / has) no house to live in.

2-1 many, much, a lot of, lots of

many books

not **many** books

much money

not **much** money

01

many, much, a lot of, lots of 등은 모두 '많은'이라는 뜻인데 many는 셀 수 있는 명사에, much는 셀 수 없는 명사에, a lot of(=lots of)는 셀 수 있는 명사나 셀 수 없는 명사에 모두 사용한다.

① 수를 나타내는 형용사(많은)

many
a number of 　⟩ + 셀 수 있는 명사

② 양을 나타내는 형용사(많은)

much
a great deal of 　⟩ + 셀 수 없는 명사
a large amount of

③ 수와 양을 모두 나타내는 형용사(많은)

a lot of
lots of 　⟩ + 셀 수 있는 명사 / 셀 수 없는 명사(둘 다 가능)
plenty of

I haven't seen Brian for **many** years. 난 오랫동안 Brian을 보지 못했어.
There are **many** people on the street. 길에 사람들이 많이 있다.

A large number of tickets were sold immediately. 많은 표가 금방 팔렸다.
You're under **a great deal of** stress. 당신은 스트레스를 상당히 많이 받고 있다.

We have **a lot of** homework to do. 우린 해야 할 숙제가 많이 있다.
You always have **a lot of** secrets. 넌 항상 비밀이 많더라.
There are **plenty of** places to go and see. 가 볼 만한 장소가 많이 있다.
There is **plenty of** milk in the fridge. 냉장고에 우유가 많이 있다.

14

서술형 기초다지기

정답 p. 2

Challenge 1 다음 괄호 안의 단어 중에서 알맞은 것을 고르세요.

01. I don't have (many / much) books about history.

02. There is (many / much) snow on the roof.

03. We don't have (many / much) water in the fridge.

04. Do you drink (many / much) coffee?

05. How (many / much) oranges does your brother have?

06. How (many / much) bread is there in the bread drawer?

Challenge 2 다음 밑줄 친 부분을 many 또는 much로 바꾸어 문장을 다시 써 보세요.

01. Bob has a lot of problems.

    → _____

02. People in the office waste a great deal of paper.

    → _____

03. We usually have a large amount of homework.

    → _____

04. Are there plenty of roses in the vase?

    → _____

05. My mom uses a lot of salt for cooking.

    → _____

06. We didn't take lots of pictures when we were on vacation last winter.

    → _____

07. You can get plenty of information on how to stay healthy in magazines.

    → _____

2-2 some, any, no, none

We love this place. We can get **some** peace and quiet here.
There aren't **any** cars. There aren't **any** cell phones.
There isn't **any** noise.
우리는 이곳이 좋다. 이곳에서 우리는 평온함과 고요함을 얻을 수 있다.
차도 한 대 없다. 어떤 휴대전화도 없다. 조금의 소음도 없다.

01 some과 any는 '몇몇의, 약간의, 조금의'라는 뜻으로 우리가 어떤 것에 대해 정확한 개수와 양을 모를 때 사용한다. some과 any는 셀 수 있는 명사나 셀 수 없는 명사 모두와 함께 쓸 수 있다.

some	any
① **주로 긍정문**에 쓴다. She needs **some** water to drink. 그녀는 마실 물이 좀 필요하다. ② **부탁이나 권유의 의문문**에 쓰인다. Would you have **some** more cake? 케이크 좀 더 먹을래요?	① **주로 부정문과 의문문**에 쓴다. Are there **any** flowers in the park? 공원에 꽃들이 좀 있나요? – No, there aren't **any** flowers. There are some trees. 아니오, 꽃들이 조금도 없어요. 나무들이 약간 있어요. ② **긍정문에 쓰일 때는 '어떤~라도'의 뜻**이 된다. She can play **any** instruments. 그녀는 어떤 악기라도 연주할 수 있다.

02 no와 none (of)은 셀 수 있는 명사와 셀 수 없는 명사에 모두 사용한다. 둘 다 '전혀 없다'는 뜻인데, **no는 형용사**처럼 쓰이고 **none은 대명사**로 쓰인다.

I have **no** idea. 난 전혀 모르겠다.
I have **no** brothers and sisters. 나는 형제자매가 없다.
None of my friends call me any more. 이제 더 이상 어떤 친구도 나한테 전화하지 않는다.

03 부정문에 쓰인 any는 no로 바꾸어 쓸 수 있으며, '조금도[아무(것)도] 없는'의 의미이다.

There aren't **any** students in the class. 교실에는 학생들이 아무도 없다.
= There are **no** students in the class.

She doesn't know **anything** about it. 그녀는 그것에 관해 조금도 모른다.
= She knows **nothing** about it.

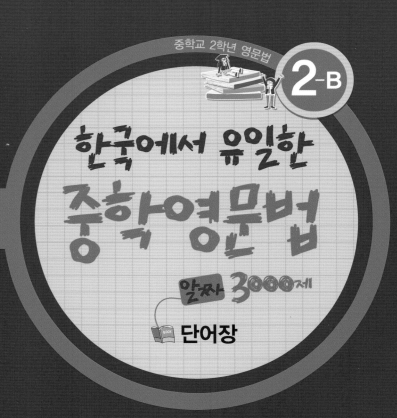

중학교 2학년 영문법

2-B

한국에서 유일한

중학영문법

알짜 3000제

📖 단어장

I am books

중학교 2학년 영문법

2-B

한국에서 유일한

중학영문법

알짜 3000제

BOOK 단어장

Iam books

과학적 암기 비법인 쪽지 접기 메모리를 활용하세요.

(반드시 읽고 단어 암기장을 활용하세요!)

1️⃣ 단어와 한글 뜻을 보면서 단어를 암기합니다.

2️⃣ 맨 왼쪽 ①번을 접어서 영단어가 보이지 않게 합니다. 세 번째 칸의 한글 뜻을 보면서 영어 단어를 다시 쓰되, 이번에는 맨 밑에서부터 반대로 적어 올라갑니다.

3️⃣ 다시 ②번 선을 접어 한글 뜻 부분을 안보이게 합니다.

4️⃣ 자신이 적은 영단어 뜻을 보면서 마지막 칸에 다시 한글 뜻을 적는데, 이번에는 중간 부터 아래 위로 하나씩 올라갔다 내려갔다 하면서 써봅니다. (또는 한글만 보고 소리 내어 영단어를 말하면서 최종 확인을 합니다.)

5️⃣ 어휘를 암기한 후, 원어민이 녹음한 MP3 파일을 들으면서 빈칸에 영단어 또는 숙어 표현을 적고, 자신이 받아 적은 단어의 뜻을 다시 한글로 적어 봅니다.

(MP3 파일 다운 : www.iambooks.co.kr)

> ①
> 단어 암기 후 이 부분을 접어
> 한글만 보고 다시 영어로 쓰세요.

Chapter 01 시제

001	take place	발생하다, 열리다		
002	study	ⓥ 공부하다		
003	live	ⓥ 살다		
004	teach	ⓥ 가르치다		
005	speak	ⓥ 말하다		
006	work	ⓝ 직장, 회사		

> ② 다시 이 부분을 접고
> 자신이 적은 영단어를 보고 아래서부터
> 위로 한글 뜻을 써보세요.

001	weather	ⓝ 날씨		
002	serious	ⓐ 심각한, 진지한		
003	soldier	ⓝ 군인		
004	drunken	ⓐ 술취한, 만취한		
005	be afraid of	~을 무서워하다		
006	by oneself	혼자서, 홀로		
007	scary	ⓐ 무서운, 두려운		
008	guest	ⓝ 손님, 특별 출연자		
009	over there	저쪽에, 저기에		
010	asleep	ⓐ 잠이 든, 자고 있는		
011	economy	ⓝ 경제		
012	twins	ⓝ 쌍둥이		
013	the disabled	신체 장애인들		
014	have a date	데이트를 하다		
015	particular	ⓐ 특별한		
016	fur	ⓝ 모피, 부드러운 털		
017	donate	ⓥ 기부하다		
018	the unemployed	실직자들		
019	interesting	ⓐ 재미있는		
020	afford to ⓥ	~할 여유가 있다		
021	injured	ⓐ 부상당한		
022	the homeless	집 없는 사람들		
023	secret	ⓝ 비밀		
024	immediately	ⓐⓓ 즉각, 즉시로		
025	plenty of	많은		

녹음된 문장을 듣고 빈칸에 단어 또는 표현을 쓰고, 그 뜻도 써보세요.

001 It's cold _____ today. 뜻 _____

002 We have _____ problems. 뜻 _____

003 He looks like a _____. 뜻 _____

004 The _____ man was lying on the bench. 뜻 _____

005 She _____ _____ _____ snakes. 뜻 _____

006 David watched a movie _____ _____. 뜻 _____

007 David watched a _____ movie by himself. 뜻 _____

008 She was a _____ on a live TV show. 뜻 _____

009 Look at the small car _____ _____. 뜻 _____

010 The children are _____ on the bed. 뜻 _____

011 What is the main problem in the Korean _____? 뜻 _____

012 The _____ look alike. 뜻 _____

013 We should protect the rights of _____ _____. 뜻 _____

014 Jane _____ _____ _____ with someone humorous. 뜻 _____

015 I have nothing _____ to say. 뜻 _____

016 This _____ is not the real thing. 뜻 _____

017 We should _____ money for the poor. 뜻 _____

018 The Government created more jobs for _____ _____. 뜻 _____

019 I found nothing _____ in the book. 뜻 _____

020 Rich people can _____ _____ travel a lot. 뜻 _____

021 You'd better take care of _____ people first. 뜻 _____

022 _____ _____ have no house to live in. 뜻 _____

023 You always have a lot of _____. 뜻 _____

024 A large number of tickets were sold _____. 뜻 _____

025 There are _____ _____ places to go and see. 뜻 _____

026	a great deal of	많은, 다량의 (양)		
027	a large amount of	많은 (양)		
028	information	ⓝ 정보		
029	quiet	ⓐ 평온한, 고요한		
030	refrigerator	ⓝ 냉장고		
031	nap	ⓝ 낮잠		
032	selfish	ⓐ 이기적인		
033	closet	ⓝ 벽장		
034	briefcase	ⓝ 서류가방		
035	disappoint	ⓥ 실망시키다		
036	confuse	ⓥ 혼란시키다		
037	murderer	ⓝ 살인자		
038	throw	ⓥ 던지다		
039	imagine	ⓥ 상상하다		
040	go abroad	외국에 가다		
041	be satisfied with	~에 만족하다		
042	detective story	탐정 소설		
043	hardly	ⓐⓓ 거의 ~ 않는		
044	citizen	ⓝ 시민		
045	experiment	ⓝ 실험		
046	cupboard	ⓝ 식기장		
047	be fascinated by	~에 매료되다		
048	vase	ⓝ 꽃병		
049	exhausted	ⓐ 지친		
050	receive	ⓥ 받다		

녹음된 문장을 듣고 빈칸에 단어 또는 표현을 쓰고, 그 뜻도 써보세요.

026 You're under _____ _____ _____ _____ stress.   뜻 _____

027 We have _____ _____ _____ _____ homework.   뜻 _____

028 You can get plenty of _____ on how to stay.   뜻 _____

029 We can get some peace and _____ here.   뜻 _____

030 Is there any milk in the _____?   뜻 _____

031 You'd better take a little _____.   뜻 _____

032 You are so _____ and rude.   뜻 _____

033 There are a few shirts in the _____.   뜻 _____

034 The woman carrying her _____ is my mother.   뜻 _____

035 We were _____ in the film.   뜻 _____

036 I was _____ by her words.   뜻 _____

037 The _____ was arrested.   뜻 _____

038 They _____ stones at a bus.   뜻 _____

039 Living in a foreign country can be more exciting than you _____.   뜻 _____

040 Lots of people _____ _____ last year.   뜻 _____

041 We _____ _____ _____ the result.   뜻 _____

042 How many _____ _____ does your brother read?   뜻 _____

043 There was _____ any food left when we got there.   뜻 _____

044 The _____ were shocked.   뜻 _____

045 Did you find the _____ interesting?   뜻 _____

046 There is some coffee in the _____.   뜻 _____

047 Jessica _____ _____ _____ the characters.   뜻 _____

048 Are there plenty of roses in the _____?   뜻 _____

049 Look at the _____ people.   뜻 _____

050 I _____ a letter written in French.   뜻 _____

001	accurately	@d 정확하게		
002	driver	ⓝ 운전자		
003	fast	@d 빠르게		
004	worm	ⓝ 벌레		
005	autumn	ⓝ 가을		
006	kite	ⓝ 연		
007	quickly	@d 빨리		
008	arrive at	~에 도착하다		
009	final exam	기말 시험		
010	hardly	@d 거의 ~않는		
011	lately	@d 최근에		
012	close	@a 가까이, 가까운		
013	closely	@d 주의 깊게, 면밀히		
014	highly	@d 매우, 높이 평가하여		
015	nearly	@d 거의		
016	occur	ⓥ 발생하다, 생기다		
017	heart attack	심장마비		
018	each other	서로		
019	get promoted	승진하다		
020	pupil	ⓝ 학생, 제자		
021	neighbor	ⓝ 이웃		
022	cliff	ⓝ 절벽, 낭떠러지		
023	disappear	ⓥ 사라지다		
024	suddenly	@d 갑자기		
025	memorize	ⓥ 암기[기억]하다		

001 Basketball players throw the ball _____ into the net.   뜻 _____

002 Jennifer is a fast _____.   뜻 _____

003 Jennifer drives _____.   뜻 _____

004 The early bird catches the _____.   뜻 _____

005 It was late _____.   뜻 _____

006 The _____ flew high.   뜻 _____

007 She eats food _____.   뜻 _____

008 We _____ _____ the station.   뜻 _____

009 She studied hard for the _____ _____.   뜻 _____

010 I can _____ believe what you said.   뜻 _____

011 _____ I've lost my appetite.   뜻 _____

012 A ghost came _____ to me.   뜻 _____

013 The professor read my report _____.   뜻 _____

014 Mr. James was a _____ successful salesman.   뜻 _____

015 It took _____ two hours to get here.   뜻 _____

016 The accident _____ in late summer.   뜻 _____

017 High cholesterol is a cause of _____ _____.   뜻 _____

018 We hardly see _____ _____ these days.   뜻 _____

019 He works hard to _____ _____.   뜻 _____

020 He is highly respected by his _____.   뜻 _____

021 _____ are the people who live near us.   뜻 _____

022 She nearly fell over the _____.   뜻 _____

023 He _____ very quickly.   뜻 _____

024 _____, the old man fell to the ground.   뜻 _____

025 You must often _____ English words.   뜻 _____

026	spicy food	매운 음식		
027	cheetah	ⓝ 치타		
028	suitcase	ⓝ 여행 가방		
029	tight	ⓐ 꼭 끼이는, 꽉 죄는		
030	friendly	ⓐ 친절한, 정다운		
031	breathe	ⓥ 숨 쉬다		
032	break up	헤어지다		
033	company	ⓝ 회사		
034	accommodate	ⓥ 수용하다		
035	put on	~을 입다[쓰다, 걸치다]		
036	pick up	~을 집다, 들어 올리다		
037	wash the dishes	설거지를 하다		
038	exhausted	ⓐ 지칠 대로 지친		
039	garlic	ⓝ 마늘		
040	sequel	ⓝ 속편, 후편		
041	almost	ⓐⓓ 거의, 하마터면		
042	cholesterol	ⓝ 콜레스테롤		
043	these days	요즘에는		
044	breakfast	ⓝ 아침 식사		
045	on time	제시간에, 정각에		
046	watch	ⓝ 시계		
047	already	ⓐⓓ 이미, 벌써		
048	air-conditioner	ⓝ 에어컨		
049	movie theater	극장		
050	department store	백화점		

녹음된 문장을 듣고 빈칸에 단어 또는 표현을 쓰고, 그 뜻도 써보세요.

026 I don't eat _____ _____.   뜻 _____

027 The _____ is much faster than the tiger.   뜻 _____

028 The _____ is too heavy.   뜻 _____

029 The jeans are very _____, but she can wear them.   뜻 _____

030 People in this village are very _____.   뜻 _____

031 There's too much smoke in here, so I can't _____.   뜻 _____

032 We _____ _____ six months ago but I still miss her.   뜻 _____

033 Are you still working for the same _____?   뜻 _____

034 This classroom is big enough to _____ 50 students.   뜻 _____

035 My mom asked me to _____ _____ the trousers.   뜻 _____

036 She _____ _____ a coin on the floor.   뜻 _____

037 Where does your mom _____ _____ _____?   뜻 _____

038 He is too _____ to go on a picnic.   뜻 _____

039 I don't like _____, either.   뜻 _____

040 The first movie was much funnier than the _____.   뜻 _____

041 She drove badly and _____ had an accident.   뜻 _____

042 High _____ is a cause of heart attacks.   뜻 _____

043 We hardly see each other _____ _____.   뜻 _____

044 Kelly sometimes doesn't eat _____.   뜻 _____

045 Peter comes to work _____ _____.   뜻 _____

046 Your _____ is much better than mine.   뜻 _____

047 I've _____ finished my homework.   뜻 _____

048 I turned the _____ off.   뜻 _____

049 Have you got enough time to go to the _____ _____?   뜻 _____

050 I bought it at a _____ _____.   뜻 _____

001	health	ⓝ 건강		
002	wound	ⓝ 상처		
003	vegetable	ⓝ 야채		
004	the latter part	후반부		
005	summit	ⓝ 정상, 절정		
006	field	ⓝ 분야, 들판, 경기장		
007	individuality	ⓝ 개인, 특성, 인격		
008	the latest fashion	최신 패션		
009	philosophy	ⓝ 철학		
010	abroad	ⓐⓓ 해외로, 국외로		
011	job	ⓝ 직업, 직장, 일자리		
012	fresh	ⓐ 신선한, 새로운		
013	thoughtful	ⓐ 사려 깊은, 생각이 깊은		
014	air pollution	대기오염		
015	complex	ⓐ 복잡한		
016	serious	ⓐ 심각한, 진지한		
017	blow	ⓥ (바람이) 불다		
018	land animal	육상[육지] 동물		
019	February	2월		
020	Antarctica	ⓝ 남극 대륙		
021	fashion designer	패션 디자이너		
022	as ~ as possible	가능한 ~한		
023	ocean	ⓝ 대양, 바다		
024	turtle	ⓝ 거북이		
025	North Korea	북한		

녹음된 문장을 듣고 빈칸에 단어 또는 표현을 쓰고, 그 뜻도 써보세요.

001 _____ is more important than money. 뜻 _____

002 The _____ was worse than I thought. 뜻 _____

003 You should eat more _____ and less meat. 뜻 _____

004 _____ _____ _____ of the movie is very exciting. 뜻 _____

005 You have to go farther to reach the _____ of the mountain. 뜻 _____

006 You are the best in this _____. 뜻 _____

007 With fewer students, there would be greater _____. 뜻 _____

008 Lucy is interested in _____ _____ _____. 뜻 _____

009 _____ is often more complex than science. 뜻 _____

010 More and more people go _____ to study. 뜻 _____

011 It's becoming harder and harder to get a _____. 뜻 _____

012 The _____ the fruit is, the better it tastes. 뜻 _____

013 Jim is less _____ than Jennifer. 뜻 _____

014 _____ _____ is becoming more and more serious. 뜻 _____

015 Philosophy is often more _____ than science. 뜻 _____

016 Air pollution is becoming more and more _____. 뜻 _____

017 If we climb the mountain high, the wind _____ hard. 뜻 _____

018 Cheetahs can run the fastest of all the _____ _____. 뜻 _____

019 _____ is the shortest month of the year. 뜻 _____

020 _____ is the coldest place in the world. 뜻 _____

021 Andre Kim was one of the most famous _____ _____. 뜻 _____

022 I walked to school _____ fast _____ _____. 뜻 _____

023 A river isn't as big as an _____. 뜻 _____

024 _____ live twice as long as elephants. 뜻 _____

025 South Korea has twice as many people as _____ _____. 뜻 _____

026	Europe	ⓝ 유럽		
027	similar	ⓐ 비슷한		
028	different from	~와 다른		
029	similar to	~와 비슷한		
030	salary	ⓝ 월급[봉급, 급여]		
031	cost	ⓥ (비용이) 들다		
032	balloon	ⓝ 풍선, 기구		
033	left-handed	왼손잡이의		
034	type	ⓥ 타자를 치다		
035	collect	ⓥ 모으다, 수집하다		
036	price	ⓝ 가격		
037	watermelon	ⓝ 수박		
038	expect	ⓥ 기대하다		
039	meat	ⓝ 고기		
040	herd	ⓝ 가축의 떼, 무리		
041	weigh	ⓥ 무게가 나가다		
042	among	~의 사이에, ~가운데에		
043	wealth	ⓝ 재산, 부		
044	mammal	ⓝ 포유동물		
045	horse	ⓝ 말		
046	nickname	ⓝ 별명, 애칭		
047	activity	ⓝ 활동		
048	kite	ⓝ 연		
049	boring	ⓐ 지루한		
050	digital camera	디지털 카메라		

녹음된 문장을 듣고 빈칸에 단어 또는 표현을 쓰고, 그 뜻도 써보세요.

026 Africa is four times as large as _____. 뜻 _____

027 Susan and Lucy have _____ hats. 뜻 _____

028 Girls are _____ _____ boys. 뜻 _____

029 A rectangle is _____ _____ a square. 뜻 _____

030 His _____ is three times as high as mine. 뜻 _____

031 This T-shirt _____ twice as much as that one. 뜻 _____

032 I saw a _____ which was as big as a house. 뜻 _____

033 _____ people tend to be better at driving. 뜻 _____

034 I can _____ twice as fast as you. 뜻 _____

035 Sunny _____ as many stamps as possible. 뜻 _____

036 The smaller the phones are, the higher the _____ gets. 뜻 _____

037 _____ are the biggest fruit in the store. 뜻 _____

038 Mt. Halla was more beautiful than I _____. 뜻 _____

039 The doctor advised me to eat less _____. 뜻 _____

040 It lives with other buffalos in groups or _____. 뜻 _____

041 It _____ as much as 2,000 pounds. 뜻 _____

042 _____ the animals, giraffes are the tallest. 뜻 _____

043 Health is more important than _____. 뜻 _____

044 The blue whale is the biggest animal of _____. 뜻 _____

045 The cheetah is faster than the _____. 뜻 _____

046 Did you know her _____? 뜻 _____

047 He likes two _____. 뜻 _____

048 One is riding a bike, the other is flying a _____. 뜻 _____

049 The latter part of the game was _____. 뜻 _____

050 A _____ _____ is pretty expensive. 뜻 _____

001	iced tea	차가운 차, 냉차	
002	prescription	ⓝ 처방전	
003	go out	외출하다, 밖으로 나가다	
004	attend	ⓥ 참석[출석]하다	
005	press	ⓥ 누르다; 강요하다	
006	be responsible for	~에 책임이 있다	
007	weapon	ⓝ 무기	
008	terrorist	ⓝ 테러리스트	
009	helpless	ⓐ 어찌할 수 없는, 무력한	
010	fish	ⓝ 어류, 물고기	
011	realize	ⓥ 깨닫다, 이해하다	
012	cause	ⓥ 일으키다, 야기하다	
013	scholar	ⓝ 학자	
014	copyright	ⓝ 저작권	
015	various	ⓐ 다양한, 많은	
016	obvious	ⓐ 명백한, 분명한	
017	certain	ⓐ 확실한	
018	prohibit	ⓥ 금지하다	
019	break out	발발하다, 발생하다	
020	laptop	ⓝ 휴대용 컴퓨터	
021	dinosaur	ⓝ 공룡	
022	measure	ⓥ 측정하다, 재다	
023	submit	ⓥ 제출[제시]하다	
024	transportation card	교통카드	
025	be absent from	~에 결석[결근]하다	

녹음된 문장을 듣고 빈칸에 단어 또는 표현을 쓰고, 그 뜻도 써보세요.

001 Do you want _____ _____ or hot tea? 뜻 _____

002 I saw the doctor, and he gave me a _____. 뜻 _____

003 Do you want to _____ _____? 뜻 _____

004 Bob couldn't _____ the meeting, for he was sick. 뜻 _____

005 If you _____ the button, the door will open. 뜻 _____

006 Either you or I _____ _____ _____ the result. 뜻 _____

007 The knives were used for cooking or _____. 뜻 _____

008 Neither the _____ nor the police survived the explosion. 뜻 _____

009 Not only you but also I was _____ at that moment. 뜻 _____

010 Whales are not _____ but mammals. 뜻 _____

011 Brian _____ that he had made a mistake. 뜻 _____

012 That smoking can _____ cancer is a fact. 뜻 _____

013 I think that he is a great _____. 뜻 _____

014 MP3 files can break an artist's _____. 뜻 _____

015 We have _____ kinds of bags. How about that? 뜻 _____

016 It is _____ that he finished the work himself. 뜻 _____

017 It is _____ that he will win the game. 뜻 _____

018 Smoking in public places should be _____. 뜻 _____

019 Do you know when the Korean War _____ _____? 뜻 _____

020 I don't know where Victoria bought her _____. 뜻 _____

021 Do you know why _____ became extinct? 뜻 _____

022 I can _____ how deep this lake is. 뜻 _____

023 The important part is if Karen will _____ the report. 뜻 _____

024 I lost my _____ _____. 뜻 _____

025 Jim _____ _____ _____ the class. 뜻 _____

026	planet	ⓝ 행성		
027	impatient	ⓐ 성급한, 참을성이 없는		
028	go out	(불 등이) 꺼지다		
029	make sure	반드시 (~하도록) 하다		
030	as soon as	~하자마자		
031	instead	ⓐⓓ 대신에		
032	can't afford to	(시간, 금전적으로) ~할 여유가 없다		
033	break up with	~와 헤어지다		
034	personality	ⓝ 성품, 성격, 인격		
035	due to	~때문에 (=because of)		
036	go skiing	스키 타러 가다		
037	temperature	ⓝ 온도		
038	fluently	ⓐⓓ 유창하게		
039	in spite of	~임에 불구하고(=despite)		
040	deny	ⓥ 부인[거절]하다		
041	passport	ⓝ 여권		
042	regularly	ⓐⓓ 규칙[정기]적으로		
043	lonely	ⓐ 외로운		
044	continue	ⓥ 계속하다		
045	burst into laughter	웃음을 터뜨리다		
046	selfish	ⓐ 이기적인		
047	vegetarian	ⓝ 채식주의자		
048	typhoon	ⓝ 태풍		
049	mop	ⓥ 닦다, 청소하다		
050	extinct	ⓐ 멸종된		

녹음된 문장을 듣고 빈칸에 단어 또는 표현을 쓰고, 그 뜻도 써보세요.

026 I wonder if there's life on other _____.   뜻 _____

027 Kevin's trouble is that he's too _____.   뜻 _____

028 When I was studying, the light _____ _____.   뜻 _____

029 _____ _____ to turn off the TV before you go to bed.   뜻 _____

030 _____ _____ _____ she arrives, she will put on clothes.   뜻 _____

031 Because I was tired, my wife drove the car _____.   뜻 _____

032 Jennifer _____ _____ _____ buy a car.   뜻 _____

033 I _____ _____ _____ my girlfriend again.   뜻 _____

034 I like Lucy because of her good _____.   뜻 _____

035 The baseball game was cancelled _____ _____ rain.   뜻 _____

036 We can _____ _____ every Saturday.   뜻 _____

037 If the _____ falls below zero, water turns to ice.   뜻 _____

038 She speaks English _____.   뜻 _____

039 _____ _____ _____ the traffic, we arrived on time.   뜻 _____

040 In spite of the fact, he _____ he had done it.   뜻 _____

041 Unless you have a _____, you can't travel abroad.   뜻 _____

042 Unless you exercise _____, you won't lose weight.   뜻 _____

043 The future will be a _____ place to live because of computers.   뜻 _____

044 Though it rained, we _____ to play soccer.   뜻 _____

045 As soon as I saw her face, I _____ _____ _____.   뜻 _____

046 If people are _____, they haven't got many friends.   뜻 _____

047 I only eat salad because I am a _____.   뜻 _____

048 They had to cancel the flight to London because of the _____.   뜻 _____

049 Are are you going to _____ the floor?   뜻 _____

050 Do you know why dinosaurs became _____?   뜻 _____

001	marry	ⓥ ~와 결혼하다	
002	trust	ⓥ 믿다, 신뢰하다	
003	next door	옆집에	
004	elementary school	초등학교	
005	life	ⓝ 목숨, 생명	
006	be injured	다치다, 부상을 입다	
007	bedroom	ⓝ 침실	
008	recently	ⓐ 최근에	
009	on one's own	혼자서, 단독으로	
010	be covered with	~로 덮여 있다	
011	photo	ⓝ 사진	
012	hill	ⓝ 언덕	
013	journalist	ⓝ 기자, 언론인	
014	be stolen	도난당하다	
015	movie star	유명 영화배우	
016	blonde	ⓐ 금발의	
017	meaning	ⓝ 의미	
018	recommend	ⓥ 추천하다, 권하다	
019	garage	ⓝ 차고	
020	cheerleader	ⓝ 치어리더	
021	look for	~를 찾다, 구하다	
022	self-confidence	자신감	
023	top	ⓝ 정상, 꼭대기	
024	make a speech	연설하다	
025	used to ⓥ	~하곤 했(었)다	

001 He _____ a woman who was from Vietnam.   뜻 _____

002 I have a boyfriend who(m) I can _____.   뜻 _____

003 The woman who lives _____ _____ is a doctor.   뜻 _____

004 I met friends who I've known since _____ _____.   뜻 _____

005 This is the man who saved her _____.   뜻 _____

006 The girl who _____ _____ in the accident is in the hospital.   뜻 _____

007 This is the house which has 9 _____.   뜻 _____

008 This is the book which I have written _____.   뜻 _____

009 I can't solve the problems _____ _____ _____.   뜻 _____

010 Look at the house which _____ _____ _____ snow.   뜻 _____

011 Kathy has some _____ that I took.   뜻 _____

012 I saw an old castle which stood on the _____.   뜻 _____

013 I met a person whose job is a _____.   뜻 _____

014 The man whose car _____ _____ called the police.   뜻 _____

015 I know a girl whose brother is a _____ _____.   뜻 _____

016 I saw a girl whose hair is _____.   뜻 _____

017 There are many words whose _____ I don't know.   뜻 _____

018 The library Kevin _____ was closed.   뜻 _____

019 This is the key which opens the _____.   뜻 _____

020 I hate the _____ you played with.   뜻 _____

021 I never found the book which I was _____ _____.   뜻 _____

022 What you really need is _____.   뜻 _____

023 She is the first woman that arrived at the _____.   뜻 _____

024 He _____ _____ _____ on the customs in Africa.   뜻 _____

025 That is the library where we _____ _____ study.   뜻 _____

026	the disabled	신체 장애인들(복수취급)		
027	work	ⓥ 작동하다, 움직이다		
028	be held	개최되다		
029	escape	ⓥ 탈출하다, 달아나다		
030	go through	경험하다		
031	quit	ⓥ 그만두다, 떠나다		
032	avoid	ⓥ 피하다, 막다		
033	get fired	해고되다		
034	break into	~에 침입하다		
035	be good at	~을 잘하다		
036	take place	발생하다		
037	break down	고장나다		
038	source	ⓝ 근원, 원천		
039	necklace	ⓝ 목걸이		
040	rescue	ⓥ 구출[구조]하다		
041	grow up	자라다		
042	painter	ⓝ 화가		
043	invent	ⓥ 발명하다		
044	the other day	일전에, 며칠 전에		
045	take care of	~을 돌보다		
046	play	ⓝ 연극		
047	procedure	ⓝ 진행, 절차, 순서		
048	crash	ⓥ 갑자기 기능을 멈추다		
049	plant	ⓥ 심다, 이식하다		
050	anthropology	ⓝ 인류학		

녹음된 문장을 듣고 빈칸에 단어 또는 표현을 쓰고, 그 뜻도 써보세요.

026 This is the place where only _____ _____ can park.   뜻 _____

027 The clerk explained how the DVD _____.   뜻 _____

028 In 2002 Korea-Japan World Cup _____ _____.   뜻 _____

029 She told me how she _____ from the bus.   뜻 _____

030 He made a speech on the customs that he _____ _____ in Africa.   뜻 _____

031 Do you know the reason why Brian is _____ his job?   뜻 _____

032 This is the way that Michael _____ the accident.   뜻 _____

033 I can't understand the reason why I _____ _____.   뜻 _____

034 I don't know how the thief _____ _____ my house.   뜻 _____

035 I know the girls who _____ _____ _____ French.   뜻 _____

036 That is the place where the car accident _____ _____.   뜻 _____

037 We helped a woman whose car had _____ _____.   뜻 _____

038 Mother Earth is the _____ of life.   뜻 _____

039 He gave me the _____ he bought yesterday.   뜻 _____

040 It _____ people who are in danger.   뜻 _____

041 This is the house where I _____ _____.   뜻 _____

042 I have a friend whose mother is a famous _____.   뜻 _____

043 Do you know the reason why he _____ this machine?   뜻 _____

044 Is this the book you were looking for _____ _____ _____?   뜻 _____

045 A dentist is a person who _____ _____ _____ your teeth.   뜻 _____

046 An actress is a person who acts in a _____.   뜻 _____

047 A flight attendant looks after the flight's safety _____.   뜻 _____

048 The computer I bought has already _____ several times.   뜻 _____

049 The trees we _____ last year have doubled in size.   뜻 _____

050 _____ in which I'm interested is the study of people and society.   뜻 _____

001	gas station	주유소		
002	fly	ⓝ 파리		
003	autumn	ⓝ 가을(=fall)		
004	come out	~로 밝혀지다		
005	jar	ⓝ 병, 단지, 항아리		
006	sound	ⓥ ~처럼 들리다		
007	ring	ⓝ 반지		
008	pianist	ⓝ 피아니스트		
009	kite	ⓝ 연		
010	figure skater	피겨 스케이팅 선수		
011	promise	ⓝ 약속(하다)		
012	bodyguard	ⓝ 경호원		
013	allow	ⓥ 허락하다		
014	comic book	만화책		
015	wash the dishes	설거지를 하다		
016	repair	ⓥ 수리[수선]하다		
017	shaking	ⓐ 흔들리는		
018	order	ⓥ 명령[주문]하다		
019	healthy	ⓐ 건강한		
020	turn off	(전기, 기계 등을) 끄다		
021	ringing	ⓐ 울리는		
022	burning	ⓐ 불타는		
023	cello	ⓝ 첼로		
024	salt	ⓝ 소금		
025	green tea	녹차		

녹음된 문장을 듣고 빈칸에 단어 또는 표현을 쓰고, 그 뜻도 써보세요.

001 Is there a _____ _____ near here?　　　뜻 _____

002 There are two _____ on the wall.　　　뜻 _____

003 In _____ the leaves turn yellow.　　　뜻 _____

004 The report _____ _____ true the next morning.　　　뜻 _____

005 There is some sugar in the _____.　　　뜻 _____

006 Her story _____ strange.　　　뜻 _____

007 I gave her the gold _____.　　　뜻 _____

008 My sister is a famous _____.　　　뜻 _____

009 My dad will make a _____ for me.　　　뜻 _____

010 My dad made me a famous _____ _____.　　　뜻 _____

011 I want you to keep your _____.　　　뜻 _____

012 He ordered the _____ to protect the president.　　　뜻 _____

013 My dad _____ me to go to the party.　　　뜻 _____

014 My mom didn't let me read _____ _____.　　　뜻 _____

015 My mom made me _____ _____ _____.　　　뜻 _____

016 I had Scott _____ the bicycle.　　　뜻 _____

017 I felt the ground _____.　　　뜻 _____

018 He _____ the bodyguards to protect the president.　　　뜻 _____

019 Exercising regularly will keep you _____.　　　뜻 _____

020 I asked my little sister to _____ _____ the TV.　　　뜻 _____

021 I heard the alarm _____ loudly.　　　뜻 _____

022 Jane smelled something _____ in the oven.　　　뜻 _____

023 Who is playing the _____?　　　뜻 _____

024 Pass me the _____, will you?　　　뜻 _____

025 Would you like coffee or _____ _____?　　　뜻 _____

026	brave	ⓐ 용감한		
027	creative	ⓐ 창조[창의]적인		
028	rush	ⓥ 서두르게 하다		
029	boring	ⓐ 지루한		
030	airplane	ⓝ 비행기		
031	office	ⓝ 사무실		
032	guess	ⓥ 추측[짐작]하다		
033	roof	ⓝ 지붕		
034	grade	ⓝ 성적, 등급		
035	toothache	ⓝ 치통		
036	cook	ⓥ 요리하다		
037	fan club	팬클럽, 후원회		
038	pull out	끄집어내다, 뽑다		
039	crawl	ⓥ 기어가다		
040	force	ⓥ ~을 억지로 시키다		
041	secretary	ⓝ 비서		
042	recover	ⓥ 회복하다		
043	advice	ⓝ 충고, 조언		
044	laugh	ⓥ 웃다		
045	electrical outlet	전기코드		
046	memorize	ⓥ 암기[기억]하다		
047	go on a diet	다이어트를 (시작)하다		
048	warn	ⓥ 경고하다		
049	try on	입어[신어] 보다		
050	price tag	가격표		

녹음된 문장을 듣고 빈칸에 단어 또는 표현을 쓰고, 그 뜻도 써보세요.

026 He is a _____ man.   뜻 _____

027 You are very _____.   뜻 _____

028 Let's not _____ it.   뜻 _____

029 It was a very _____ film.   뜻 _____

030 Do you know how _____ fly?   뜻 _____

031 Can you tell me if Kate is in her _____?   뜻 _____

032 What do you _____ it means?   뜻 _____

033 There is a lot of snow on the _____.   뜻 _____

034 Kathy got a good _____ in the English test.   뜻 _____

035 You have a _____, don't you?   뜻 _____

036 My mom _____ us a great dinner.   뜻 _____

037 There are many members in her _____ _____.   뜻 _____

038 I had my tooth _____ _____.   뜻 _____

039 She felt the ants _____ up her leg.   뜻 _____

040 I will _____ them to start tonight.   뜻 _____

041 She had her _____ type the letter.   뜻 _____

042 They helped me to _____ soon.   뜻 _____

043 He gives us some useful _____.   뜻 _____

044 The Gag Concert makes me _____.   뜻 _____

045 Tom warned me not to touch the _____ _____.   뜻 _____

046 My English teacher had me _____ English words.   뜻 _____

047 The doctor advised me to _____ _____ ___ _____.   뜻 _____

048 Tom _____ me not to touch the electrical outlet.   뜻 _____

049 You are _____ _____ a jacket.   뜻 _____

050 You're looking at a _____ _____, which is very high.   뜻 _____

001	bus stop	버스 정류장		
002	pocket	ⓝ 호주머니		
003	traffic light	(교통) 신호등		
004	pick up	~를 (차에) 태우러 가다		
005	grass	ⓝ 풀, 잔디		
006	on the way to + ⓝ	~로 가는 길에		
007	wall	ⓝ 벽		
008	floor	ⓝ 바닥, 층		
009	along	ⓟⓡⓔ ~을 따라서		
010	through	ⓟⓡⓔ ~을 관통하여		
011	out of	ⓟⓡⓔ ~밖으로		
012	bakery	ⓝ 제과점		
013	across from	맞은편		
014	anywhere	ⓐⓓ 아무데도, 어디든지		
015	try to + ⓥ	~하려고 노력하다		
016	Why don't you + ⓥ	~하는 게 어때?		
017	sunrise	ⓝ 일출, 해돋이		
018	toss and turn	뒤척이다		
019	half an hour	반시간, 30분		
020	bravely	ⓐⓓ 용감하게		
021	sign	ⓥ 사인[서명]하다		
022	driver's license	운전 면허증		
023	credit card	신용카드		
024	death penalty	사형		
025	be afraid of	~을 무서워하다		

녹음된 문장을 듣고 빈칸에 단어 또는 표현을 쓰고, 그 뜻도 써보세요.

001 People are standing at the _____ _____.　　　　　뜻 _____

002 The cell phone is in her _____.　　　　　뜻 _____

003 The car is waiting at the _____ _____.　　　　　뜻 _____

004 I will _____ you _____ at the airport tomorrow.　　　　　뜻 _____

005 Don't sit on the _____.　　　　　뜻 _____

006 I met Lucy _____ _____ _____ _____ school.　　　　　뜻 _____

007 There is a clock on the _____.　　　　　뜻 _____

008 There is a carpet on the _____.　　　　　뜻 _____

009 He jogs _____ the river.　　　　　뜻 _____

010 They walked _____ the forest.　　　　　뜻 _____

011 He took his PDA _____ _____ his backpack.　　　　　뜻 _____

012 There is a bus stop in front of the _____.　　　　　뜻 _____

013 Sunny is sitting _____ _____ Kevin.　　　　　뜻 _____

014 Don't go _____. I'll be back in ten minutes.　　　　　뜻 _____

015 People _____ _____ keep the peace.　　　　　뜻 _____

016 _____ _____ _____ go to the movies on Friday?　　　　　뜻 _____

017 She likes to take a walk around _____.　　　　　뜻 _____

018 I _____ _____ _____ all through the night.　　　　　뜻 _____

019 I waited for you for _____ _____ _____.　　　　　뜻 _____

020 They fought _____ for their country.　　　　　뜻 _____

021 Please _____ your name with a pen.　　　　　뜻 _____

022 You can get a _____ _____ at 18.　　　　　뜻 _____

023 Will you pay by _____ _____?　　　　　뜻 _____

024 Are you for or against the _____ _____?　　　　　뜻 _____

025 He _____ _____ _____ dogs.　　　　　뜻 _____

026	be good at	~을 잘하다
027	be poor at	~을 못하다
028	be crowded with	~로 붐비다[가득 차다]
029	be different from	~와 다르다
030	be interested in	~에 흥미가 있다, 관심이 있다
031	be jealous of	~을 질투하다
032	be similar to	~와 비슷하다
033	be dependent on	~에 의존하다
034	be famous for	~로 유명하다
035	mistake	ⓝ 실수, 오류
036	wait for	~을 기다리다
037	laugh at	~을 보고 웃다[비웃다]
038	consist of	~로 구성되다
039	selfish	ⓐ 이기적인
040	apply for	~에 지원하다
041	enormous	ⓐ 거대한, 엄청난
042	heart attack	심장마비
043	wedding anniversary	결혼기념일
044	be sure to ⓥ	반드시 ~하다
045	experience	ⓥ 경험하다
046	cultural heritage	문화유산
047	take a walk	산책하다
048	keep in touch	연락을 (유지)하다
049	be responsible for	~에 책임이 있다
050	belong to + ⓝ	~에 속하다

026 Sunny _____ _____ _____ playing the violin. 뜻 _____

027 He _____ _____ _____ swimming. 뜻 _____

028 The roads in Korea _____ _____ _____ cars. 뜻 _____

029 The movie _____ _____ _____ what I'd expected. 뜻 _____

030 _____ you _____ _____ art? 뜻 _____

031 You _____ always _____ _____ other people. 뜻 _____

032 Your opinion _____ _____ _____ mine. 뜻 _____

033 I don't want to _____ _____ _____ anybody. 뜻 _____

034 What _____ Korea _____ _____? 뜻 _____

035 The letter I wrote was full of _____. 뜻 _____

036 She is _____ _____ me in the car. 뜻 _____

037 Everybody will _____ _____ you. 뜻 _____

038 The test _____ _____ writing and speaking. 뜻 _____

039 Nancy is _____. 뜻 _____

040 Are you going to _____ _____ the company? 뜻 _____

041 We had an _____ meal. It consisted of eight courses. 뜻 _____

042 Bob died of a _____ _____. 뜻 _____

043 My _____ _____ is on May 26th. 뜻 _____

044 _____ _____ _____ come back by 5 o'clock. 뜻 _____

045 While I was in Korea, I _____ interesting things. 뜻 _____

046 Koreans take pride in their unique _____ _____. 뜻 _____

047 She likes to _____ _____ _____ around sunrise. 뜻 _____

048 We will _____ _____ _____ by e-mail. 뜻 _____

049 Who _____ _____ _____ all that noise last night? 뜻 _____

050 Does this iPhone _____ _____ you? 뜻 _____

001	go fishing	낚시하러 가다		
002	freeze	ⓥ 얼음이 얼다		
003	sleepy	ⓐ 졸리는		
004	put on weight	체중이 늘다		
005	sneeze	ⓥ 재채기하다		
006	nail	ⓝ 손톱		
007	mark	ⓝ 성적, 점수		
008	temperature	ⓝ 온도		
009	break into	~에 침입하다		
010	cost	ⓥ 비용이 들다		
011	address	ⓝ 주소; 연설		
012	yacht	ⓝ 요트		
013	hire	ⓥ 고용하다		
014	west	ⓝ 서쪽		
015	millionaire	ⓝ 백만장자		
016	go on a vacation	휴가를 가다		
017	invite	ⓥ 초대[초청]하다		
018	weather report	일기예보		
019	check	ⓥ 확인하다		
020	have the accident	사고가 나다		
021	punish	ⓥ 벌하다		
022	bake	ⓥ 굽다		
023	view	ⓝ 경치		
024	go to the movies	영화 보러 가다		
025	job	ⓝ 직업, 일		

녹음된 문장을 듣고 빈칸에 단어 또는 표현을 쓰고, 그 뜻도 써보세요.

001 If it is fine tomorrow, I will _____ _____. 뜻 _____

002 If the temperature doesn't fall below zero, water doesn't _____. 뜻 _____

003 If I have a big lunch, it makes me _____. 뜻 _____

004 If you eat too much, you will _____ _____ _____. 뜻 _____

005 If people _____, they close their eyes. 뜻 _____

006 If you break _____, it grows back again. 뜻 _____

007 If I get good _____, my parents will be happy. 뜻 _____

008 If the _____ reaches −15℃, the lake freezes. 뜻 _____

009 I saw someone _____ _____ your house. 뜻 _____

010 If we stayed in a hotel, it would _____ too much money. 뜻 _____

011 If I knew your _____, I could write you a letter. 뜻 _____

012 As I'm not rich, I can't buy a _____. 뜻 _____

013 If she spoke English well, we would _____ her. 뜻 _____

014 The sun doesn't rise in the _____. 뜻 _____

015 If I were a _____, I could have an airplane. 뜻 _____

016 We will _____ _____ _____ _____. 뜻 _____

017 If I knew her well, I could _____ her to the party. 뜻 _____

018 I had heard the _____ _____. 뜻 _____

019 I _____ the e-mail. 뜻 _____

020 As it snowed, we _____ _____ _____. 뜻 _____

021 He _____ _____ because he broke the window. 뜻 _____

022 I _____ a cake. 뜻 _____

023 The _____ was wonderful. 뜻 _____

024 We can _____ _____ _____ _____ tonight. 뜻 _____

025 Tiffany wishes she had a good _____. 뜻 _____

026	take a shower	샤워하다		
027	interrupt	ⓥ 방해하다		
028	pilot	ⓝ 조종사		
029	college	ⓝ 대학교		
030	secret	ⓝ 비밀		
031	musical instrument	악기		
032	bring	ⓥ 가져오다		
033	at once	즉시		
034	have a cold	감기에 걸리다		
035	waste	ⓥ 낭비[허비]하다		
036	listen carefully	귀를 기울이다		
037	climb	ⓥ (기어) 오르다		
038	answer	ⓝ 해답		
039	fasten	ⓥ 잠그다, 묶다		
040	crash	ⓝ 충돌(사고)		
041	exercise	ⓥ 운동하다		
042	alarm clock	자명종, 알람시계		
043	thoughtful	ⓐ 생각이 깊은		
044	promise	ⓝ 약속		
045	relax	ⓥ 휴식을 취하다		
046	weather	ⓝ 날씨		
047	fall off	떨어지다		
048	go on holiday	휴가를 가다		
049	be in trouble	어려움에 처하다		
050	lie	ⓝ 거짓말		

녹음된 문장을 듣고 빈칸에 단어 또는 표현을 쓰고, 그 뜻도 써보세요.

026 I wish he were going to _____ _____ _____. 뜻 _____

027 I wish you wouldn't keep _____ me. 뜻 _____

028 I wish that he were a _____. 뜻 _____

029 I wish I had gone to _____ after high school. 뜻 _____

030 Robert wishes he hadn't told the _____. 뜻 _____

031 Bob had learned to play a _____ _____. 뜻 _____

032 She didn't _____ her digital camera. 뜻 _____

033 I wish the woman had been saved _____ _____. 뜻 _____

034 Since I _____ ___ bad _____, I didn't attend the meeting. 뜻 _____

035 I am sorry I _____ my time when I was young. 뜻 _____

036 _____ _____, or you won't understand it. 뜻 _____

037 It snowed yesterday, so we didn't _____ the mountain. 뜻 _____

038 I don't know the _____. 뜻 _____

039 She _____ a seat belt. 뜻 _____

040 She wasn't injured in the _____. 뜻 _____

041 If he _____ _____, he would have been healthy. 뜻 _____

042 I had set my _____ _____ not to be late for the meeting. 뜻 _____

043 I should be more _____ to understand him. 뜻 _____

044 I wish you had kept your _____ yesterday. 뜻 _____

045 She doesn't have time to _____. 뜻 _____

046 If the _____ were fine, we could go on a picnic. 뜻 _____

047 Scott didn't _____ _____ his bike. 뜻 _____

048 If you feel tired, you should _____ _____ _____. 뜻 _____

049 If you write on the desk, you'll _____ _____ _____. 뜻 _____

050 I wish I hadn't told a _____ to my teacher. 뜻 _____

서술형 기초다지기

정답 p. 2

Challenge 1   다음 빈칸에 some과 any 중에 알맞은 것을 쓰세요.

01. After lunch we usually eat _____ ice cream for dessert.

02. There isn't _____ pizza. Who ate all of my pizza?

03. I have _____ money today, but yesterday I didn't have _____ money.

04. Is there _____ milk in the refrigerator?

05. Could you give me _____ soup, please?

06. Would you like _____ tea?

07. I will wash my hair. Is there _____ shampoo?

Challenge 2   다음 문장을 의문문과 부정문으로 바꿔 쓰세요.

01. My brother likes some cheese.

(의문문) → _____

(부정문) → _____

02. There are some flowers in the garden.

(의문문) → _____

(부정문) → _____

Challenge 3   「not ~ any」를 no로 바꿔 문장을 다시 써 보세요.

01. There aren't any students in the library.

→ _____

02. We didn't see anybody.

→ _____

03. She didn't have any pencils to write with.

→ _____

2-3 (a) few, (a) little

Laura runs **a few** miles every day.
로라는 매일 몇 마일을 달린다.

She drinks a lot of milk and eats **a little** fruit.
그녀는 많은 우유를 마시고, 약간의 과일을 먹는다.

01 **a few vs. a little**

a few는 셀 수 있는 명사 앞에 써서 '**조금의, 몇 개의**' 뜻으로 많지 않은 **수**를 나타내며 긍정의 의미가 담겨 있다.

a little은 셀 수 없는 명사 앞에 써서 '**약간의**' 뜻으로 많지 않은 **양**을 나타내며 긍정의 의미가 담겨 있다.

I have **a few** things to tell you. 너한테 할 얘기가 몇 가지 있어.

You'd better take **a little** nap. 너는 낮잠을 좀 자는 게 좋겠어.

They will come back in **a few** days. 그들은 며칠 후에 돌아올 것이다.

This sauce needs **a little** salt. 이 소스에는 소금이 좀 필요하다.

02 **few vs. little**

few는 셀 수 있는 명사 앞에 써서 '**거의 없는 (수)**'이라는 부정의 의미를 내포하고 있다.

little은 셀 수 없는 명사 앞에 써서 '**거의 없는 (양)**'이라는 부정의 의미를 내포하고 있다.

I have **little** time. I must hurry. 나는 시간이 거의 없다. 나는 서둘러야 한다.

You are so selfish and rude. That's why you have **few** friends.
너는 너무 이기적이고 무례해. 그래서 친구가 거의 없는 거야.

It's raining. There are **few** people in the street. 비가 온다. 거리에 사람들이 거의 없다.

She uses **little** salt in her food. 그녀는 음식에 소금을 거의 사용하지 않는다.

서술형 기초다지기

정답 p. 2

Challenge 1   다음 빈칸에 a few 또는 a little을 쓰세요.

01. There was _____ food in the refrigerator.

02. Lisa drinks _____ glasses of juice every day.

03. There are _____ shirts in the closet.

04. We have _____ rain this year.

05. I've got _____ eggs. I can make an omelette.

06. I know _____ Japanese. I can understand Japanese people.

Challenge 2   다음 빈칸에 few와 little 중 알맞은 것을 쓰세요.

01. I have _____ friends in England and I feel quite lonely.

02. We had _____ snow last year.

03. We use _____ salt for cooking.

04. He eats _____ sweets for his teeth.

Challenge 3   다음 빈칸에 a few, few, a little, little 중 알맞은 것을 쓰세요.

01. A: Do you need _____ help?

   B: Yes, please. There are _____ questions I can't answer.

02. He knows _____ English, so he's going to take _____ English classes.

03. _____ students didn't pass the test; they said they had _____ time.

Unit 03 형용사로 쓰이는 분사

3-1 분사의 형용사 역할

The news was **surprising**.
그 소식은 놀라웠다.

I was **surprised** to hear the news.
나는 그 소식을 듣고 놀랐다.

01 현재분사와 과거분사는 형용사처럼 **명사를 앞에서 수식하거나 연결동사(be동사) 뒤에 쓴다.**

I will never see this **boring** movie again in my life! 내 인생에서 다시는 이런 지루한 영화를 보지 않을 것이다.
I was **bored** to see this movie. 나는 이 영화를 봐서 지루했다.
Look at the **exhausted** people. 그 지친 사람들을 봐라.
They are **exhausted**. 그들은 지쳐 있다.

02 현재분사와 과거분사 뒤에 **다른 수식어구가 붙는 경우 명사를 뒤에서 꾸미는 형용사 역할**을 한다.

I'm going to take the train **leaving** in the early morning. 나는 아침 일찍 떠나는 기차를 탈 거야.
The woman **carrying** her briefcase is my mother. 서류 가방을 들고 있는 저분이 내 어머니야.
Look at the girls **frightened** by the dog. 그 개에 놀란 소녀들을 봐라.
I received a letter **written** in French. 나는 불어로 쓰인 편지를 받았다.

03 형용사로 쓰이는 현재분사와 과거분사는 분명한 의미 차이를 갖는다. **현재분사의 수식을 받는 명사는 그 행위를 하는 주체라 명사와는 능동의 관계이고, 과거분사의 수식을 받는 명사는 그 행위를 받는 대상이라 명사와는 수동의 관계**이다.

The film was **disappointing**. 그 영화는 실망스러웠다.
We were **disappointed** in the film. 우리는 그 영화에 실망했다.

Her words were **confusing**. 그녀의 말은 혼란스러웠다.
I was **confused** by her words. 나는 그녀의 말로 인해 혼란스러웠다.

We saw a man **beating** a boy. 우리는 한 남자가 소년을 때리는 것을 보았다.
We saw a man **beaten** by a boy. 우리는 한 남자가 소년에게 맞는 것을 보았다.

서술형 기초다지기

Challenge 1 다음 문장을 읽고 현재분사와 과거분사를 이용한 문장으로 완성하세요.

> **보기** The game excites us.
> → The game is _exciting_. We are _excited_ to see the game.

01. This film bores me.

→ This film is _____. I am _____ with this film.

02. The news shocked the citizens.

→ The news was _____. The citizens were _____.

03. The story moved me.

→ The story was _____. I was _____.

04. Computer games excite us.

→ Computer games are _____. We are _____.

Challenge 2 다음 괄호 안의 표현을 이용하여 문장을 다시 써 보세요.

01. The book is mine. (written in English)

→ _____

02. They threw stones at a bus. (moving)

→ _____

03. There is a man. (breaking into the house)

→ _____

04. The woman was put into an ambulance. (injured)

→ _____

01 출제 100% - 연결동사 뒤에 형용사를 찾아라!

출제자의 눈 be동사류의 연결동사(look, seem, appear, smell, feel, taste) 뒤에는 반드시 형용사가 온다는 것을 잊지 말자. 해석상 부사와 의미가 비슷하여 부사를 써 놓고 틀린 것을 고르라는 문제가 자주 출제된다. 단, 명사가 보어로 올 경우에는 「연결동사 + like + 명사」로 쓴다.

Ex 1.

My teacher seemed _____ because I was late.

(a) angrily   (b) angry   (c) anger   (d) happy

Ex 2.

What beautiful roses! They smell _____.

(a) good   (b) nicely   (c) well   (d) better

02 출제 100% - some과 any를 반드시 구별하라!

출제자의 눈 some은 긍정문, any는 부정문과 의문문에 쓴다. 권유나 부탁 의문문에 some을 쓰기도 하고, '어떤 ~라도'의 의미로 any를 긍정문에 쓰기도 한다. 이 둘을 구별하는 문제가 자주 출제된다. 또한, many와 much 뒤에 오는 알맞은 명사를 묻는 문제나 many, much, a lot of, lots of를 바르게 쓸 줄 아는지 묻는 문제가 많이 출제된다.

Ex 3.

Would you like _____ orange juice?

(a) any   (b) no   (c) some   (d) much

Ex 4.

I live in a small town in Australia. There aren't _____ there.

(a) much house   (b) many house

(c) much houses   (d) many houses

03 출제 100% - 형용사는 -thing류의 대명사 앞에서 수식할 수 없다.

 출제자의 눈 -thing, -body, -one으로 끝나는 대명사는 반드시 형용사가 뒤에서 수식한다. 이를 물어보는 어순 문제가 많이 출제된다. few나 a few는 뒤에 셀 수 있는 명사가 오고, little이나 a little은 뒤에 셀 수 없는 명사가 온다는 것 역시 자주 출제된다. 상황에 따라 긍정의 의미이면 a few와 a little을 쓰고 부정의 의미일 때는 few, little을 쓴다는 다소 어려운 문제도 출제된다.

Ex 5.

We have _____ you.

(a) new nothing to tell   (b) nothing new to tell

Ex 6.

It's September but there are still _____ tourists on the island.

(a) few   (b) a little   (c) little   (d) a few

04 출제 100% - 보어 역할을 하는 분사를 확실히 이해해 두자!

 출제자의 눈 행위를 직접적으로 하거나 감정을 직접 전달하는 경우 현재분사(V-ing)를 쓰고, 행위를 당하거나 감정을 받는 대상 즉, 수동의 의미일 경우 과거분사(V-ed)를 쓴다. 이 둘을 혼동하게 하는 문제가 집중적으로 출제된다. 또한, 「the + 형용사」는 자체가 복수 명사이므로 동사는 언제나 복수 형태를 취한다. 단수형 동사를 주고 틀린 것을 찾는 문제가 출제될 수 있다.

Ex 7.

I think living in a foreign country can be more _____ than you might imagine.

(a) excited   (b) exciting   (c) excite   (d) excites

Ex 8.

틀린 곳을 찾아 고치시오.

The young is interested in foreign languages.

_____ → _____

1. 다음 문장의 밑줄 친 부분과 바꿔 쓸 수 있는 것은?

> We should buy <u>some</u> milk and bread at the E-Mart.

❶ few   ❷ little   ❸ a few
❹ a little   ❺ many

2. 다음 중 어법상 옳지 <u>않은</u> 문장은?

❶ The baby fell asleep in the cradle.
❷ I saw a drunken man lying on the street.
❸ My elder brother is very tall.
❹ I want to eat hot something.
❺ He has a large number of books.

3. 다음 빈칸에 들어갈 말이 바르게 짝지어진 것은?

> A: What did you do over the weekend?
> B: I saw a movie.
> A: Did you find it _____?
> B: No, I didn't. It was very _____.

❶ exciting − bored   ❷ excited − bored
❸ excited − boring   ❹ exciting − boring
❺ excite − boring

4. 우리말과 같은 뜻이 되도록 주어진 단어를 올바른 순서로 배열하시오.

> A: What's the longest river in the world?
> B: Isn't it the Mississippi?
> A: I'm _____.
>   (wrong / you / are / afraid)
>   네가 틀린 것 같은데.

5. 다음 빈칸에 들어갈 말이 순서대로 바르게 짝지어진 것은?

> A: What's wrong with you? You look so
>   _____.
> B: I made too many _____ in my
>   English exam.

❶ happy − mistakes   ❷ down − mistakes
❸ down − mistake   ❹ angrily − mistake
❺ happily − mistakes

6. 다음 두 사람의 대화 중 어법상 <u>틀린</u> 것은?

❶ A: How are you doing?
   B: Special nothing. And you?
❷ A: What's the matter with you?
   B: Well, I am so tired.
❸ A: I'm worried about the exam.
   B: Don't worry. You will do fine.
❹ A: I don't feel good. I have a cold.
   B: You should take a rest.
❺ A: Do you often draw pictures?
   B: Yes, I do. I am in the Art Club.

7. 다음 밑줄 친 부분을 괄호 안의 단어와 바꿔 쓸 수 <u>없는</u> 것은?

❶ She drinks <u>lots of</u> coffee. (= much)
❷ We had <u>a lot of</u> snow last winter. (= much)
❸ I visited <u>a lot of</u> cities in the United States and Canada. (= much)
❹ I usually have <u>a lot of</u> homework, so I only have a little free time. (= much)
❺ There is <u>lots of</u> fresh air up there. (= much)

오답 노트 만들기

★틀린 문제 : _____   ★다시 공부한 날 : _____

(1) 문제를 왜? 틀렸는지 곰곰이 생각하고 그 이유를 적어본다.

(2) 핵심 개념을 적는다.

(3) 자신이 몰랐던 단어와 숙어 표현이 있으면 정리한다.

(4) 해설집에서 필요한 부분을 골라 풀이 해법을 정리한다.

★틀린 문제 : _____   ★다시 공부한 날 : _____

(1) 문제를 왜? 틀렸는지 곰곰이 생각하고 그 이유를 적어본다.

(2) 핵심 개념을 적는다.

(3) 자신이 몰랐던 단어와 숙어 표현이 있으면 정리한다.

(4) 해설집에서 필요한 부분을 골라 풀이 해법을 정리한다.

★틀린 문제 : _____   ★다시 공부한 날 : _____

(1) 문제를 왜? 틀렸는지 곰곰이 생각하고 그 이유를 적어본다.

(2) 핵심 개념을 적는다.

(3) 자신이 몰랐던 단어와 숙어 표현이 있으면 정리한다.

(4) 해설집에서 필요한 부분을 골라 풀이 해법을 정리한다.

★틀린 문제 : _____   ★다시 공부한 날 : _____

(1) 문제를 왜? 틀렸는지 곰곰이 생각하고 그 이유를 적어본다.

(2) 핵심 개념을 적는다.

(3) 자신이 몰랐던 단어와 숙어 표현이 있으면 정리한다.

(4) 해설집에서 필요한 부분을 골라 풀이 해법을 정리한다.

[1-2] 다음 문장을 아래와 같이 바꿔 쓰시오.

> This is a pretty doll.
> → <u>The doll is pretty.</u>

1. These are not very useful books.

→ _____

2. They are very kind nurses.

→ _____

3. **다음 문장에서 <u>어색한</u> 부분을 찾아 바르게 고치시오.**

> When I was a child, I liked to listen to a bedtime story before I fell sleep.

_____ → _____

4. **다음 밑줄 친 부분 중 쓰임이 <u>어색한</u> 것은?**

❶ I have <u>few</u> friends to play with.
❷ They had <u>some</u> money to buy food.
❸ <u>Lots of</u> people went abroad last year.
❹ There isn't <u>much</u> water in this river.
❺ There were <u>little</u> sunny days last month.

5. **다음 빈칸에 들어갈 말로 알맞은 것은?**

> She isn't very popular. She has very
> _____ friends.

❶ much ❷ a few ❸ few
❹ a little ❺ any

6. **우리말과 같은 뜻이 되도록 주어진 단어를 올바른 순서로 배열하시오.**

> 볼만한 중요한 것이 없었다.
> = There was _____
> _____ .
> (see / to / nothing / important)

7. **다음 중 밑줄 친 부분의 쓰임이 <u>잘못된</u> 것은?**

❶ The movie was very <u>exciting</u>.
❷ I was <u>surprising</u> at the news.
❸ The comic books are <u>interesting</u>.
❹ I think that it's a <u>boring</u> book.
❺ We were <u>satisfied</u> with the result.

8. 다음 대화에서 어색한 부분을 찾아 고치시오.

> A : How many detective stories does your brother read every summer?
> B : Oh, I don't know. He reads much books. He even reads on the beach!

_____ → _____

오답노트

[9-11] 다음 대화를 읽고 물음에 답하시오.

> A : Christina, do you have ___(A)___ money?
> B : Well, a little bit. Why?
> A : This Friday is Nancy's birthday. She invited me to her party. But ⓐ I'm broke.
> B : I have ___(B)___ money, but I ⓑ (a book / buy / to / have). I don't buy gifts. I usually make them.

9. 윗글 (A)와 (B)에 들어갈 말로 알맞은 것은?

❶ no – any
❷ some – any
❸ any – any
❹ any – some
❺ any – no

10. 밑줄 친 ⓐ가 의미하는 것으로 알맞은 것은?

❶ 선물을 깨뜨렸어.
❷ 돈이 하나도 없어.
❸ 약속을 어겼어.
❹ 초대를 받았어.
❺ 돈을 잃어 버렸어.

11. 밑줄 친 ⓑ를 알맞게 배열하시오.

→ _____

오답노트

12. 다음 문장 중 어법상 어색한 것은?

❶ I feel so tired today.
❷ That sounds good to me.
❸ Bob looks a little surprising.
❹ This cookie tastes so delicious.
❺ This soup smells good.

오답노트

[13-15] 다음 중 틀린 부분을 모두 찾아 바르게 고치시오.

13. His ideas are very difficult, but few people understand them.

_____ → _____

14. How many butter are there in the refrigerator?

_____ → _____

15. There was hardly some food left by the time we got there.

_____ → _____

오답노트

16. 다음 문장 중 어법상 어색한 문장은?

❶ I've already finished my lunch.
❷ There is something mysterious in this town.
❸ A few people are coming for tea.
❹ Have you heard good news? You look happily.
❺ We had little snow this winter.

오답노트

17. 다음 빈칸에 들어갈 말로 알맞지 <u>않은</u> 것은?

> Jessica is a _____ woman.

❶ politely   ❷ careful   ❸ rude
❹ beautiful   ❺ friendly

오답노트

[18-20] 다음 빈칸에 들어갈 말로 바르게 짝지어진 것은?

18.

> · The rich _____ not always happy.
> · The old often _____ of the past.

❶ is – thought   ❷ was – thinks
❸ is – think   ❹ are – think
❺ are – thinks

오답노트

19.

> · He is a _____ man.
> · _____ bird was caught.

❶ drunk – An alive
❷ drunken – An alive
❸ drunk – A live
❹ drunken – A live
❺ drinking – Living

오답노트

20.

> · Wake up the _____ student.
> · My mom and I are _____ in many ways.

❶ asleep – alike   ❷ asleep – like
❸ sleeping – alike   ❹ sleeping – like
❺ asleep – like

오답노트

21. 다음 우리말을 영어로 바르게 옮긴 것은?

> 오늘 밤 TV에 재미있는 거라도 있니?

❶ Is there interesting on TV tonight?
❷ Is there interesting something on TV tonight?
❸ Is there something interesting on TV tonight?
❹ Is there anything interesting on TV tonight?
❺ Is there interesting anything on TV tonight?

오답노트

22. 다음 문장 중 어법상 어색한 것은?

❶ Something smells good!
❷ He is taking care of sleeping children.
❸ Is there a lot of paper on the desk?
❹ His mistake made his classmates angrily.
❺ I borrowed a few books from the library.

오답노트

23. 빈칸에 알맞은 단어를 쓰시오.

> People who have a lot of money can afford to travel a lot.
> = _____ _____ can afford to travel a lot.

> We should do more for people who don't have enough money.
> = We should do more for _____ _____.

[24-26] 다음 문장을 읽고 현재분사와 과거분사를 사용하여 문장을 완성하시오.

24.
> The movie wasn't as good as we had expected. (disappoint)
> → The movie was _____.
> → We were _____ in the movie.

25.
> Sunny teaches young children. It's a very hard job. (exhaust)
> → Her job is _____.
> → She is often _____.

26.
> It's been raining all day. I hate this weather. (depress)
> → This weather is _____.
> → This weather makes me _____.

27. 다음 밑줄 친 말과 바꾸어 쓸 수 있는 것은?

> There are a number of tigers in this zoo.

❶ few   ❷ a lot   ❸ many
❹ lot of   ❺ much

28. 다음 괄호 안에 들어갈 말로 가장 알맞은 것은?

> Red Devils were very ( ) when the Korean soccer team lost the game.
> *Red Devils: 붉은 악마

❶ happy   ❷ excited
❸ disappointed   ❹ interesting
❺ satisfied

29. 괄호 안에 들어갈 말이 바르게 짝지어진 것은?

> · Are you ( ) in movies?
>   = 너 영화에 관심이 있니?
> · Did you find the experiment ( )?
>   = 너 그 실험이 재미있었니?

❶ interesting − interested
❷ interested − interesting
❸ to interest − interested
❹ interesting − interesting
❺ interested − to interest

A. excite를 이용하여 다음 문장을 완성하시오.

1.

People were so _____.

2.

The soccer game was very _____.

B. 다음 우리말을 영어로 옮긴 문장에서 <u>잘못된</u> 부분을 찾아 바르게 고쳐 쓰시오.

1. Please give me a few orange juice. (저에게 오렌지 주스 좀 주세요.)

→ _____

2. There is new nothing in today's newspaper. (오늘 신문에는 새로운 것이 없다.)

→ _____

3. I saw strange something there. (나는 저기서 무언가 이상한 것을 보았다.)

→ _____

C. 빈칸에 a few, few, a little, little 중 알맞은 것을 써서 문장을 완성하시오.

1. It's raining. There are _____ people in the park now.

2. There's _____ milk in the fridge. I'm going to the shop to get some.

3. Olivia spoke very little Korean before she took _____ courses.

4. I know _____ English. I can understand English people.

실전 서술형 평가문제

정답 p. 4

 출제의도 정보를 이용한 문장 생성 능력
평가내용 some과 any를 구분하여 문장 완성하기

A. 〈보기〉와 같이 주어진 표현과 some과 any를 활용하여 완전한 문장으로 만드시오. (전치사 in 또는 on을 사용할 것)   [서술형 유형 : 10점 / 난이도 : 중]

> | 보 기 | apples / refrigerator → oranges (X) |
> |---|---|
> | | → *There are some apples in the refrigerator but there aren't any oranges.* |

1. bananas / table → milk (X)

→ _____

2. orange juice / refrigerator → yoghurt (X)

→ _____

3. bread / table → sugar (X)

→ _____

4. coffee / cupboard → rice (X)

→ _____

5. tomatoes / refrigerator → carrots (X)

→ _____

실전 서술형 평가문제

출제의도 감각동사 look을 활용하여 묘사하기
평가내용 「look + 형용사」를 이용한 문장 구성

B. 다음 그림을 보고 look을 이용한 완전한 문장으로 묘사하시오.

[서술형 유형 : 6점 / 난이도 : 하]

보기		How does she look in this picture? → *She looks thirsty.*

1.

How does she look in this picture?

→ _____

2.

How do the men look in this picture?

→ _____

3.

How do they look in this picture?

→ _____

출제의도 -ing 또는 -ed로 끝나는 분사의 형용사 역할
평가내용 현재분사 또는 과거분사의 역할 이해

C. 다음 그림을 보고 괄호 안의 단어를 알맞은 형태의 형용사로 고쳐 쓰시오.　　　[서술형 유형 : 16점 / 난이도 : 하]

Jessica is reading a book.
She really likes it. She can't
put it down. She has to keep
reading.

1. Reading the book is really _____. (interest)

2. Jessica is really _____. (interest)

3. Reading the story is _____. (excite)

4. Jessica is _____ about the story. (excite)

5. Jessica is _____ by the characters in the book. (fascinate)

6. The characters in the story are _____. (fascinate)

7. Jessica doesn't like to read books when she is _____ and _____.
(bore / confuse)

8. Jessica didn't finish the last book she started because it was _____ and
_____. (bore / confuse)

실전 서술형 평가문제

정답 p. 4

 출제의도 주어진 정보를 보고 문장 완성하기
평가내용 (a) few / (a) little을 사용하여 문장 완성하기

D. 〈보기〉와 같이 질문에는 many 또는 much를, 대답에는 (a) few, (a) little, any 중 하나를 이용하여 그림을 묘사하시오. [서술형 유형 : 10점 / 난이도 : 하]

보 기	Q : *Is there much butter on the table?* (butter)
	A : No, *there is a little butter.* (on the table)

1. Q : _____ (eggs)

　　A : No, _____ .

2. Q : _____ (coffee)

　　A : No, _____ .

3. Q : _____ (orange juice)

　　A : No, _____ .

4. Q : _____ (cheese)

　　A : No, _____ .

5. Q : _____ (pencils)

　　A : No, _____ .

Chapter 2

부사 (Adverbs)

Unit 01 부사의 형태

1-1 부사 만들기

Basketball players throw the ball **quickly** and **accurately** into the net.
농구선수들은 공을 그물 안으로 빠르고 정확하게 던진다.

01 부사는 대개 형용사에 -ly를 붙여 만든다.

① 대부분의 형용사 : 형용사에 -ly를 붙임	slow 느린 – slowly 느리게 safe 안전한 – safely 안전하게 kind 친절한 – kindly 친절하게 quick 빠른 – quickly 빠르게 beautiful 아름다운 – beautifully 아름답게 sudden 갑작스러운 – suddenly 갑자기 careful 조심스러운 – carefully 조심스럽게
② 「자음 + y」로 끝나는 단어 : -y를 -i로 고치고 -ly를 붙임	easy 쉬운 – easily 쉽게 happy 행복한 – happily 행복하게 angry 화난 – angrily 화나게 lucky 운 좋은 – luckily 운 좋게도 busy 바쁜 – busily 바쁘게 heavy 무거운 – heavily 무겁게
③ -le로 끝나는 단어 : -e를 없애고 -y만 붙임	idle 게으른 – idly 게으르게 terrible 무서운 – terribly 무섭게 simple 간단한 – simply 간단히 visible 눈에 보이는 – visibly 눈에 보이게 reasonable 합리적인 – reasonably 합리적으로 comfortable 편안한 – comfortably 편안하게
④ -ue로 끝나는 단어 : -e를 없애고 -ly를 붙임	true 진실의 – truly 진실로 due 적절한 – duly 적절하게
⑤ -ll로 끝나는 단어 : -y만 붙임	full 충분한 – fully 충분(완전)히 dull (우)둔한 – dully (우)둔하게
⑥ -ic로 끝나는 단어 : -ical로 바꾸고 -ly를 붙임	basic 기초의 – basically 기본적으로 dramatic 극적인 – dramatically 극적으로

정답 p. 5

Challenge 1 다음 단어를 부사로 고쳐 쓰세요.

01. slow → _____   02. quick → _____

03. clear → _____   04. nice → _____

05. safe → _____   06. quiet → _____

07. sincere → _____   08. sudden → _____

09. angry → _____   10. easy → _____

11. happy → _____   12. lucky → _____

13. heavy → _____   14. busy → _____

15. simple → _____   16. terrible → _____

17. idle → _____   18. reasonable → _____

19. visible → _____   20. comfortable → _____

21. true → _____   22. due → _____

23. full → _____   24. dull → _____

25. basic → _____   26. dramatic → _____

Memo

1-2 형용사와 모양이 같은 부사

Jennifer is a **fast** driver. (형용사)
Jennifer는 빠른 운전자이다.

Jennifer drives **fast**. (부사)
Jennifer는 빠르게 운전한다.

01 형용사와 형태가 같은 부사이다. 형태는 같지만 의미와 문장에서의 역할이 다르므로 구분해야 한다.

hard	형 열심인, 힘든	He is a **hard** worker. 그는 열심히 일하는 사람이다.
	부 열심히, 힘들게	He works **hard**. 그는 열심히 일한다.
fast	형 빠른	Mike is a **fast** reader. Mike는 속독가이다.
	부 빠르게, 빨리	Mike reads **fast**. Mike는 책을 빨리 읽는다.
early	형 이른	The **early** bird catches the worm. 일찍 일어나는 새가 먹이(벌레)를 잡는다.
	부 이르게, 일찍	I get up **early** in the morning. 나는 아침에 일찍 일어난다.
late	형 늦은	It was **late** autumn. 늦가을이었다.
	부 늦게	He came five minutes **late**. 그는 5분 늦게 왔다.
high	형 높은	You can see a **high** building on the right. 우측으로 고층 건물을 볼 수 있다.
	부 높게, 높이	The kite flew **high**. 그 연은 높이 날았다.
last	형 마지막인	We missed the **last** bus of the day. 그는 막차를 놓쳤다.
	부 마지막으로	I saw him **last** two years ago. 2년 전에 그를 마지막으로 보았다.
long	형 오래된, 긴	He's been ill for a **long** time. 그는 오랫동안 아팠다.
	부 오래	Everybody wants to live **long**. 누구나 오래 살고 싶어 한다.

※ 형용사 good의 부사는 well(잘, 좋게)이고 반대말은 각각 bad와 badly이다. 참고로, well이 형용사로 쓰이면 '건강한'(in good health)의 뜻이며 이때의 반대말은 ill(아픈)이다.

서술형 기초다지기

Challenge 1 다음 괄호 안의 단어 중에서 알맞은 것을 고르세요.

01. She eats food (quick / quickly).

02. Sunny runs (fast / fastly).

03. He plays the piano (good / well).

04. This homework is (hard / hardly).

05. We arrived at the station (late / lately).

06. They are (happy / happily).

Challenge 2 다음 부사의 형용사 형태를 쓰세요.

01. late (늦게) → _____ (늦은)

02. long (길게) → _____ (긴)

03. well (잘) → _____ (좋은)

04. fast (빠르게) → _____ (빠른)

05. high (높게) → _____ (높은)

06. early (일찍) → _____ (이른)

07. hard (열심히) → _____ (어려운)

08. last (마지막으로) → _____ (마지막인)

Challenge 3 다음 빈칸에 공통으로 들어갈 단어를 찾아 쓰세요.

hard	fast	high	last

01. Laura runs very _____ . She is a _____ runner.

02. It's almost time for the _____ subway. When did you see your son _____ ?

03. The mountain is _____ and steep. She's aiming _____ in her exams.

04. Mike had a _____ day. Don't hit it so _____ .

1-3 -ly가 붙으면 의미가 달라지는 부사

They arrived in the meeting late.
그들은 회의에 늦게 도착했다.

Have you seen any movies lately?
최근에 영화 본 적 있니?

01 형용사에 -ly를 붙여 형용사와 모양이 비슷하지만 완전히 뜻이 달라지는 부사가 있다. 부사로 쓰인 hard는 '열심히'라는 의미이지만 -ly를 붙여서 만든 부사 hardly는 '거의 ~ 않는'이라는 다른 의미의 부사가 된다.

hard	㈜ 열심히, 힘들게	She studied **hard** for the final exam. 그녀는 기말시험을 위해 열심히 공부했다.
hardly	㈜ 거의 ~ 않는	I can **hardly** believe what you said. 나는 네가 말한 것을 좀처럼 믿을 수 없다.
late	㈜ 늦게	She has to study **late** tonight. 그녀는 오늘밤 늦게까지 공부해야 한다.
lately	㈜ 최근에	**Lately** I've lost my appetite. 최근에 나는 식욕을 잃었다.
close	㈜ 가까이	A ghost came **close** to me. 귀신이 나에게 가까이 다가왔다.
closely	㈜ 주의깊게, 면밀히	The professor read my report **closely**. 교수님은 나의 리포트를 면밀히 읽었다.
high	㈜ 높이, 높게	The frog jumped **high** from the ground. 개구리는 땅에서 높이 뛰었다.
highly	㈜ 높이 평가하여, 매우	Mr. James was a **highly** successful salesman. James 씨는 매우 성공한 영업사원이었다.
near	㈜ 가까이	The summer vacation is drawing **near**. 여름방학이 다가오고 있다.
nearly	㈜ 거의	It took **nearly** two hours to get here. 여기까지 오는 데 거의 두 시간이 걸렸다.

서술형 기초다지기

정답 p. 5

Challenge 1　다음 문장에서 밑줄 친 단어의 품사와 뜻을 쓰세요.

01. Michael was a <u>highly</u> successful businessman.　　품사 : _____　뜻 : _____

02. This homework is <u>hard</u>.　　품사 : _____　뜻 : _____

03. She married in her <u>late</u> thirties.　　품사 : _____　뜻 : _____

04. We arrived at the airport <u>late</u>.　　품사 : _____　뜻 : _____

05. <u>High</u> cholesterol is a cause of heart attacks.　　품사 : _____　뜻 : _____

06. We <u>hardly</u> see each other these days.　　품사 : _____　뜻 : _____

Challenge 2　다음 문장의 빈칸에 들어갈 알맞은 부사를 괄호 안에서 골라 쓰세요.

01. He works _____ to get promoted. (hard / hardly)

02. There was such a crowd that we could _____ move. (hard / hardly)

03. He is _____ respected by his pupils. (high / highly)

04. There are many _____ buildings in Seoul. (high / highly)

05. It's already 2 o'clock. You are _____ again. (late / lately)

06. Have you heard from your sister _____? (late / lately)

07. The day when we start for our journey is drawing _____. (near / nearly)

08. She _____ fell over the cliff. (near / nearly)

Unit 02 다양한 부사의 활용

2-1 부사의 위치

She is **really** beautiful.
그녀는 정말로 아름답다.

They are **always** on time. 그들은 항상 제시간에 도착한다.
They **always** catches their train at 7 a.m.
그들은 항상 오전 7시 열차를 탄다.

---

01 부사의 기본 위치

① 목적어가 없는 자동사 뒤

Kevin will arrive **soon**. Kevin은 곧 도착할 것이다. ▶ 자동사 arrive 수식

She goes to school **early**. 그녀는 학교에 일찍 간다.

② 타동사의 목적어 뒤

She plays the violin **well**. 그녀는 바이올린 연주를 잘한다.

③ 형용사나 부사 앞

I feel **really** happy, but I don't know why. 정말 행복하게 느끼지만 왜 그런지는 모르겠다. ▶ 형용사 happy 수식

He disappeared **very** quickly. 그는 매우 빨리 사라졌다. ▶ 부사 quickly 수식

④ 문장 맨 앞

Suddenly, the old man fell to the ground. 갑자기 노인이 넘어졌다. ▶ 문장 전체 수식

---

02 **빈도부사는 일반동사 앞 또는 be동사나 조동사 뒤에 쓴다.** 빈도부사의 빈도 정도에 따라 아래와 같이 분류할 수 있다.

always	–	usually	–	often	–	sometimes	–	seldom	–	rarely	–	never
(항상)		(주로)		(자주, 종종)		(가끔, 때때로)		(거의 ~아닌)		(거의 ~않는)		(결코 ~않는)

100% ←――――――――――――――――― 50% ―――――――――――――――――→ 0%

---

03 **부정문에서 빈도부사는 부정형 동사 앞에 쓰고 (단, always는 부정형 동사 뒤) 의문문에서는 항상 주어 뒤에 쓴다.**

Kelly **sometimes** doesn't eat breakfast. Kelly는 가끔 아침을 먹지 않는다.

Does Kelly **usually** eat breakfast? Kelly는 주로 아침을 먹니?

Sunny doesn't **always** read the newspaper. Sunny는 신문을 항상 읽지는 않는다.

서술형 기초다지기

Challenge 1 다음 괄호 안의 부사가 들어갈 알맞은 곳을 찾아 다시 써 보세요.

01. The bus was dirty. (really)

→ _____

02. He is running fast. (very)

→ _____

03. My mother drives her car. (carefully)

→ _____

Challenge 2 다음 괄호 안의 빈도부사를 알맞은 곳에 넣어 문장을 다시 쓰세요.

01. Peter comes to work on time. (always)

→ _____

02. She doesn't work on Saturday. (usually)

→ _____

03. Jane goes to a rock concert. (seldom)

→ _____

04. I'm happy to be with you. (always)

→ _____

05. You must memorize English words. (often)

→ _____

06. Is she late for work? (sometimes)

→ _____

07. Do you drink tea with dinner? (often)

→ _____

08. Maria doesn't watch TV. (always)

→ _____

2-2 very, much, too, either

It's **very** cold today. 오늘 매우 춥다.
It's **too** cold for a picnic. 소풍을 가기에는 너무 춥다.

01 부사 very와 too는 모두 형용사 앞에 써서 '너무[아주] ~한'의 뜻이다. 뜻은 같지만 **very**는 '**어려움이나 문제가 있지만 가능하다**'인 반면, **too**는 '**어려움이나 문제가 있어 불가능하다**'라는 부정의 의미를 담고 있다.

The shoes are **too** big for her. 그 신발은 그녀에게 너무 크다. (She cannot put them on.)
Lucy is **too** young to drive. Lucy는 운전하기에 너무 어리다. (She cannot drive.)
This chair is **very** heavy, but she can carry it. 이 의자는 아주 무겁지만, 그녀가 옮길 수 있다.

02 **too가 긍정문의 맨 끝에 올 경우에는** '역시, 또한'이라는 **동의의 의미**이다. 부정문에는 too 대신 either를 쓴다.

She likes horror movies. I like horror movies, **too**. 그녀는 공포 영화를 좋아한다. 나 역시 공포 영화를 좋아한다.
I didn't see the accident. He didn't, **either**. 나는 그 사고를 보지 못했다. 그도 보지 못했다.

A: I don't eat spicy food. 나는 매운 음식을 먹지 않는다.
B: Me, **neither**. 나도 마찬가지야.

※ neither는 not ~ either를 줄인 표현

03 very와 much의 차이

very	much
형용사/부사의 원급을 수식하여 '매우'의 의미	형용사/부사의 비교급을 수식하여 '훨씬'의 의미

That story was **very** exciting. 그 이야기는 매우 흥미진진했다. ▶ 형용사 원급 exciting을 수식
She speaks English **very** well. 그녀는 영어를 매우 잘한다. ▶ 부사의 원급 well을 수식

This box is **much** heavier than that one. 이 상자가 저 상자보다 훨씬 더 무겁다. ▶ 형용사의 비교급 heavier를 수식
The cheetah run **much** faster than the tiger. 치타가 호랑이보다 훨씬 더 빠르다. ▶ 부사의 비교급 faster를 수식

It is **pretty** cold. 꽤 추운 날씨이다.
※ pretty는 보통 긍정문에서 형용사와 다른 부사를 수식하여 '꽤, 상당히, 매우'의 의미이다.

44

서술형 기초다지기

정답 p. 5

Challenge 1 다음 상황에 맞게 빈칸에 very 또는 too를 쓰세요.

01. The suitcase is _____ heavy, but she can lift it.

02. The suitcase is _____ heavy. She can't lift it.

03. The jeans are _____ tight, but she can wear them.

04. The shoes are _____ big. He can't wear them.

Challenge 2 다음 빈칸에 too, either, neither 중 알맞은 것을 써 넣으세요.

01. A: We need pencils.   B: We need paper, _____.

02. A: I can speak English very well.   B: Me, _____.

03. If you don't want to go, I won't, _____.

04. He can swim well and I can, _____.

05. A: Bob doesn't have any brothers.   B: I don't have any, _____.

06. A: I am not watching TV.   B: Me, _____.

Challenge 3 다음 빈칸에 very와 much 중 알맞은 것을 골라 쓰세요.

01. The dress is _____ beautiful. I'll buy it.

02. Your watch is _____ better than mine.

03. I am _____ interested in a detective story.

04. Today is _____ colder than yesterday.

05. People in this village are _____ friendly.

2-3 already, yet, still / too many, too much

I've **already** finished my homework.
나는 이미 숙제를 끝냈다.

There is **too much** noise.
너무 시끄럽다.

01 already, yet, still

already	긍정문 – 이미 He has **already** started. 그는 이미 출발했다. 의문문 – 벌써(놀라움) Has she come **already**? 그녀가 벌써 왔다구?
yet	부정문 – 아직 Haven't you finished it **yet**? 그것을 아직 못 끝냈니? 의문문 – 벌써, 이미, 이제 Have you seen the movie **yet**? 벌써 그 영화를 봤니? ※ 주로 문장 끝에 쓰임
still	긍정/부정/의문문 – 여전히, 아직도 She is **still** angry. 그녀는 아직도 화가 나 있다. I **still** can't buy the house. 나는 여전히 그 집을 살 수 없다. Do you **still** have her phone number? 너는 아직도 그녀의 전화번호를 가지고 있니?

02 too many와 too much는 **지나치게 많은 수나 양**을 나타내며, **too many 뒤에는 셀 수 있는 명사**가 오고 **too much 뒤에는 셀 수 없는 명사**가 온다.

There were **too many** guests and **too much** food. 너무 많은 손님들과 음식이 있었다.

There's **too much** smoke in here. I can't breathe. 여기에 연기가 너무 많아. 나는 숨을 쉴 수가 없다.

There are **too many** students in the library. 도서관에 너무 많은 학생들이 있다.

서술형 기초다지기

Challenge 1   다음 빈칸에 already, yet, still 중 알맞은 것을 쓰세요.

01. You don't have to do it. I've _____ done it.

02. I've had no time. I haven't done it _____.

03. Don't wake him. He's _____ asleep.

04. I've _____ told you what to do. Listen carefully this time.

05. The plane has _____ arrived. It was really early.

06. We broke up six months ago but I _____ miss her.

07. Are you _____ working for the same company?

08. I bought it seven years ago and I haven't had any problems _____.

09. I'm feeling lazy. I'm _____ in bed.

Challenge 2   다음 괄호 안의 단어 중에서 알맞은 것을 고르세요.

01. There are (too many / too much) people here.

02. Kathy drinks (too many / too much) milk.

03. (There is / There are) too much pollution.

04. Lisa buys (too many / too much) books.

2-4 주의해야 할 부사의 위치

She **put** her hat **on**. (O) 그녀는 모자를 썼다.
She **put on** her hat. (O)

She **put** it **on**. (O) 그녀는 그것을(모자를) 썼다.
She **put on** it. (X)

01 「동사 + 부사」로 이루어진 동사구에는 목적어가 반드시 필요한데, **목적어가 '명사'일 때는 부사 뒤에 쓰거나 동사와 부사 사이에 쓸 수 있다.**

I **turned on** the radio. (O) 나는 라디오를 켰다.
I **turned** the radio **on**. (O)

02 **목적어가 '대명사'일 때는 반드시 동사와 부사 사이에 쓴다.** 즉, 「동사＋목적어＋부사」의 어순으로만 쓴다.

She picked up the pencil. 그녀는 연필을 집었다.
→ She **picked** it **up**. (O)
→ She **picked up** it. (X)

03 일반적으로 부사가 형용사나 다른 부사를 수식할 때는 수식하는 형용사나 부사 앞에 온다. 그러나 **enough**가 부사로 쓰일 때는 수식하는 **형용사나 부사 뒤**에 위치한다.

This classroom is big **enough** to accommodate 50 students.

이 교실은 50명의 학생을 수용할 정도로 크다. ▶ 부사 enough가 형용사(big)를 뒤에서 수식

He is old **enough** to go to school. 그는 학교에 갈 정도로 나이가 들었다. ▶ 부사 enough가 형용사(old)를 뒤에서 수식

※ euough가 형용사로 명사를 수식할 때는 보통 형용사와 마찬가지로 명사 앞에서 수식한다.

I have **enough** money to buy a bicycle. 나는 자전거를 살 충분한 돈을 가지고 있다.
▶ 형용사 enough가 명사(money)를 앞에서 수식

48

서술형 기초다지기

정답 p. 6

Challenge 1   다음 괄호 안의 주어진 단어를 어순에 맞게 쓰세요.

01. I'll _____ at the airport at 7.
    (up / pick / you)

02. My mom asked me to _____, so I put them on.
    (the trousers / on / put)

03. Kevin _____ in the room.
    (off / it / took)

04. She _____ on the floor.
    (a coin / up / picked)

05. I turned the air-conditioner off, but soon I had to _____ again.
    (it / on / turn)

06. When my hair caught on fire, my friend _____ immediately.
    (it / out / put)

07. _____ if you feel cold.
    (your sweater / on / put)

Challenge 2   다음 괄호 안의 단어 중에서 알맞은 것을 고르세요.

01. The soup is too warm. It is not (enough cool / cool enough).

02. Have you got (time enough / enough time) to go to the movie theater?

03. The little boy is not (enough old / old enough) to walk.

04. I can't buy a car. I haven't got (enough money / money enough).

05. The table is too small. It is not (enough big / big enough).

06. Have you got (eggs enough / enough eggs) to make an omelette?

2-5 의문부사

When do you go to school? 너는 언제 학교에 가니?
(= **What time** do you go to school?)
- At 8 o'clock. (= I go to school at 8 o'clock.) 8시에 학교 가.

01 **When** : 궁금한 것이 **'언제 /때(시간)'**일 때 when을 사용한다. what time도 같은 뜻이다.

A : **When** do you go to bed? 넌 언제 잠을 자니?
B : I go to bed at 11:00. 11시에 자.

02 **Where** : 궁금한 것이 **'장소'** 또는 **'위치'**일 때 where를 사용한다.

A : **Where** did you buy your iPhone? 넌 아이폰을 어디에서 샀니?
B : I bought it at a department store. 백화점에서 샀어.

03 **Why** : 궁금한 것이 **'왜?'**라는 이유나 원인인 경우에 why를 쓴다.

A : **Why** did you break the window? 넌 왜 그 창문을 깼니?
B : (Because) I didn't have the key. 열쇠가 없었기 때문이야.

04 **How** : 궁금한 것이 **'어떻게'**라는 방법인 경우에는 how를 쓴다.

A : **How** do I carry this big box? 어떻게 내가 이 큰 상자를 옮기지?
B : I will help you. 내가 너를 도와줄게.

05 How는 아래와 같이 수량, 길이, 횟수, 크기 등을 나타내는 형용사나 부사와 결합하여 '얼마나 ~한가?'라고 정도를 물어볼 수 있다.

How many + 셀 수 있는 명사 ~? 얼마나 많은지	**How many** books do you have? 넌 얼마나 많은 책을 가지고 있니?
How much + 셀 수 없는 명사 ~? 얼마나 많은지	**How much** milk do you drink? 넌 얼마나 많은 우유를 마시니?
How long ~? 얼마나 긴(오래)	**How long** is the fish? 그 물고기는 길이가 얼마나 되니?
How far ~? 얼마나 멀리	**How far** is it from here to the post office? 여기서 우체국까지 거리가 얼마나 되니?
How often ~? 얼마나 자주(횟수, 빈도)	**How often** do you go shopping? 얼마나 자주 쇼핑하니?
How old ~? 얼마나 나이 든, 얼마나 오래된	**How old** is she? 그녀는 몇 살이니?
How tall ~? 얼마나 높은, 얼마나 큰	**How tall** is he? 그는 키가 얼마니?

서술형 기초다지기

Challenge 1 다음 의문부사를 이용하여 의문문으로 바꿔 쓰세요.

01. He teaches music to his students. (how)

→ _____

02. Jessica and Scott learn Korean. (why)

→ _____

03. Your mom washes the dishes. (where)

→ _____

04. She takes a walk. (when)

→ _____

Challenge 2 B의 대답에 상응하는 A의 질문으로 알맞은 것을 골라 쓰세요.

· How often do you use your car?　　　· How old is your father?

· How tall are you?　　　· How high is Mt. Everest?

· How far is it from here to the airport?

---

01. A: _____ B: I'm 180 centimeters tall.

02. A: _____ B: 3 times a week.

03. A: _____ B: He's 45 years old.

04. A: _____ B: About 17 kilometers.

05. A: _____ B: Almost 9,000 meters.

이것이 시험에 출제되는 영문법이다!

01 출제 100% - 빈도부사의 위치를 묻는 문제는 반드시 출제된다.

 출제자의 눈 빈도부사의 위치는 조동사나 be동사 뒤 또는 일반동사 앞이다. 부정문에서 빈도부사는 부정형 동사 앞에 쓰고(단, always는 부정형 동사 뒤) 의문문에서는 항상 주어 뒤에 쓴다. 어순을 물어보거나 빈도부사를 이용한 간단한 영작 문제가 서술형으로 출제될 수 있다.

> **Ex 1.**
>
> 빈도부사의 위치가 <u>틀린</u> 것은?
>
> (a) You sleep sometimes in class.　　(b) I am never late for class.
>
> (c) He usually plays soccer after school.　　(d) It is often hot.
>
> (e) He will never meet her again.

02 출제 100% - too와 either를 반드시 구별하라!

출제자의 눈 문장 맨 끝에서 '역시, 또한'의 의미로 긍정문에는 too를 쓰고, 부정문에서는 either를 쓴다. 줄여서 Me, too와 Me, neither를 쓰는 것도 암기해 두어야 한다.

> **Ex 2.**
>
> A: I haven't been to the United States.
>
> B: I haven't, _____.
>
> (a) too　　　　(b) neither　　　　(c) very　　　　(d) either

> **Ex 3.**
>
> A: I like the decor and atmospheres.
>
> B: And I do, _____.
>
> (a) so　　　　(b) too　　　　(c) such　　　　(d) either

> **Ex 4.**
>
> A: Have you ever been to Tokyo?
>
> B: No, I haven't. Have you?
>
> A: _____.
>
> (a) Me, too　　(b) I haven't, too　　(c) Me, neither　　(d) I am, too

03 출제 100 % - 목적어가 대명사일 때 어순에 주의하라.

 출제자의 눈 put on, put off, turn on처럼 「동사 + 부사」로 이루어진 동사구의 경우 목적어가 대명사일 때는 반드시 「동사 + 대명사 + 부사」의 어순으로 써야 한다. (영어에서는 중요한 정보를 뒤에 두는 것이 일반적이므로, 이미 알고 있는 정보인 대명사를 뒤에 두어 강조할 필요가 없기 때문이다.) 이러한 어순을 물어보는 문제가 수능에서도 출제되었고, 내신에서도 반드시 출제된다.

Ex 5.

어법상 <u>어색한</u> 곳을 골라 고쳐 쓰시오.
A: Please turn off the coffee maker before you leave.
B: I've already turned off it.

_____ → _____

04 출제 100 % - very와 much를 구별하라!

출제자의 눈 very는 (형용사나 부사의) 원급과 현재분사를 수식할 수 있고, much는 비교급과 과거분사를 수식할 수 있다.

Ex 6.

I like tea _____ better than coffee.
(a) very　　　　　(b) too　　　　　(c) much　　　　　(d) more

Ex 7.

A: Did you enjoy the movie?
B: No. It was _____ boring.
(a) much　　　　　(b) very　　　　　(c) too　　　　　(d) either

1. 다음 밑줄 친 단어의 쓰임이 나머지 넷과 다른 것은?

   ❶ This computer is pretty fast.
   ❷ It's already pretty dark.
   ❸ Jennifer is wearing a pretty dress.
   ❹ The basketball player is pretty tall.
   ❺ That house is pretty big.

2. 다음 중 밑줄 친 단어의 쓰임이 바른 것은?

   ❶ 나도 마늘을 좋아하지 않아.
     = I don't like garlic, too.
   ❷ 저 연 좀 봐. 높이 날아가고 있어.
     = Look at the kite. It is flying high.
   ❸ 그는 버스를 놓쳤기 때문에 늦게 왔다.
     = He came lately because he missed the bus.
   ❹ 기차가 20분 늦게 도착했다.
     = The train arrived 20 minutes lately.
   ❺ 나는 저녁 식사 후에 TV를 거의 보지 않아.
     = I hard ever watch TV after dinner.

3. 다음 밑줄 친 단어의 위치가 어색한 것은?

   ❶ In my house I never watch TV.
   ❷ A bookstore usually sells books.
   ❸ I sometimes ride a bicycle.
   ❹ We often find bottles by the sea.
   ❺ John always is early for school.

4. 다음 밑줄 친 단어의 쓰임이 어색한 것은?

   ❶ Isn't she friendly?
   ❷ Don't treat him so badly.
   ❸ The prince and the princess lived happily ever after.
   ❹ She is nearly as tall as her mother.
   ❺ We play usually baseball on weekends.

5. 다음 도서관과 박물관 방문 빈도표를 보고 내용과 일치하는 것을 고르면?

	library	museum
Sunny	∨∨	∨∨
Lisa	∨	∨∨
Jim	∨∨∨	∨

   (∨ : seldom, ∨∨ : sometimes, ∨∨∨ : often)

   ❶ Sunny seldom goes to the library and sometimes goes to the museum.
   ❷ Lisa often goes to the library.
   ❸ Jim sometimes goes to the museum.
   ❹ Sunny sometimes goes to the library and the museum.
   ❺ Jim seldom goes to the library.

6. 다음 문장의 밑줄 친 much와 의미가 다른 것은?

   Kathy studies much harder than anyone else.

   ❶ My mom gets up much earlier than anyone of us.
   ❷ Tom is much shorter than me.
   ❸ We enjoyed the party very much.
   ❹ My new apartment is much closer to my work than my old one.
   ❺ We found the house much smaller than we imagined.

7. 다음 대화의 빈칸에 들어갈 말로 알맞은 것은?

   A : Can you speak Korean?
   B : No, I can't. How about you?
   A : _____. But I'm going to take a Korean class this summer vacation.

   ❶ I don't, too   ❷ Me, too
   ❸ Me, either   ❹ Me, neither
   ❺ I can, either

오답 노트 만들기

※ 틀린 문제에는 빨간색으로 V표시를 한다.
※ 두세 번 정도 반복해서 복습하고 완전히 알 때에만 O표를 한다.

★틀린 문제 : _____ ★다시 공부한 날 : _____

(1) 문제를 왜? 틀렸는지 곰곰이 생각하고 그 이유를 적어본다.

(2) 핵심 개념을 적는다.

(3) 자신이 몰랐던 단어와 숙어 표현이 있으면 정리한다.

(4) 해설집에서 필요한 부분을 골라 풀이 해법을 정리한다.

★틀린 문제 : _____ ★다시 공부한 날 : _____

(1) 문제를 왜? 틀렸는지 곰곰이 생각하고 그 이유를 적어본다.

(2) 핵심 개념을 적는다.

(3) 자신이 몰랐던 단어와 숙어 표현이 있으면 정리한다.

(4) 해설집에서 필요한 부분을 골라 풀이 해법을 정리한다.

★틀린 문제 : _____ ★다시 공부한 날 : _____

(1) 문제를 왜? 틀렸는지 곰곰이 생각하고 그 이유를 적어본다.

(2) 핵심 개념을 적는다.

(3) 자신이 몰랐던 단어와 숙어 표현이 있으면 정리한다.

(4) 해설집에서 필요한 부분을 골라 풀이 해법을 정리한다.

★틀린 문제 : _____ ★다시 공부한 날 : _____

(1) 문제를 왜? 틀렸는지 곰곰이 생각하고 그 이유를 적어본다.

(2) 핵심 개념을 적는다.

(3) 자신이 몰랐던 단어와 숙어 표현이 있으면 정리한다.

(4) 해설집에서 필요한 부분을 골라 풀이 해법을 정리한다.

1. 다음 중 always가 들어갈 위치로 적절한 곳은?

> Bob ❶ eats ❷ oranges ❸ for ❹ dessert,
> ❺ but this evening he's eating apples.

오답노트

2. 다음 대화의 빈칸에 들어갈 말로 알맞은 것은?

> A: I haven't been to the zoo for a long
>   time.
> B: I haven't, _____. (나도 그래.)

❶ also ❷ too ❸ either
❹ often ❺ neither

오답노트

3. 다음 중 형용사와 부사의 연결이 바르지 <u>않는</u> 것은?

❶ good − well
❷ polite − politely
❸ reasonable − reasonably
❹ hard − hardly
❺ happy − happily

오답노트

4. 다음 빈칸에 들어갈 말로 알맞지 <u>않은</u> 것은?

> She spoke _____.

❶ more slowly ❷ quietly
❸ fast ❹ very loudly
❺ good

오답노트

5. 다음 빈칸에 들어갈 말로 알맞은 것은?

> A: Scott hasn't been to London. How
>   about Kathy?
> B: She has never been there, _____.

❶ too ❷ either ❸ often
❹ neither ❺ yet

오답노트

6. 다음 빈칸에 들어갈 말로 알맞은 것은?

> A: _____ much milk do you want in
>   your coffee?
> B: I'll have black coffee.

❶ When ❷ How ❸ Why
❹ Where ❺ How far

오답노트

7. 우리말과 같은 뜻이 되도록 주어진 단어들을 바르게 배열하시오.

> 그녀는 언제나 회의에 늦는다.
>
> = _____
>
> (meeting / always / is / for / the / she / late)

오답노트

10. 다음 빈칸에 들어갈 말로 알맞은 것은?

> A: _____ did you get to the airport?
> B: I went there by bus.

❶ Who   ❷ When
❸ Where   ❹ What
❺ How

오답노트

[8-9] 다음 빈칸에 들어갈 말이 바르게 짝지어진 것은?

8.

> · I haven't stopped smoking _____.
> · Have you seen the movie _____?

❶ yet − still   ❷ still − yet
❸ yet − yet   ❹ already − ago
❺ already − already

오답노트

11. 다음 빈칸에 쓸 수 없는 것은?

> The first movie was _____ funnier than the sequel.

❶ much   ❷ even   ❸ far
❹ still   ❺ very

오답노트

9.

> · He is not a dentist and I'm not, _____.
> · You have to listen to them _____ carefully.

❶ too − very   ❷ either − much
❸ neither − very   ❹ too − much
❺ either − very

오답노트

12. 다음 문장 중 어법상 어색한 것은?

❶ I never swim after a big meal.
❷ She always will love you.
❸ I often tell funny stories.
❹ It will sometimes rain this summer.
❺ I'm never late.

오답노트

[13-16] 두 문장이 같은 뜻이 되도록 빈칸에 알맞은 말을 쓰시오.

13. He is a good swimmer.

= He swims _____.

14. Lisa is a fast learner.

= Lisa learns _____.

15. We're careful examiners.

= We examine _____.

16. He's a slow worker.

= He works _____.

오답노트

17. 다음 빈칸에 들어갈 말로 알맞은 것은?

A: How _____ do you have your hair cut?

B: About once a month.

❶ many   ❷ long   ❸ far
❹ often   ❺ usually

오답노트

18. 다음 괄호 안의 단어를 사용하여 질문에 대한 대답을 쓰시오.

A: Why didn't you come to the party?

B: Because _____.

                   (sick)

오답노트

19. 다음 빈칸에 공통으로 들어갈 말은?

· The shoes are _____ big. He can't wear them.

· He will help us, and Peter will, _____.

❶ so   ❷ too   ❸ either
❹ much   ❺ also

오답노트

20. 다음 괄호 안에 들어갈 말로 알맞은 것은?

Laura _____ the comic books.

❶ does not always read
❷ does not read always
❸ always read does not
❹ read always does not
❺ does always not read

오답노트

21. 다음 중 어법상 옳지 <u>않은</u> 것은?

❶ I picked the bread up at once, but it was dirty.
❷ I picked up the bread at once, but it was dirty.
❸ I picked it up at once, but it was dirty.
❹ I picked up it at once, but it was dirty.
❺ I picked them up at once, but they were dirty.

오답노트

22. 다음 빈칸에 알맞은 말을 쓰시오.

> The park was so noisy that I couldn't rest.
>
> = The park was _____ noisy for me to rest.

23. 다음은 Alaska의 날씨 빈도를 나타낸 것이다. 표를 보고 빈칸에 알맞은 말을 고르면?

rain	snow	cold	hot
∨	∨∨	∨∨∨	X

(∨: sometimes, ∨∨: often, ∨∨∨: always, X: never)

> · In Alaska, it _____ rains and it _____ snows.
> · It is _____ cold but it is _____ hot.

❶ often − sometimes − always − never
❷ always − often − sometimes − never
❸ sometimes − often − always − never
❹ never − sometimes − often − always
❺ sometimes − always − often − never

24. 다음 괄호 안의 단어를 알맞게 배열하시오.

> He is such a tall man that he can reach the ceiling.
>
> = He is _____ the ceiling. (reach / enough / to / tall)

25. 다음 빈칸에 들어갈 알맞은 단어를 순서대로 나열한 것은?

> · I have _____ done all the reading.
> · Kevin hasn't come to class _____.
> · We lived in Seoul ten years _____.
> · Her daughter _____ lives in the United States.

❶ already − ago − yet− still
❷ already − yet − ago − still
❸ yet − already − ago − still
❹ yet − still − ago − already
❺ ago − still − already − yet

26. 다음 빈칸에 공통으로 들어갈 말을 쓰시오.

> · Hercules is _____ stronger than Zeus.
> · He is _____ interested in studying English.

A. 다음 빈칸에 알맞은 형용사를 찾아 부사형과 함께 문장을 완성하시오.

happy	fast	noisy	good

1.

Jason is a _____ dancer. He dances very _____.

2.

The children are very _____. They play _____.

3.

Laura is a _____ runner. She runs _____.

4.

Tina and Karen are _____ girls. They always smile _____.

B. 다음은 하루 일과를 나타낸 것이다. 빈도부사를 이용하여 자신의 일과를 써 보시오.

1. I get up early in the morning.

→ _____

2. I walk to school.

→ _____

3. I watch TV.

→ _____

4. I go to bed after doing my homework.

→ _____

실전 서술형 평가문제

정답 p. 7

 출제의도 정보를 이용한 문장 생성
평가내용 빈도부사를 활용하여 문장 완성하기

A. 다음은 Nancy가 얼마나 자주 무엇을 하는지를 나타낸 표이다. 주어진 표를 참고하여 빈도부사를 넣어 문장을 서술하시오.

[서술형 유형 : 8점 / 난이도 : 중하]

	always	usually	often	sometimes	seldom
eat hamburgers for breakfast					∨
meet friends				∨	
listen to music		∨			
go to the Internet cafe	∨				
go shopping with her mother			∨		

보기	*Nancy always goes to the Internet cafe.*

1. _____

2. _____ _____

3. _____

4. _____

실전 서술형 평가문제

출제의도 주어진 정보의 활용
평가내용 의문부사의 활용과 부사, 빈도부사를 이용한 문장 완성하기

B. 다음 글을 읽고 주어진 단어를 이용하여 질문을 만들고 그 질문에 해당하는 대답을 찾아 서술하시오.

[서술형 유형 : 10점 / 난이도 : 중]

 Laura is a very careful person. She goes to work on time. She sometimes takes a subway. She works hard at home and at work. She drives her car very carefully. She doesn't drive very fast, and she stops at all the red lights. But, on her way home yesterday evening, she drove badly and almost had an accident.

보기	What kind / of person / Laura / ?
	Q : *What kind of person is Laura?* A : *She is a very careful person.*

1. she / work / hard / ?

Q : _____ A : _____

2. she / usually / drive / how / ?

Q : _____ A : _____

3. she / take a subway / how often / ?

Q : _____ A : _____

4. How / she / drive / yesterday evening / ?

Q : _____ A : _____

5. she / had an accident / ?

Q : _____ A : _____

출제의도 부사 too의 이해
평가내용 실생활에서의 too의 정확한 의미와 활용

C. 「too + 형용사」 구문을 이용하여 〈보기〉와 같이 문장을 영작하시오.   [서술형 유형 : 6점 / 난이도 : 중하]

| 보기 | 
(heavy) | Why can't she lift the box?
→ *She can't lift it because it is too heavy.* |

1.
(big)

Why can't she wear the hat?

→ _____

2.
(sleepy)

Why can't she finish her homework?

→ _____

3.
(hot)

Why can't she eat the pizza?

→ _____

서술형 평가문제	채 점 기 준	배 점	나의 점수
A		2점×4문항=8점	
B	표현이 올바르고 문법, 철자가 모두 정확한 경우	2점×5문항=10점	
C		2점×3문항=6점	
D		2점×4문항=8점	
공통	문법(빈도부사의 위치, 시제 등), 철자가 1개씩 틀린 경우	각 문항당 1점씩 감점	
	내용과 전혀 일치하지 않거나 답을 기재하지 못한 경우	0점	

실전 서술형 평가문제

출제의도 빈도부사의 이해
평가내용 실생활에서의 빈도부사의 쓰임과 문장 완성하기

D. 빈도부사를 이용하여 다음 질문에 답하시오.

[서술형 유형 : 8점 / 난이도 : 중하]

1.

0%(never)

2.

100%(always)

3.

about 50%(sometimes)

4.

about 90%(usually)

1. How often does your mother wash clothes by hand?

   → _____

2. How often does Kelly drink milk?

   → _____

3. How often do they go shopping on Sunday?

   → _____

4. How often does Susan take the school bus?

   → _____

Chapter 3

비교급과 최상급
(Comparatives and Superlatives)

Unit 01 비교급, 최상급 만들기

1-1 비교급 만드는 방법

Jason is tall. Jason은 키가 크다.
Jason is taller than Lucy.
Jason은 Lucy보다 키가 더 크다.

Health is important. 건강은 중요하다.
Health is more important than money.
건강은 돈보다 더 중요하다.

---

01 형용사나 부사의 음절이 **1음절이면 -er**을 붙인다. **-e로 끝나는 경우 -r**만 붙이면 된다.

old – old**er** than	tall – tall**er** than	cheap – cheap**er** than
short – short**er** than	high – high**er** than	kind – kind**er** than
wise – wis**er** than	nice – nic**er** than	large – larg**er** than

---

02 단어가 **-y로 끝나면 -y를 - i로 바꾸고 -er**을 붙인다.

easy – eas**ier** than	pretty – prett**ier** than	happy – happ**ier** than
heavy – heav**ier** than	healthy – health**ier** than	early – earl**ier** than

---

03 1음절 단어의 경우 「단모음 + 단자음」으로 끝날 때 **맨 끝에 자음을 한 번 더 쓰고 -er**을 붙인다.

hot – hot**ter** than	fat – fat**ter** than
thin – thin**ner** than	big – big**ger** than

---

04 **2음절 이상의 형용사는 more를 형용사 앞에 쓴다.**(단, -y로 끝나는 2음절 형용사는 제외.) 분사 형태의 형용사에도 more를 붙여 비교급을 만든다.

famous – **more** famous than	difficult – **more** difficult than
interesting – **more** interesting than	boring – **more** boring than
shocking – **more** shocking than	expensive – **more** expensive than

---

05 **-ly로 끝나는 부사 앞에는 more를 붙인다.**(단, early는 예외: early – earlier)

slowly – **more** slowly than	quickly – **more** quickly than
beautifully – **more** beautifully than	easily – **more** easily than
fluently – **more** fluently than	

서술형 기초다지기

정답 p. 8

Challenge 1 다음 단어의 비교급을 써 보세요. (than도 붙일 것)

01. young   – _____
02. long   – _____
03. tall   – _____
04. large   – _____
05. warm   – _____
06. smart   – _____
07. small   – _____
08. fast   – _____
09. fresh   – _____
10. old   – _____

Challenge 2 다음 단어의 비교급을 써 보세요. (than도 붙일 것)

01. easy   – _____
02. pretty – _____
03. big   – _____
04. busy   – _____
05. hot   – _____
06. healthy – _____
07. heavy   – _____
08. thin   – _____
09. lazy   – _____
10. happy   – _____

Challenge 3 다음 단어의 비교급을 써 보세요. (than도 붙일 것)

01. difficult   – _____
02. quickly   – _____
03. helpful   – _____
04. shocking   – _____
05. beautifully – _____
06. boring   – _____
07. fluently   – _____
08. slowly   – _____

1-2 최상급 만드는 방법

Mt. Everest is **the highest** mountain in the world.
에베레스트산은 세계에서 가장 높은 산이다.

01 규칙 변화

규칙 변화	원급 (~한/~하게)	비교급 (더 ~한/~하게)	최상급 (가장 ~한/~하게)
① 대부분의 경우 : 형용사/부사 끝에 -est를 붙임	long strong fast	longer stronger faster	the long**est** the strong**est** the fast**est**
② -e로 끝나는 경우 : -st를 붙임	large wise	larger wiser	the large**st** the wise**st**
③ 「자음 + y」로 끝나는 경우 : -y를 -i로 고치고 -est를 붙임	happy pretty early	happier prettier earlier	the happ**iest** the prett**iest** the earl**iest**
④ 「단모음 + 단자음」으로 끝나는 경우 : 마지막 자음을 한 번 더 쓰고 -est를 붙임	big hot sad	bigger hotter sadder	the big**gest** the hot**test** the sad**dest**
⑤ -ful, -less, -ive, -ous, -ing로 끝나는 2음절 단어나 3음절 이상의 긴 단어 : 형용사/부사 앞에 most를 붙임	famous difficult carefully interesting expensive	more famous more difficult more carefully more interesting more expensive	the **most** famous the **most** difficult the **most** carefully the **most** interesting the **most** expensive

서술형 기초다지기

Challenge 1 다음 단어의 비교급과 최상급을 쓰세요.

01. young – _____ – _____   **02.** slow – _____ – _____

03. big – _____ – _____   **04.** long – _____ – _____

05. old – _____ – _____   **06.** happy – _____ – _____

07. hot – _____ – _____   **08.** thin – _____ – _____

09. smart – _____ – _____   **10.** healthy – _____ – _____

11. early – _____ – _____   **12.** high – _____ – _____

13. heavy – _____ – _____   **14.** dirty – _____ – _____

15. popular – _____ – _____

16. slowly – _____ – _____

17. expensive – _____ – _____

18. serious – _____ – _____

19. excited – _____ – _____

20. useful – _____ – _____

21. foolish – _____ – _____

22. patient – _____ – _____

Jane is my **elder** sister, but she looks younger than me.
Jane은 나의 언니이지만 나보다 더 어려 보인다.

01 비교급, 최상급의 불규칙 변화

원급	비교급	최상급
good 좋은	better 더 좋은	the best 가장 좋은
well 잘	better 더 잘	(the) best 가장 잘하는
bad 나쁜	worse 더 나쁜	the worst 가장 나쁜
ill 병든, 건강이 나쁜	worse 더 병든, 더 건강이 나쁜	the worst 가장 건강이 나쁜
many (수) 많은	more 더 많은	the most 가장 많은
much (양) 많은	more 더 많은	the most 가장 많은
few (수) 적은	fewer 더 적은	the fewest 가장 적은
little (양) 적은	less 더 적은	the least 가장 적은

This bicycle is **better** than that one. 이 자전거가 저 자전거보다 더 좋다.

The wound was **worse** than I thought. 그 상처는 내가 생각했던 것보다 더 심했다.

You should eat **more** vegetables and **less** meat. 너는 채소를 더 많이 먹고 고기를 덜 먹어야 한다.

02 비교급과 최상급이 각각 두 개씩이고 그 의미가 다른 경우가 있다.

원급	비교급	최상급
old	older (나이)	the oldest 가장 나이가 많은
	elder (서열)	the eldest 가장 손위의
late	later (시간)	the latest 최근의
	latter (순서)	the last 마지막의
far	farther (거리)	the farthest 거리가 가장 먼
	further (정도)	the furthest 정도가 가장 많이

She arrived in Seoul **later** than I expected. 그녀는 내가 기대했던 것보다 서울에 더 늦게 도착했다.

The **latter** part of the movie is very exciting. 이 영화의 후반부는 매우 흥미진진하다.

You have to go **farther** to reach the summit of the mountain.
산 정상에 도달하기 위해서는 더 멀리 가야 합니다.

Please visit our website for **further** information. 더 자세한 정보를 원하시면 우리 웹사이트를 방문해 주시기 바랍니다.

Challenge 1 다음 형용사나 부사의 비교급과 최상급을 써 보세요.

01. good   – _____ – _____   02. old (나이)   – _____ – _____

03. old (손위의) – _____ – _____   04. many   – _____ – _____

05. much   – _____ – _____   06. ill   – _____ – _____

07. bad   – _____ – _____   08. little   – _____ – _____

09. late (순서) – _____ – _____   10. far (거리)   – _____ – _____

11. far (정도) – _____ – _____   12. late (시간) – _____ – _____

Challenge 2 다음 우리말과 같도록 빈칸에 알맞은 말을 쓰세요.

01. 이 분야에서는 네가 최고야.

= You are the _____ in this field.

02. 그는 내가 가진 것보다 더 많은 책을 가지고 있다.

= He has _____ books than I have.

03. 그 경기의 후반부는 지루했다.

= The _____ part of the game was boring.

04. 만일 우리가 교수당 학생 수가 더 적었다면 더 훌륭한 소규모 교육이 가능했었을 것이다.

= If we had _____ students per teacher, there would be greater individuality.

05. Lucy는 최신 패션에 관심이 있다.

= Lucy is interested in the _____ fashion.

Unit 02 비교급

2-1 비교급의 쓰임

Janet's hair is **longer than** Kevin's hair.
Janet의 머리가 Kevin의 머리보다 더 길다.

01

두 명의 사람이나 두 개의 대상을 놓고 서로 비교하는 말을 '비교급'이라고 한다. 우리말에는 '~보다 더'라는 말이 있지만 영어에는 이런 말이 없어서 **형용사나 부사의 끝에 보통 -er을 붙여 우리말의 '더'라는 말을,** than은 **우리말의 '~보다'**라는 말을 대신한다.

Susan is **taller than** me. Susan은 나보다 더 키가 크다.
China is **larger than** America. 중국은 미국보다 더 넓다.
This pen is **better than** that one. 이 펜이 저것보다 더 좋다.

02

형식을 갖추는 영어에서는 **than 뒤에 비교 대상을 주격 대명사로 쓰지만 일상 영어에서는 거의 목적격으로 쓴다.**

My mom was happier than I.
→ My mom was happier than **me**. 엄마가 나보다 더 기뻐하셨다.

He worked harder than **she** did.
→ He worked harder than **her**. 그는 그녀보다 더 열심히 일했다.

03

형용사의 음절이 **2음절 이상이거나 -ly로 끝나는 부사 앞에는 more**를 붙여 비교급을 만든다.

She looked **more beautiful than** a flower. 그녀는 꽃보다 더 아름다웠다.
Introducing myself was **more difficult than** taking exams.
나 자신을 소개하는 것이 시험 치는 것보다 더 어려웠다.
Philosophy is often **more complex than** science. 철학은 종종 과학보다 더 복잡하다.
Scott drives **more carefully than** I do. Scott은 나보다 더 조심스럽게 운전한다.

Challenge 1 | 다음 괄호 안의 단어 중에 알맞은 것을 고르세요.

01. I am (older / more old) than you.

02. Kathy is (beautifuler / more beautiful) than Lucy.

03. This camera is (expensive / more expensive) than that one.

04. This bicycle is (more cheap / cheaper) than that one.

05. This morning I got up (more early / earlier) than yesterday.

06. The first movie was (funnier / more funny) than the sequel.

Challenge 2 | 다음 단어를 이용하여 비교급 문장을 완성하세요.

01.

(old / young)

I am _____ my grandmother.

My grandmother is _____ me.

02.

(tall / short)

Wilson is _____ Nancy.

Nancy is _____ Wilson.

03.

(big / small)

The soccer ball is _____ the baseball.

The baseball is _____ the soccer ball.

2-2 비교급 강조 / 열등 비교(less + 원급 + than)

You look **even** more beautiful than usual.
너는 평소보다 훨씬 더 아름다워 보인다.

Nancy is **less fat than** her sister.
Nancy는 그녀의 언니보다 덜 뚱뚱하다.

01 비교급을 강조하여 '훨씬 ~한/~하게'란 뜻을 표현하려면 비교급 앞에 **much, still, even, far, a lot, very much, a little bit**(약간) 등을 쓴다. **very**는 비교급을 강조하지 못하고 형용사와 부사의 원급을 강조한다.

I am **still** stronger than you. 나는 너보다 힘이 훨씬 더 세다.

I feel **much** happier now than before. 나는 전보다 지금이 훨씬 더 행복하다고 느낀다.

An elephant is **much** bigger than an ant. 코끼리는 개미보다 훨씬 더 크다.

Sunny did the work **a lot** better than I did. Sunny는 나보다 그 일을 훨씬 더 잘했다.

This car is **a little bit** bigger than that one. 이 차는 저 차보다 약간 더 크다.

02 '~보다 덜~하다'의 뜻인 **열등 비교**는 「**less** + 형용사/부사 + **than**」으로 쓴다. 일상 영어에서는 열등 비교 보다 원급 비교에 not을 붙인 「**not as(so)** + 형용사/부사 + **as**」를 더 자주 쓴다.

Susan is **less** happy **than** her sister. Susan은 언니보다 덜 행복하다.

= Susan is**n't as** happy **as** her sister. Susan은 언니만큼 행복하지 않다.

= Her sister is happ**ier than** Susan. Susan의 언니는 Susan보다 더 행복하다.

A cell phone is **less** expensive **than** a digital camera. 휴대폰은 디지털 카메라보다 덜 비싸다.

= A cell phone is**n't as** expensive **as** a digital camera. 휴대폰은 디지털 카메라만큼 비싸지 않다.

= A digital camera is **more** expensive **than** a cell phone. 디지털 카메라가 휴대폰보다 더 비싸다.

※ less 뒤에는 형용사나 부사의 원급을 써야 한다. 음절이 2음절 이상이더라도 less more expensive와 같이 쓰지 않는다.

서술형 기초다지기

Challenge 1 다음 괄호 안의 단어를 이용하여 빈칸에 비교급 표현을 쓰세요.

01. My grandmother is _____ me. (much / old)

02. The cheetah is _____ the deer. (far / fast)

03. My dad is _____ me. (a lot / strong)

Challenge 2 괄호 안의 단어를 알맞게 배열하여 문장을 완성하세요. (필요하면 동사 형태 바꾸기)

01. 치타는 고양이보다 훨씬 더 빠르다. (still / than / faster / a cat / is)

The cheetah _____.

02. Kevin은 다른 누구보다 훨씬 더 노래를 잘한다. (anyone else / better / than / even / sing)

Kevin _____.

03. 이것이 저것보다 훨씬 더 길다. (is / longer / that / than / much)

This _____.

Challenge 3 두 문장의 의미가 같도록 〈보기〉와 같이 「not as ~ as」를 이용하여 빈칸을 채우세요.

> 보기
> He is less strong than Superman.
> = *He isn't as strong as Superman.*

01. Steve drives less carefully than Tim.

= Steve _____.

02. Money is less important than health.

= Money _____.

2-3 비교구문을 이용한 표현

The more we have, **the more** we want.
더 많이 가지면 가질수록, 더 많이 원한다.

More and more people go aborad to study.
점점 더 많은 사람들이 공부하기 위해 해외로 간다.

---

01 변화를 강조하기 위해 「비교급(-er) + and + 비교급(-er)」 또는 「more and more」를 쓴다. '점점 더 ~하다'로 해석한다.

The world is getting **smaller and smaller**. 세계가 점점 더 좁아지고 있다.

It is getting **colder and colder** outside. 바깥 날씨가 점점 더 추워지고 있다.

It's becoming **more and more difficult** to get a job these days.
요즈음은 직장을 구하기가 점점 더 어려워지고 있다.

02 「the + 비교급, the + 비교급」은 '~하면 할수록 더 ~하다'의 뜻으로 상호 연관을 갖고 변화하고 있음을 보여 주는 표현이다. 앞의 내용이 조건이나 원인, 뒤의 내용이 결과에 해당된다.

The higher you go up Mt. Everest, **the colder** it becomes.
에베레스트산은 높이 올라가면 갈수록 날씨가 더 추워진다.

The more I exercise, **the stronger** I get. 운동을 하면 할수록 더 강해진다.

The fresher the fruit is, **the better** it tastes. 과일은 신선하면 신선할수록 더 맛이 있다.

03 「Which/Who ~ 비교급, A or B?」는 「A와 B 중 어느 것이/누가 더 ~하니?」라는 의미이다.

Which do you like **better**, summer **or** winter? 여름과 겨울 중 어느 계절을 더 좋아하니?

Who is **taller**, Jason **or** Bob? Jason과 Bob 중에 누가 더 키가 크니?

서술형 기초다지기

Challenge 1 우리말과 같아지도록 괄호 안의 단어를 알맞게 고쳐 쓰세요.

01. Scott은 나보다 더 학교에 일찍 왔다.

= Scott came to school _____ I did. (early)

02. Jim은 Jennifer보다 덜 사려 깊다.

= Jim is _____ Jennifer. (thoughtful)

03. Sunny와 Kathy 중 누가 더 뚱뚱하니?

= Who is _____, Sunny _____ Kathy? (fat)

04. 대기 오염이 점점 더 심각해지고 있다.

= Air pollution is becoming _____. (serious)

05 태양과 지구 중 어느 것이 더 크니?

= Which is _____, the Sun _____ the Earth? (big)

06 어두워지면 어두워질수록 우리는 더 공포를 느꼈다.

= _____ it grew, _____ we felt. (dark, scared)

Challenge 2 다음 문장을 읽고 빈칸을 「the + 비교급, the + 비교급」 문장으로 완성해 보세요.

보기	If the fruit is fresh, it tastes good. → *The fresher* the fruit is, *the better* it tastes.

01. We got close to the fire. We felt warm.

→ _____ we got to the fire, _____ we felt.

02. If we climb the mountain high, the wind blows hard.

→ _____ we climb the mountain, _____ the wind blows.

03. As I listened to the music longer, I became angry.

→ _____ I listened to the music, _____ I became.

Chapter 3 – 비교급과 최상급 · 77

Unit 03 최상급

3-1 최상급의 활용

Peter is **the tallest** of the three.
Peter가 셋 중에서 가장 키가 크다.

The blue whale is **the largest** animal in the world.
흰긴수염고래가 세상에서 가장 큰 동물이다.

01 **최상급은 셋 이상의 사람이나 사물을 비교**해서 그 중에 '**누가 가장 ~한/~하게**'라는 뜻을 나타내는 표현이다.

This is **the most** expensive car in the shop. 이것이 상점에서 가장 비싼 자동차이다.
Cheetahs can run **the fastest** of all the land animals. 치타는 모든 육상 동물들 중에서 가장 빨리 달릴 수 있다.

02 최상급 뒤에는 비교 범위를 정해주는 말이 함께 나온다. in[~안에서(범위)] 뒤에는 장소나 단체(this class, the world, my family)의 단수 명사를 쓰고, of(~중에서) 뒤에는 복수 명사(all the students, four seasons, all the cities 등)를 쓴다. 형용사절을 써서 최상급의 명사를 수식하기도 한다.

The Nile is the longest river **in the world.** 나일강은 세계에서 가장 긴 강이다.
Brown is the shortest **of all his friends.** Brown은 그의 친구들 중에서 가장 키가 작다.
Avatar is the best movie **that I have ever seen.** 〈아바타〉는 이제까지 내가 본 최고의 영화이다.

03 이미 앞에서 명사가 제시되어 있어 **말하지 않아도 서로 알만한 경우에는 최상급 뒤에 있는 명사를 생략**할 수 있다. 그러나 항상 명사를 생략할 수 있는 것은 아니다.

I have three books, but this one is **the best (book)** of all. 나는 세 권의 책이 있지만 이것이 최고이다.

04 일상 영어에서는 잘 쓰지 않으나 '**가장 ~하지 않은**'의 뜻인 **the least**는 the most와는 반대 의미를 나타낸다. the least 뒤에는 원급을 쓴다.

What is **the least** expensive MP3 player? 어떤 게 가장 덜 비싼 MP3 플레이어니?
= What is the cheapest MP3 player? 어떤 게 가장 싼 MP3 플레이어니? ▶ 더 자주 쓰는 표현

서술형 기초다지기

Challenge 1 다음 괄호 안의 비교급과 최상급 표현 중 알맞은 것을 고르세요.

01. The giraffe is the (taller / tallest) animal.

02. My dad is (the oldest / older) than me.

03. This is the (more expensive / most expensive) car.

04. Jennifer is (prettier / the prettiest) girl in our class.

Challenge 2 다음 괄호 안의 단어를 활용하여 빈칸을 최상급 표현으로 완성하세요.

01. Toronto is _____ in Canada. (city / large)

02. Mississippi is _____ in the USA. (river / long)

03. Russia is _____ in the world. (country / large)

04. The cheetah is _____ in the world. (animal / fast)

05. February is _____ of the year. (month / short)

06. Antarctica is _____ in the world. (place / cold)

Memo

최상급의 다양한 쓰임

He is **one of the most famous fashion designers** in the world.
그는 세계에서 가장 유명한 패션디자이너 중 한 명이다.

01 「one of the + 최상급 + 복수 명사」는 '가장 ~한 것 중의 하나'의 뜻이다.

The Amazon is **one of the longest rivers** in the world. 아마존은 세계에서 가장 긴 강 중 하나이다.
Jennifer is **one of the most intelligent students** in her school.
Jennifer는 그녀의 학교에서 가장 영리한 학생들 중의 한 명이다.

02 원급과 비교급 표현을 이용하여 최상급을 나타낼 수 있다.

> No (other) ~ as[so] + 원급 + as
> = No (other) ~ 비교급 + than
> = 비교급 + than any other + 단수 명사
> = 비교급 + than all the other + 복수 명사

Scott is **the tallest boy** in his class. Scott은 그의 반에서 가장 키가 큰 소년이다.
= **No (other)** boy is **as[so] tall as** Scott in his class.
= **No (other)** boy is **taller than** Scott in his class.
= Scott is **taller than any other boy** in his class.
= Scott is **taller than all the other boys** in his class.

Seoul is **the largest city** in Korea. 서울은 한국에서 가장 큰 도시이다.
= **No (other)** city is **as[so] large as** Seoul in Korea.
= **No (other)** city is **larger than** Seoul in Korea.
= Seoul is **larger than any other city** in Korea.
= Seoul is **larger than all the other cities** in Korea.

Challenge 1 다음 표현을 이용하여 「one of + 최상급 + 복수 명사」 형태의 문장을 완성하세요.

보 기	an expensive car in the world → A Rolls Royce *is one of the most expensive cars in the world.*

01. a beautiful city in the world

→ Seoul _____.

02. a famous man in the world

→ Gandhi _____.

03. a high mountain in Korea

→ Mt. Halla _____.

04. a pretty park in St. Louis

→ Forest Park _____.

Challenge 2 다음 최상급 문장을 괄호 안의 지시대로 고쳐 쓰세요.

01. The Han River is the longest in Seoul. (비교급 + than any other + 단수 명사)

→ _____

02. New York is the biggest city in the United Sates. (No other + as + 원급 + as)

→ _____

03. Alex is the most handsome boy in his class. (비교급 + than all the other + 복수 명사)

→ _____

04. Bill Gates is the richest man in the world. (비교급 + than any other + 단수 명사)

→ _____

Unit 04 원급을 이용한 비교 표현

4-1 as+원급+as

Karen is 150cm. Lucy is 150cm.
Karen은 150cm이다. Lucy도 150cm이다.

Karen is **as** tall **as** Lucy.
(= Karen and Lucy are the same height.)
Karen은 Lucy만큼 키가 크다.

01 비교급은 둘 중 어느 하나가 더 낫거나 못한 경우를 표현하지만 **원급 비교는 두 명의 사람이나 사물이 서로 같거나 비슷하다고 표현하는** 말이다. 「as + 형용사/부사 + as」로 나타내며 두 번째 오는 as는 '~만큼'으로 해석한다.

This box is **as** heavy **as** that one. 이 상자는 저 상자만큼 무겁다.
Can you run **as** fast **as** Tony? 너는 Tony만큼 빨리 달릴 수 있니?

02 원급 비교의 부정 표현인 「**not as[so] + 형용사/부사 + as**」는 '~만큼 ~하지 않다'의 뜻이다. 원급 비교의 부정은 「비교급 + than」의 문장으로 바꾸어 쓸 수 있다.

Sunny is **not as** tall **as** Steve. Sunny는 Steve만큼 키가 크지 않다.
= Sunny is **shorter than** Steve. Sunny는 Steve보다 더 작다.

His hair is **not as** long **as** her hair. 그의 머리는 그녀의 머리만큼 길지 않다.
= His hair is **shorter than** her hair. 그의 머리는 그녀의 머리보다 더 짧다.

03 「as + 원급 + as possible」은 '**가능한 ~한[하게]**'의 의미이다. 「as + 원급 + as + 주어 + can[could]」로 바꾸어 쓸 수 있다.

I walked to school **as fast as possible**. 나는 학교까지 가능한 빨리 걸어갔다.
= I walked to school **as fast as I could**.

I will wait for you **as long as possible**. 나는 가능한 오래 너를 기다릴 것이다.
= I will wait for you **as long as I can**.

Challenge 1 다음 괄호 안의 단어 중에서 알맞은 것을 고르세요.

01. Sunny is not as (young / younger) as Bob.

02. He says that he is (smart / smarter) than Einstein.

03. Today is as (hotter / hot) as yesterday.

04. This bag is not so (heavier / heavy) as that one.

05. Peter ran as fast as he (can / could).

06. Peter ran as fast as (could / possible).

Challenge 2 다음 문장을 「as ~ as」 또는 「not as[so] ~ as」를 이용하여 한 문장으로 만드세요.

01. My bicycle is old. Your bicycle is old, too.

　→ My bicycle _____.

02. Bob got home late. Jason got home late, too.

　→ Bob _____.

03. A river isn't big. An ocean is very big.

　→ A river _____.

Challenge 3 다음 원급의 부정 표현 문장을 비교급 문장으로 바꾸어 쓰세요.

01. This book isn't as cheap as that one.

　→ This book _____. (expensive)

02. English class isn't as easy as history class.

　→ English class _____. (difficult)

4-2 기타 비교 표현

Turtles live **twice as long as** elephants.
거북이는 코끼리보다 두 배 더 오래 산다.

Both A and B are **the same**. A와 B는 똑같다.
A is **the same as** B. A는 B와 똑같다.

01　「배수사＋as＋원급＋as ～」는 '～보다 몇 배 ～한'이라는 의미의 표현이다.

South Korea has **twice as many people as** North Korea. 남한은 북한보다 2배 더 인구가 많다.
Africa is **four times as large as** Europe. 아프리카의 넓이가 유럽의 4배이다.
This company is **twice as large as** it was a year ago. 이 회사는 1년 전보다 2배나 커졌다.

※ 배수사: one, twice(＝two times), three times, four times, etc.

02　the same, similar, different는 비교 대상과의 동일함이나 유사함, 차이점을 나타내는 형용사이다. same 은 형용사이지만 반드시 the와 함께 쓴다는 것에 유의한다.

Kevin and Peter have **the same** pencil. Kevin과 Peter는 똑같은 연필을 갖고 있다.
= Kevin's pencil and Peter's pencil are **the same**. Kevin의 연필과 Peter의 연필은 똑같다.

Susan and Lucy have **similar** hats. Susan과 Lucy는 비슷한 모자를 가지고 있다.
= Susan's hat and Lucy's hat are **similar**. Susan의 모자와 Lucy의 모자는 비슷하다.

Scott and Bob have **different** characters. Scott과 Bob은 다른 성격을 가지고 있다.
= Scott's character and Bob's character are **different**. Scott의 성격과 Bob의 성격은 다르다.

03　the same, similar, different 뒤에 비교하는 대상이 오면 각각 **the same as, similar to, different from**을 비교 대상 앞에 쓴다.

Your shoes are **the same as** mine. 너의 신발은 내 것과 똑같다.
A rectangle is **similar to** a square. 직사각형은 정사각형과 비슷하다.
Girls are **different from** boys. 여자 아이들은 남자 아이들과는 다르다.

Challenge 1 다음 괄호 안의 표현을 이용하여 문장을 완성하세요.

01. 이 상자는 저 상자보다 두 배 더 무겁다.

    = This box is _____ that one. (heavy)

02. 그의 월급은 내 월급의 세 배이다.

    = His salary is _____ mine. (high)

03. 이 티셔츠가 저 티셔츠보다 두 배 더 비싸다.

    = This T-shirt costs _____ that one. (much)

Challenge 2 다음 빈칸에 as, to, from 중 알맞은 것을 골라 써 넣으세요.

01. My coat is different _____ yours.

02. My dictionary is the same _____ yours.

03. South Korea is much different _____ North Korea.

04. Janet's hair style is similar _____ Nancy's hair style.

Challenge 3 same, similar, different 중 알맞은 것을 골라 다음 문장을 완성해 보세요.

Photo A   Photo B   Photo C   Photo D

보기   Photo C and Photo D are *the same*.

01. Photo B is _____ _____ photo C.

02. Photo B and photo C are _____.

03. Photo D is the _____ _____ photo C.

04. Photo A is _____ _____ photo D.

01 출제 100% - 원급, 비교급, 최상급의 기본에 충실하자.

 출제자의 눈 비교급과 최상급의 형태를 묻는 간단한 문제가 가장 많이 출제된다. 특히 원급 비교 (as~as)에서 as와 as 사이에 형용사나 부사의 원급을 제대로 쓸 줄 아는지 묻는 문제가 자주 출제된다. as를 틀리게 써 놓거나 more 다음에 than을 쓰지 않고 틀린 표현으로 혼동시키는 문제도 출제된다.

Ex 1.

다음 주어진 단어들의 비교급이 <u>잘못된</u> 것은?

(a) heavy - heavyer   (b) tall - taller   (c) high - higher

(d) good - better   (e) exciting - more exciting

Ex 2.

다음 중 <u>어색한</u> 문장은?

(a) Apples are the most small fruit in the store.

(b) Seo-yoon is the most wonderful lady in the world.

(c) The green jacket is more expensive than the blue one.

(d) Brian is the tallest player in our team.

(e) The yellow car is bigger than the black one.

02 출제 100% - 원급, 비교급, 최상급 영작 문제는 반드시 출제된다.

 출제자의 눈 평소에 비교 문장을 자주 써 보는 연습을 해야 한다. 비교급을 원급의 부정형인 「not as[so]~as」로 전환하는 문제, 우리말을 주고 비교급 또는 최상급 문장을 완성하는 단답형 주관식 문제가 반드시 출제된다. 그리고 much, still, far, a lot 등은 비교급을 강조하지만 very는 '매우'의 뜻으로 원급만 강조한다. 강조의 표현을 물어보는 문제가 집중적으로 출제된다.

Ex 3.

빈칸에 알맞지 <u>않은</u> 것은?

Her computer looks _____ better than mine.

(a) even   (b) still   (c) much   (d) very

Ex 4.

다음 문장의 뜻이 같도록 빈칸에 공통으로 들어갈 말을 쓰시오.

You are not as strong as I.

= You are not _____ than I. = I am _____ than you.

03 출제 100 % - 비교 구문을 이용한 표현을 주의하라.

 출제자의 눈 「the + 비교급, the + 비교급」과 「비교급 + and + 비교급」의 형태를 묻는 문제는 내신뿐 아니라 토익, 텝스에서도 자주 출제되는 항목이다. 이 형태를 반드시 암기하고 있어야 한다. 배수를 나타내는 「배수사 + as ~ as」 형태를 묻는 문제도 출제될 수 있다. 마지막으로 '가능한 ~한/하게'의 뜻인 「as ~ as possible」을 부분 영작하게 하거나, 같은 의미인 「as ~ as + 주어 + can[could]」로 바꿔 쓰거나 같은 의미의 표현을 고르는 문제가 출제된다.

Ex 5.

The faster you finish what you're doing, _____ you can go home.

(a) sooner   (b) the sooner   (c) the soonest   (d) more soon

Ex 6.

빈칸에 들어갈 알맞은 말을 한 단어로 쓰시오.

You should get home as quickly as _____.

너는 가능한 한 집에 빨리 와야 한다.

04 출제 100 % - 비교 구문을 활용한 단답형 주관식 문제는 반드시 출제된다.

 출제자의 눈 원급, 비교급, 최상급은 서술형 문제로 출제하기 가장 좋은 유형이다. 표나 그림을 주고 비교급, 최상급을 활용한 빈칸 문제나, 우리말을 영작하는 주관식 문제는 반드시 출제된다. 난이도가 조금 있는 문제로는, 최상급 구문을 같은 의미의 비교급이나 원급 구문으로 바꿔 써 보라는 문제가 출제될 수 있다.

Ex 7.

두 문장이 같은 뜻이 되도록 빈칸에 알맞은 말을 쓰시오.

She is the tallest girl in her class.

= She is _____ than any _____ _____ in her class.

Ex 8.

우리말과 같은 뜻이 되도록 빈칸에 알맞은 말을 쓰시오.

Tom은 Mike만큼 빨리 달린다.

= Tom runs _____ Mike.

1. 다음 밑줄 친 우리말을 영어로 알맞게 표현한 것은?

> In my dream, I saw a balloon which was
> <u>집만큼 큰(집채만한)</u>.

❶ like a house as big
❷ as big as a house
❸ as a house like big
❹ as a house as big
❺ as big a house as

2. 다음 문장의 빈칸에 알맞지 <u>않은</u> 것은?

> This mountain is _____ higher than your father's building.

❶ lots of　　❷ far　　❸ even
❹ still　　❺ much

3. 다음 표의 내용과 일치하지 <u>않는</u> 문장을 고르시오.

	Kevin	Lucy	Bob
나이	15	14	15
키	163	170	170
성적	90	90	70

❶ Kevin is as old as Bob.
❷ Kevin isn't as tall as Lucy.
❸ Kevin is as smart as Lucy.
❹ Lucy is as tall as Bob.
❺ Lucy isn't as smart as Bob.

4. 다음 문장 중 어법상 <u>잘못된</u> 것은?

❶ Peter is much taller than any other boy in his class.
❷ Your ring is prettier than mine.
❸ Left-handed people tend to be better at driving.
❹ This movie is more interesting than *Harry Potter*.
❺ She is less smarter than you.

5. 다음 우리말과 같도록 빈칸에 알맞은 말을 쓰시오.

> 나는 너보다 두 배 빠르게 타자를 칠 수 있다.
> = I can type _____ _____ _____ _____ you.

6. 다음 두 문장의 의미가 같도록 빈칸에 알맞은 말을 쓰시오.

> Sunny collected as many stamps as possible.
> = Sunny collected as many stamps as _____ _____.

7. 원급, 비교급, 최상급이 <u>잘못</u> 짝지어진 것은?

❶ hot − hotter − hottest
❷ many − more − most
❸ easy − easier − easiest
❹ thin − thiner − thinest
❺ exciting − more exciting − most exciting

8. 다음 빈칸에 들어갈 말을 순서대로 쓰시오.

> 당신이 더 많이 가지면 가질수록, 가난한 사람을 더 많이 도와야 한다.
> = _____ you have, _____ you must help the poor.

9. 다음 문장 중 의미가 <u>다른</u> 하나는?

❶ Russia is the largest country in the world.
❷ No country in the world is larger than Russia.
❸ Russia is not as large as any other country in the world.
❹ Russia is larger than any other country in the world.
❺ No country in the world is as large as Russia.

오답 노트 만들기

★틀린 문제 : _____   ★다시 공부한 날 : _____

(1) 문제를 왜? 틀렸는지 곰곰이 생각하고 그 이유를 적어본다.

(2) 핵심 개념을 적는다.

(3) 자신이 몰랐던 단어와 숙어 표현이 있으면 정리한다.

(4) 해설집에서 필요한 부분을 골라 풀이 해법을 정리한다.

★틀린 문제 : _____   ★다시 공부한 날 : _____

(1) 문제를 왜? 틀렸는지 곰곰이 생각하고 그 이유를 적어본다.

(2) 핵심 개념을 적는다.

(3) 자신이 몰랐던 단어와 숙어 표현이 있으면 정리한다.

(4) 해설집에서 필요한 부분을 골라 풀이 해법을 정리한다.

★틀린 문제 : _____   ★다시 공부한 날 : _____

(1) 문제를 왜? 틀렸는지 곰곰이 생각하고 그 이유를 적어본다.

(2) 핵심 개념을 적는다.

(3) 자신이 몰랐던 단어와 숙어 표현이 있으면 정리한다.

(4) 해설집에서 필요한 부분을 골라 풀이 해법을 정리한다.

★틀린 문제 : _____   ★다시 공부한 날 : _____

(1) 문제를 왜? 틀렸는지 곰곰이 생각하고 그 이유를 적어본다.

(2) 핵심 개념을 적는다.

(3) 자신이 몰랐던 단어와 숙어 표현이 있으면 정리한다.

(4) 해설집에서 필요한 부분을 골라 풀이 해법을 정리한다.

[1-2] 원급, 비교급, 최상급이 <u>잘못</u> 짝지어진 것은?

1. ❶ long – longer – longest
   ❷ happy – happier – happiest
   ❸ useful – more useful – most useful
   ❹ hot – hoter – hotest
   ❺ boring – more boring – most boring

   오답노트

2. ❶ good – better – best
   ❷ bad – worse – worst
   ❸ much – more – most
   ❹ slowly – more slowly – most slowly
   ❺ easily – easilier – easiliest

   오답노트

[3-4] 우리말에 맞게 괄호 안의 단어를 바르게 배열하시오.

3. Jennifer와 Susan 중 누가 더 키가 크니?
   (is / Jennifer / who / Susan / or / taller)
   → _____

   오답노트

4. 날이 점점 추워지고 있다.
   (it / and / colder / getting / colder / is)
   → _____

   오답노트

5. 우리말과 같은 뜻이 되도록 괄호 안의 단어를 빈칸에 알맞은 형태로 써 보시오.

   > 〈아바타〉는 이제까지 내가 본 가장 좋은 영화이다.
   > *Avatar* is _____ movie I've ever seen. (good)

   오답노트

[6-8] 다음 중 빈칸에 알맞지 <u>않은</u> 것을 고르시오.

6. Steve is as _____ as you.
   ❶ clever   ❷ old   ❸ fast
   ❹ brave   ❺ shorter

   오답노트

7. It is one of the _____ rooms in our hotel.
   ❶ largest   ❷ brightest
   ❸ better   ❹ most expensive
   ❺ nicest

   오답노트

8. She looks _____ than before.
   ❶ better   ❷ prettier   ❸ more beautiful
   ❹ taller   ❺ sader

   오답노트

9. 다음 그림의 내용과 일치하지 <u>않는</u> 것은?

❶ Mary is heavier than both Julie and Sally.
❷ The girl wearing a skirt is the shortest of the three.
❸ Julie is the tallest girl of the three.
❹ Julie's hair is longer than Sally's.
❺ Sally is as tall as Julie.

오답노트

10. 다음 도표의 내용과 일치하는 것은?

이름	Peter	Juliet	Nancy
나이	13	14	12
신장	152cm	148cm	160cm

❶ Peter is as old as Juliet.
❷ Nancy is taller than Juliet.
❸ Nancy is older than Peter.
❹ Peter is the tallest of the three.
❺ Nancy is as old as Peter.

오답노트

11. 다음 문장과 의미가 같은 것은?

> He is the tallest boy in his class.

❶ All the boys are taller than he is.
❷ He is as tall as any boys in his class.
❸ He isn't as tall as any boys in his class.
❹ He isn't taller than any boy in his class.
❺ He is taller than any other boy in his class.

오답노트

12. 다음 빈칸에 공통으로 들어갈 말을 쓰시오.

> · _____ smaller the cell phones are,
> _____ higher the price gets.
> · Who is _____ most famous soccer player in Korea?

오답노트

13. 다음 두 문장의 의미가 같도록 빈칸에 알맞은 말을 쓰시오.

> The film is not as interesting as the book.
> = The book is _____ _____ _____ the film.

오답노트

14. 다음 빈칸에 들어갈 말로 어색한 것은?

> Tiffany speaks Korean _____ better than Jason.

❶ very ❷ even ❸ far
❹ still ❺ much

오답노트

15. 다음 대화의 빈칸에 들어갈 단어가 알맞게 짝지어진 것은?

> A: _____ city is warmer, Sydney or New York?
> B: Sydney is _____ than New York.
> A: Then, is New York warmer than London?
> B: No, it isn't. New York is as _____ as London.

❶ Who − warm − warmer
❷ Which − warmer − warm
❸ Who − the warmest − the warmest
❹ What − warmer − warm
❺ Which − the warmest − warmer

오답노트

16. 다음 그림에 대한 설명이 바르지 <u>않은</u> 것은?

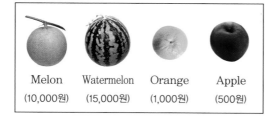

Melon	Watermelon	Orange	Apple
(10,000원)	(15,000원)	(1,000원)	(500원)

❶ Oranges are more expensive than apples.
❷ Apples are the cheapest fruit in the store.
❸ Apples are cheaper than melons.
❹ Watermelons are the biggest fruit in the store.
❺ Melons are bigger than watermelons.

오답노트

17. 다음 글과 일치하도록 물음에 대한 알맞은 답을 고르시오.

> Julie is a good dancer. Sunny dances better than Julie. Laura doesn't dance as well as Julie.

Q: Who is the best dancer of the three?
❶ Julie is.
❷ Laura is.
❸ Sunny is.
❹ Laura dances better than Julie.
❺ No girls dance well.

오답노트

[18-19] 우리말과 뜻이 같도록 괄호 안의 단어를 알맞은 순서대로 배열하시오.

18.
> 너는 수영과 스키 중에서 어느 것을 더 좋아하니?
> (like/you/better/which/do), swimming or skiing?

→ _____

오답노트

19.

한라산은 내가 기대했던 것보다 더 아름다웠다.
Mt. Halla was (than/beautiful/I/more/expected).

→ _____

오답노트

[20-22] 다음 두 문장의 의미가 같도록 빈칸에 알맞은 말을 쓰시오.

20.

This bridge is longer than that one.
= That bridge is not _____ this bridge.

오답노트

21.

As you go up higher, you will feel better.
= The _____ you go up, the _____ you will feel.

오답노트

22.

I'll do the work as hard as I can.
= I'll do the work _____ .

오답노트

[23-25] 우리말과 뜻이 같도록 빈칸에 들어갈 알맞은 단어를 고르시오.

23.

그 이야기의 후반부는 지루했다.
= The _____ part of the story was boring.

❶ late ❷ later ❸ latter
❹ last ❺ latest

오답노트

24.

그녀는 최신 패션에 관심이 있다.
= She is interested in _____ fashion.

❶ late ❷ the last ❸ the lastest
❹ lastest ❺ the latest

오답노트

25.

의사가 나에게 고기를 줄이고 채소를 더 많이 먹으라고 충고했다.
= The doctor advised me to eat _____ meat and _____ vegetables.

❶ little, more ❷ least, more
❸ little, much ❹ least, most
❺ less, more

오답노트

A. 밑줄 친 우리말과 의미가 같도록 빈칸에 알맞은 말을 쓰시오.

> 들소는 북아메리카에서 가장 큰 동물이다. It weighs as much as 2,000 pounds.
> It lives with other buffalos in groups or herds.

→ The buffalo is _____ _____ _____ _____ North America.

B. 다음 표를 보고 빈칸 ⓐ, ⓑ에 알맞은 말을 쓰시오.

	bears	giraffes	elephants
height (m)	2	5.3	3.5
weight (kg)	1,200	1,400	1,800

→ Among the animals, ⓐ _____ are the tallest and ⓑ _____ are the heaviest.

C. 우리말과 의미가 같도록 괄호 안의 단어들을 바르게 배열하시오.

1. 건강이 재산보다 중요하다.

(wealth / important / health / more / is / than)

→ _____

2. 이 휴대폰은 아이폰보다 덜 비싸다.

(expensive / is / this cell phone / the iPhone / less / than)

→ _____

3. 그 책이 그 영화보다 더 재미있다.

(is / than / the book / interesting / the movie / more)

→ _____

D. 다음 비교급 문장과 같은 의미가 되도록 괄호 안의 단어를 이용하여 not as[so]~as로 바꿔 다시 쓰시오.

1. Linda is younger than Peter. (old)

→ _____

2. Linda is shorter than Peter. (tall)

→ _____

3. Linda's hair is longer than Peter's hair. (short)

→ _____

E. 다음 두 문장의 의미가 같도록 빈칸에 알맞은 말을 쓰시오.

Mary is the wisest girl in my class.

= Mary is _____ than _____ _____ girl in my class.

F. 다음 사진을 보고 최상급의 문장으로 표현하시오.

1.　　　　　**2.**　　　　　**3.**

1. _____
(the blue whale / of mammals / big)

2. _____
(Mt. Everest / in the world / high)

3. _____
(Sunny / of the four / tall)

실전 서술형 평가문제

출제의도 최상급의 이해 및 활용
평가내용 최상급의 사용

A. 다음 질문에 대한 대답을 최상급을 활용한 문장으로 완성하시오.　　　　[서술형 유형 : 12점 / 난이도 : 하]

Steve is taller than Susan. Nancy is shorter than Susan.

1. Q : Who is the tallest?　　　A : _____ of the three.

2. Q : Who is the shortest?　　　A : _____ of the three.

Kim's bicycle is more expensive than Maria's bicycle.
Maria's bicycle is more expensive than Karen's bicycle.

3. Q : Whose bicycle is the most expensive?　　A : _____

4. Q : Whose bicycle is the cheapest?　　A : _____

Scott is faster than John. Bob is faster than Scott.

5. Q : Who is the fastest?　　A : _____ of the three.

6. Q : Who is the slowest?　　A : _____ of the three.

출제의도 비교급의 이해와 적용
평가내용 같은 의미의 원급을 비교급으로 표현하기

B. 다음 「not as~as」 문장을 같은 의미의 비교급 문장으로 2개씩 영작하시오.　　[서술형 유형 : 6점 / 난이도 : 중하]

1. This book isn't as cheap as that book.

→ _____

→ _____

2. A mouse isn't as big as an elephant.

→ _____

→ _____

3. English class isn't as easy as history class.

→ _____

→ _____

출제의도 원급, 비교급, 최상급의 이해
평가내용 원급, 비교급, 최상급을 이용한 비교 표현

C. 세 명의 선생님에 관한 글을 읽고 원급, 비교급, 최상급을 이용한 문장을 2개씩 완성해 보시오.

[논술형 유형 : 18점 / 난이도 : 중상]

Steve (English teacher)	He is 30 years old and he is the most handsome in our school. He's 180cm tall. He likes to play basketball on weekends. We love his big smile. His nickname is "Mr. Happy Guy."
Jennifer (Music teacher)	She is 30 years old and she sings very well. She's 165cm tall. She has blue eyes and is very pretty. She is always proud of herself. Her nickname is "Princess."
Brian (Music teacher)	He sings very well, too. He is 40 years old and 160cm tall. He likes two activities: one is riding a bike, the other is flying a kite. He is very ugly so his nickname is "Ugly Man."

1. _____

2. _____

3. _____

4. _____

5. _____

6. _____

서술형 평가문제	채 점 기 준	배 점	나의 점수
A	표현이 올바르고 문법, 철자가 모두 정확한 경우	2점 × 6문항 = 12점	
B		2점 × 3문항 = 6점	
C		3점 × 6문항 = 18점	
D		3점 × 4문항 = 12점	
공통	문법, 철자가 1개씩 틀린 경우	각 문항당 1점씩 감점	
	문제당 2개의 답변 중 하나만 완성한 경우(B에 해당)		
	최상급 표현을 전혀 사용하지 못한 경우	0점	
	내용과 전혀 일치하지 않거나 답을 기재하지 못한 경우		

출제의도 원급, 비교급을 활용한 문장 완성
평가내용 실생활에서의 비교 구문 활용하기

D. 〈보기〉와 같이 주어 'I'로 시작하는 원급과 비교급 문장을 최소 4개 영작하시오. (각 문장은 I think that ~으로 시작하고 아래의 형용사를 활용할 것)

[서술형 유형 : 12점 / 난이도 : 중상]

| easy | bad | good | boring |
| difficult | exciting | interesting |

(reading)

(watching TV)

(swimming)

(cycling)

(washing the car)

(doing homework)

| 보기 | *I think that reading is more interesting than watching TV.*
I think that reading isn't as interesting as watching TV. |

1. _____

2. _____

3. _____

4. _____

Chapter 4

접속사 (Conjunctions)

Unit 01 등위접속사

1-1 and, but, or

Doctors **and** nurses work in hospitals.
의사와 간호사들은 병원에서 일한다.

Wake up now, **and** you'll catch the school bus.
지금 일어나라, 그러면 너는 학교버스를 탈 수 있을 거다.

01 and(~와, 그리고), but(그러나, 하지만), or(또는, 혹은)은 **단어와 구, 절을 대등하게 연결**한다. 두 단어를 연결할 때는 쉼표(,)를 쓰지 않고, **세 개 이상의 단어를 연결할 때는 각 단어 뒤와 접속사 앞에 쉼표를 쓴다.**

I want some bread **and** orange juice. 나는 약간의 빵과 오렌지 주스를 원한다.
Kevin puts milk, sugar, **and** kiwi in his tea. Kevin은 차에 우유와 설탕, 키위를 넣는다.
Do you want iced tea **or** hot tea? 차가운 차 드실래요, 뜨거운 차 드실래요?

02 **문장과 문장을 연결할 때는 접속사 앞에 쉼표를 쓴다.**

I saw the doctor, **and** he gave me a prescription. 나는 의사의 진찰을 받았고, 그는 처방전을 주었다.
I love Kathy, **but** she doesn't love me. 나는 Kathy를 사랑하지만 그녀는 나를 사랑하지 않는다.
Do you want to watch TV, **or** do you want to go out? TV를 보고 싶니, 아니면 밖으로 나가고 싶니?

03 so(=therefore 그래서), for(=because 왜냐하면), yet(=but 그러나)은 **문장과 문장만 연결**시키며, **접속사 앞에 항상 쉼표를 쓴다.**

The movie was very long, **so** we got home late. 영화가 너무 길어서, 우리는 집에 늦게 도착했다.
Bob couldn't attend the meeting, **for** he was sick. Bob은 회의에 참석하지 못했다. 왜냐하면 아팠기 때문이다.
I washed my shirt, **yet** it didn't get clean. 나는 셔츠를 세탁했지만 깨끗해지지 않았다.

04 「**명령문 + and**」는 '~해라, 그러면'의 의미이고, 「**명령문 + or**」는 '~해라, 그렇지 않으면'의 의미이다.

Press the button, **and** the door will open. 버튼을 눌러라, 그러면 문이 열릴 것이다.
= If you press the button, the door will open.

Run to the station, **or** you won't see her. 역으로 뛰어가라, 그렇지 않으면 너는 그녀를 못 볼 것이다.
= If you don't run to the station, you won't see her.
= Unless you run to the station, you won't see her.

서술형 기초다지기

정답 p. 11

Challenge 1   다음 괄호 안의 단어 중에서 알맞은 접속사를 고르세요.

01. Would you like some water (and / but / or) some fruit juice?

02. My aunt puts milk (and / but / or) sugar in her tea.

03. Who is taller, Nancy (and / but / or) Grace?

04. Sunny is very smart, (and / but / or) her brother is very foolish.

05. We went to the restaurant, (and / but / or) it was closed.

Challenge 2   다음 빈칸에 so, for, yet 중 알맞은 것을 쓰세요.

01. I was tired, _____ I went to bed early.

02. Scott sent an e-mail to Susan, _____ she didn't get it.

03. My friend studied hard, _____ he failed the exam.

04. We didn't go swimming, _____ it was so cold.

05. It started to rain, _____ she opened her umbrella.

Challenge 3   두 문장이 같은 뜻이 되도록 「명령문＋and／or」의 문장으로 완성해 보세요.

01. If you don't speak louder, nobody will hear you.

    = _____ louder, _____ nobody will hear you.

02. If you help each other, the world will be better.

    = _____ each other, _____ the world will be better.

03. If you don't come home early, your mother will be angry.

    = _____ home early, _____ your mother will be angry.

04. If you are honest, everybody will like you.

    = _____ honest, _____ everybody will like you.

Unit 02 상관접속사

2-1 상관접속사의 종류

Both Jane **and** I like to ride a bicycle.
Jane과 나는 둘 다 자전거 타기를 좋아한다.

She is **not only** a writer **but also** an English teacher.
그녀는 작가일 뿐만 아니라 영어선생님이기도 하다.

01 **both A and B**: 「A와 B 둘 다(부가 additive)」의 뜻이다. 주어로 쓸 때는 복수 취급하여 복수형의 동사를 쓴다. 상관접속사는 등위접속사와 비슷한 뜻이지만 **상관접속사는 주로 강조**하기 위해 사용된다.

Sunny can speak Korean **and** Japanese. Sunny는 한국어와 일본어를 할 수 있다.
→ Sunny can speak **both** Korean **and** Japanese. (강조)
→ Sunny can speak **not only** Korean **but also** Japanese. (더 강한 어조)

02 **either A or B**: 「A와 B 둘 중에 하나 (양자택일 alternative)」의 뜻이다. 주어 자리에 쓸 때 동사의 수는 B에 일치시켜야 한다.

Either you **or** I am responsible for the result. 너와 나 둘 중의 한 명은 그 결과에 책임이 있다.
The knives were used **either** for cooking **or** for weapons. 칼은 요리용이나 무기 둘 중의 하나로 사용되었다.

03 **neither A nor B**: 「A와 B도 ~ 아닌 (양자부정 negative)」의 뜻으로 쓴다. 주어 자리에 쓸 때 동사의 수는 B에 일치시켜야 한다. 「not ~ either A or B」와 의미가 같다.

Neither the terrorist **nor** the police survived the explosion.
테러리스트와 경찰 둘 다 그 폭발에서 살아남지 못했다.
= **Not either** the terrorist **or** the police survived the explosion.

04 **not only A but (also) B**: 「A뿐만 아니라 B도(B를 강조)」의 뜻이다. 주어 자리에 쓸 때 동사의 수는 B에 일치시켜야 한다. 「B as well as A」와 같은 의미이다. also를 생략하고 but만 쓰는 경우도 많다.

Not only you **but also** I saw the ghost. 너뿐만 아니라 나도 그 귀신을 봤다.
= I **as well as** you saw the ghost.

05 **not A but B**: 「A가 아니라 B」의 뜻이다. B에 수를 일치시킨다.

Not Emily **but** I am going to London to study. Emily가 아니라 내가 런던에 공부하러 갈 거다.

서술형 기초다지기

정답 p. 11

Challenge 1   다음 문장을 읽고 빈칸에 알맞은 말을 쓰세요.

01. I know her. He knows her, too.

→ _____ I _____ he know her.

02. Kathy is going to watch TV. Or she is going to watch the movie.

→ Kathy is going to watch _____ TV _____ the movie.

03. Nancy doesn't play the piano. She doesn't play the cello, either.

→ Nancy plays _____ the piano _____ the cello.

04. I don't play computer games. I don't play video games, either.

→ I _____ play computer games _____ play video games.

05. I don't want to go out to dinner. I don't want to see a movie, either.

→ I don't want to _____ go out to dinner _____ see a movie.

Challenge 2   다음 두 문장이 같은 의미가 되도록 빈칸에 알맞은 말을 쓰세요.

01. Peter usually takes the dog out for a walk. If he can't do it, his sister does.

= _____ Peter _____ his sister takes the dog out for a walk.

02. I as well as you was helpless at that moment.

= _____ _____ you _____ _____ I was helpless at that moment.

Challenge 3   우리말과 의미가 같도록 괄호 안의 단어들을 바르게 배열하세요.

01. 나는 뜨거운 커피뿐만 아니라 냉커피도 좋아한다. (but also / hot coffee / iced coffee / not only)

→ I like _____.

02. 고래는 어류가 아니라 포유류이다. (fish / but / not / mammals)

→ Whales are _____.

Unit 03 명사절

3-1 명사절로 쓰이는 that

Brian realized **that** he had made a mistake.
Brian은 그가 실수를 저질렀다는 것을 알았다.

He hopes **that** people won't notice.
그는 사람들이 눈치 못 채길 바란다.

---

01 「접속사 + S + V」의 덩어리가 문장에서 명사 역할을 하기 때문에 명사절이라고 한다. 따라서 that으로 시작하는 **명사절**은 문장에서 **주어 역할**을 할 수 있다.

That smoking can cause cancer is a fact. 흡연이 암을 유발할 수 있다는 것은 사실이다.
That he is a genius is believable. 그가 천재라는 것은 믿을 만하다.

02 영어는 주어가 길어지는 것을 싫어한다. **명사절이 주어 자리에 쓰일 경우** 주어가 너무 길어지므로 그 자리에 **가주어 it을 쓰고 전부 뒤로 보낸다.**

That Scott is an excellent student is true. Scott이 우수한 학생이라는 것은 사실이다.
= It is true **that Scott is an excellent student.**

03 동사의 목적어로 (대)명사를 쓰지만 「S + V」를 쓰려면 명사절을 쓴다. 목적어 자리에 명사절을 쓸 때 that은 생략할 수 있다.

I think (**that**) he is a great scholar. 나는 그가 위대한 학자라고 생각한다.
He knows (**that**) his brother will marry this year. 그는 올해 그의 형이 결혼할 것이라는 걸 안다.

04 be동사의 보어로 명사나 형용사 이외에 명사절이 올 수 있다. **보어로 쓰일 때는 명사절을 이끄는 접속사 that은 생략하지 않는다.**

The truth is **that Lucy wasn't here last week.** 사실은 Lucy가 지난주에 여기에 없었다는 것이다.
One problem with MP3 files is **that they can break an artist's copyright.**
MP3 파일이 가진 한 가지 문제점은 그것들이 예술가의 저작권을 침해할 수 있다는 것이다.

서술형 기초다지기

정답 p. 12

Challenge 1 다음 밑줄 친 that의 쓰임에 해당되는 곳에 V 표 하세요.

01. We have various kinds of bags. How about <u>that</u>?　　대명사 _____ 접속사 _____

02. It is obvious <u>that</u> he finished the work himself.　　대명사 · _____ 접속사 _____

03. This is Mr. Brown. <u>That</u> is his wife, Mrs. Brown.　　대명사 _____ 접속사 _____

04. Everyone knows <u>that</u> the Earth is round.　　대명사 _____ 접속사 _____

Challenge 2 다음 문장을 가주어 It을 사용하여 다시 쓰세요.

01. That he will win the game is certain.

　　= _____

02. That Tiffany hasn't been able to make any friends is a pity.

　　= _____

03. That a cat isn't able to taste sweet things is true.

　　= _____

Challenge 3 다음 문장을 괄호 안의 표현을 이용하여 〈보기〉와 같이 바꿔 써 보세요.

보기	Smoking in public places should be prohibited. (feel / don't feel). = *I feel[don't feel] that smoking in public places should be prohibited.*

01. People can live without light. (don't believe)

　　→ _____

02. There will be peace in the world soon. (doubt / don't doubt)

　　→ _____

03. It is difficult for some people to learn languages. (think)

　　→ _____

3-2 의문사로 시작하는 명사절(간접의문문)

I don't know. + What is the answer?
→ I don't know **what the answer is**.
나는 답이 무엇인지 모르겠다.

01 의문사가 있는 의문문(직접의문문)이 문장의 명사 자리(주어, 목적어, 보어)에 들어가 명사 역할을 한다. 이때는 **반드시 「의문사 + S + V」의 어순으로 순서를 바꿔 쓴다.**

What color was the car? 그 차는 어떤 색이었나요?
→ I can't remember **what color it was**. 나는 그것이 어떤 색이었는지 기억이 안 난다.

Where is he going? 그가 어디로 가고 있나요?
→ I don't know **where he is going**. 나는 그가 어디로 가고 있는지 모른다.

02 직접의문문이 간접의문문(의문사 + S + V~?)으로 바뀌어 명사 자리에 오면 문장 끝에 물음표(?)를 쓰지 않는다. 다만 **주절이 의문문일 때는 물음표를 쓴다.**

I wonder where he is going. 나는 그가 어디로 가는지 궁금하다. ▶ 마침표 대신 물음표를 쓰면 안 됨
Can you tell me what time it is**?** 몇 시인지 나에게 말해 줄 수 있나요? ▶ 주절이 의문문이므로 물음표를 씀

03 간접의문문을 만들 때 직접의문문에 쓰인 do, does, did가 없어지고, 대신 **주어에 따라 동사의 수와 시제를 일치시킨다.** 의문사 자신이 주어인 경우에는 「의문사 + 동사」의 어순으로 쓴다.

Do you know? + when did they leave?
→ Do you know **when they left**? 그들이 언제 떠났는지 아니? ▶ 의문문에 쓰인 did가 없어지고 leave의 과거형이 옴

Please tell me. + Who is coming to the party?
→ Please tell me **who is coming to the party**. 누가 파티에 올지 말해 줘.
　　　　　　　　　　　　　　　　　　　　　　▶ 의문사 who가 주어로 쓰여 「의문사 + 동사」의 어순이 됨

04 직접의문문 대신 **간접의문문을 쓰는 이유**는 간접적으로 물어봄으로써 더욱 **예의 바른 표현**이 되기 때문이다. 따라서 친구나 가족과 같이 가까운 사이가 아닌, 다소 거리가 있는 사람에게 쓰게 된다.

What time is it? 몇 시니? ▶ 일반적
Can you tell me **what time it is**? 몇 시인지 말해 줄 수 있나요? ▶ 정중

서술형 기초다지기

Challenge 1   다음 두 문장을 〈보기〉와 같이 한 문장으로 바꾸세요.

> **보기**
> Can you tell me? + How much is it?
> → *Can you tell me how much it is?*

01. Please tell me. + How old is your father?

→ _____

02. Tell me. + What did you buy?

→ _____

03. Do you know? + When did the Korean War break out?

→ _____

Challenge 2   〈보기〉와 같이 빈칸을 완성하세요.

> **보기**
> A: Where does she live?
> B: I don't *know where she lives*.

01. A: Why is Jessica laughing?

     B: I don't know. Does anybody know _____ ?

02. A: How long do penguins live?

     B: I don't know _____ .

03. A: Where did Victoria buy her laptop?

     B: I don't know _____ .

Challenge 3   우리말과 일치하도록 괄호 안의 단어를 알맞게 배열하세요.

01. 공룡들이 왜 멸종했는지 너는 아니? (dinosaurs / extinct / became / why)

→ Do you know _____ ?

02 나는 이 호수가 얼마나 깊은지를 측정할 수 없다. (this lake / how deep / is)

→ I can't measure _____ .

3-3 if/whether로 시작하는 명사절

I wonder. + Did Alice go to Chicago?
→ I wonder **if Alice went to Chicago.**
나는 Alice가 시카고에 갔는지 안 갔는지가 궁금하다.

---

01 직접의문문에 '의문사'가 없는 경우 if 또는 whether를 명사절 접속사로 하여 명사절을 만든다. if나 whether로 시작하는 명사절은 **직접의문문이 간접의문문으로 바뀐 것이므로 반드시** 「if / whether + S + V」 의 어순으로 쓴다. 일상 영어에서는 if를 더 많이 쓰고, 둘 다 '~인지 아닌지'의 뜻이다.

I wonder. + Is Eric at home?
→ I wonder **if Eric is at home.** 나는 Eric이 집에 있는지 없는지 궁금하다.

The important part is. + Will Karen submit the report?
→ The important part is **if[whether] Karen will submit the report.**
중요한 부분은 Karen이 보고서를 제출할 것인가, 안 할 것인가이다.

---

02 '~인지 아닌지'의 명사절을 **주어로 쓸 경우 whether가 이끄는 명사절만이 가능하다.** if는 (be)동사 뒤에 쓴다. if나 whether 모두 뒤에 or not을 쓰거나 생략할 수 있다.

Will she come? + It isn't uncertain.
→ **Whether she will come or not** is uncertain.
그녀가 올 건지 안 올 건지는 불확실하다. ▶ whether ~ or not은 주어 역할

I don't know. + Are they angry?
→ I don't know **if[whether] they are angry (or not).**
그들이 화가 났는지 안 났는지 잘 모르겠다. ▶ if[whether] 이하는 know의 목적어 역할

I don't know **whether[if]** he is honest (or not). 나는 그가 정직한지 아닌지 모르겠다.
= I don't know **whether or not** he is honest.

Challenge 1 다음 직접의문문을 if나 whether가 이끄는 명사절로 바꿔 보세요.

> 보기
> Did I lock the door?
> → I don't know *if[whether] I locked the door.*

01. Is she coming?
→ I wonder _____ .

02. Has Jane finished medical school yet?
→ I don't know _____ .

03. Is the flight on time?
→ Can you tell me _____ ?

04. Is there enough gas in the car?
→ Do you know _____ ?

05. Did Jennifer change jobs?
→ I don't know _____ .

Challenge 2 접속사 if를 사용하여 명사절 문장을 완성하세요.

> 보기
> A: Are you going to need help moving furniture to your new apartment?
> B: I don't know *if I'm going to need help.* Thanks for asking. I'll let you know.

01. A: Does Kevin have to come with us?
B: Shhh. Don't ask _____ with us. Of course he does.
He's your brother!

02. A: Do penguins ever get cold?
B: That's an interesting question. I don't know _____ cold.

03. A: Are you tired?
B: Why do you want to know _____ tired?
A: You look tired. I'm worried about you.

"출제자가 노리는 급소" 이것이 시험에 출제되는 영문법이다!

01 출제 100% - 등위접속사의 의미를 정확하게 파악하라.

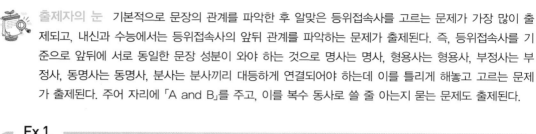 **출제자의 눈** 기본적으로 문장의 관계를 파악한 후 알맞은 등위접속사를 고르는 문제가 가장 많이 출제되고, 내신과 수능에서는 등위접속사의 앞뒤 관계를 파악하는 문제가 출제된다. 즉, 등위접속사를 기준으로 앞뒤에 서로 동일한 문장 성분이 와야 하는 것으로 명사는 명사, 형용사는 형용사, 부정사는 부정사, 동명사는 동명사, 분사는 분사끼리 대등하게 연결되어야 하는데 이를 틀리게 해놓고 고르는 문제가 출제된다. 주어 자리에 「A and B」를 주고, 이를 복수 동사로 쓸 줄 아는지 묻는 문제도 출제된다.

Ex 1.

I lost my transportation card, _____ I couldn't take the bus or the subway.

(a) but   (b) and   (c) or   (d) so

Ex 2.

My brother stayed at home and _____ TV.

(a) to watch   (b) watching   (c) watched   (d) watch

02 출제 100% - 상관접속사를 주의하라.

출제자의 눈 서로 짝을 이루는 상관접속사를 틀리게 해놓은 문제가 출제된다. both는 and와, either는 or과, neither는 nor와 함께 반드시 짝을 이뤄야 한다. 특히 상관접속사가 주어로 쓰인 경우 동사의 수일치는 and, or, but, but also 뒤에 있는 명사에 일치시킨다는 점을 꼭 알아두어야 한다. 마지막으로 상관접속사를 이용한 주관식 문제가 출제될 수 있으니 반드시 문장 전환 연습을 해 두어야 한다.

Ex 3.

Not only you _____ Jim was absent from the class.

(a) and   (b) but   (c) not   (d) or

Ex 4.

주어진 문장과 의미가 같도록 상관접속사를 이용한 문장을 완성하시오.

Bob doesn't play soccer. He doesn't play tennis, either.

= Bob plays _____.

03 출제 100% - 명령문과 함께 쓰이는 and와 or을 구별하라.

 출제자의 눈 '~해라, 그러면'의 뜻인 「명령문 + and」, '~해라, 그렇지 않으면'의 뜻인 「명령문 + or」에서 and와 or를 구별하는 문제가 출제된다. 또한 명령문을 If가 이끄는 조건절 문장으로 전환하는 서술형 문제도 반드시 출제된다.

Ex 5.

Hurry up, _____ you won't be late for the meeting.
(a) or   (b) but   (c) for   (d) and

Ex 6.

다음 문장을 if와 unless를 이용한 문장으로 각각 쓰시오.
Get some sleep, or you'll feel tired all afternoon.
= _____, you'll feel tired all afternoon.
= _____, you'll feel tired all afternoon.

04 출제 100% - 간접의문문의 어순에 주의하자!

 출제자의 눈 that이 대명사인지 명사절을 이끄는 접속사인지 구분하는 문제나, 관계사와 명사절로 쓰이는 that을 빈칸에 넣는 문제가 자주 출제된다. 특히 의문사가 있는 직접의문문을 간접의문문으로 바꿔 명사절로 영작하라든가, 의문사가 없을 때 if나 whether를 사용해서 명사절로 만들라는 주관식 문제는 반드시 출제된다.

Ex 7.

빈칸에 공통으로 들어갈 말을 쓰시오.
· Do you think _____ they will arrive before noon?
· Seoul is a city _____ attracts tourists.

Ex 8.

다음 두 문장을 명사절을 이용한 한 문장으로 완성하시오.
I wonder. + Is there life on other planets?
= _____

1. 다음 빈칸에 들어갈 말이 나머지와 다른 것은?

❶ Both Jason _____ Justin made a mistake.

❷ Not only Lucy _____ also Julia is pretty.

❸ My sister _____ I are teachers.

❹ Think hard, _____ you will get to know the answer.

❺ I can both speak _____ write French.

2. 두 문장이 같은 뜻이 되도록 빈칸에 알맞은 단어를 쓰시오.

> If you don't hurry up, you'll miss the start of the movie.
> = Hurry up, _____ you'll miss the start of the movie.

3. 다음 빈칸에 공통으로 들어갈 말로 알맞은 것은?

> · I don't believe _____ there is life on Mars.
> · Kevin's trouble is _____ he's too impatient.

❶ when　　　❷ if　　　❸ why

❹ that　　　❺ whether

4. 다음 문장과 의미가 같도록 상관접속사를 이용하여 문장을 완성하시오.

> She bought a car. She also bought a house.
> → She _____
> _____ .

[5-6] 다음 괄호 안의 접속사를 이용하여 명사절 문장을 완성하시오.

5.

> Does she like Chinese food?　+　I don't know. (if ~ or not)

→ _____
_____

6.

> Does the bus stop here?　+　I want to know. (whether ~ or not)

→ _____
_____

7. 다음 문장 중 빈칸에 들어갈 접속사가 나머지 넷과 다른 하나는?

❶ I believe _____ he is an honest boy.

❷ She said _____ she was there yesterday.

❸ I think _____ bulgogi is delicious.

❹ I know _____ you like Nancy.

❺ I studied very hard for the exam, _____ I got a poor grade.

8. 우리말과 의미가 같아지도록 빈칸에 들어갈 말이 바르게 짝지어진 것은?

> · She is not a nurse _____ a dentist.
> (그녀는 간호사가 아니라 치과의사이다.)
> · Treat others with respect, _____ you can expect others to respect you.
> (다른 사람들을 존중해라, 그러면 당신도 다른 사람이 당신을 존중해 줄 것을 기대할 수 있다.)

❶ and – that　　　❷ and – so

❸ either – nor　　　❹ but – or

❺ but – and

오답 노트 만들기

★틀린 문제 : _____   ★다시 공부한 날 : _____

(1) 문제를 왜? 틀렸는지 곰곰이 생각하고 그 이유를 적어본다.

(2) 핵심 개념을 적는다.

(3) 자신이 몰랐던 단어와 숙어 표현이 있으면 정리한다.

(4) 해설집에서 필요한 부분을 골라 풀이 해법을 정리한다.

★틀린 문제 : _____   ★다시 공부한 날 : _____

(1) 문제를 왜? 틀렸는지 곰곰이 생각하고 그 이유를 적어본다.

(2) 핵심 개념을 적는다.

(3) 자신이 몰랐던 단어와 숙어 표현이 있으면 정리한다.

(4) 해설집에서 필요한 부분을 골라 풀이 해법을 정리한다.

★틀린 문제 : _____   ★다시 공부한 날 : _____

(1) 문제를 왜? 틀렸는지 곰곰이 생각하고 그 이유를 적어본다.

(2) 핵심 개념을 적는다.

(3) 자신이 몰랐던 단어와 숙어 표현이 있으면 정리한다.

(4) 해설집에서 필요한 부분을 골라 풀이 해법을 정리한다.

★틀린 문제 : _____   ★다시 공부한 날 : _____

(1) 문제를 왜? 틀렸는지 곰곰이 생각하고 그 이유를 적어본다.

(2) 핵심 개념을 적는다.

(3) 자신이 몰랐던 단어와 숙어 표현이 있으면 정리한다.

(4) 해설집에서 필요한 부분을 골라 풀이 해법을 정리한다.

Unit 04 부사절

4-1 시간을 나타내는 접속사

After I eat dinner, I brush my teeth.
저녁 식사 후에 나는 이를 닦는다.

When I was young, I wanted to be Superman.
어렸을 때 나는 슈퍼맨이 되고 싶어했다.

01 when은 '~할 때'의 의미로 **어느 한 시점이나 기간을** 뜻한다. while은 '~하는 동안에, ~하는 사이에'의 뜻으로 **비교적 긴 시간에 걸쳐 동시에 일어나는 일을** 표현할 때 사용한다.

When I was studying, the light went out. 내가 공부하고 있을 때, 불이 나갔다.
My mom cooked dinner **while** I did my homework. 내가 숙제를 하는 동안에 엄마는 저녁을 요리했다.

02 as는 '~할 때, ~함에 따라'의 의미로 **두 가지 동작이 동시에 변화하고 있음을** 나타낼 때 사용한다.
as soon as는 '~하자마자'(=on+-ing)의 뜻이다.

Tiffany sometimes listens to music **as** she studies. Tiffany는 공부를 하면서 때때로 음악을 듣는다.
As we climbed higher, it became colder. 우리가 더 올라갈수록 더 추워졌다.
As soon as you get home, you should wash your feet. 집에 오자마자 발을 씻어야 한다.

03 그밖에도 before(~하기 전에), after(~한 후에), until(~할 때까지), since(~한 이래로, 이후로)가 있다.
특히 since는 완료시제와 함께 사용된다.

The Korean War broke out **before** I was born. 내가 태어나기 전에 한국 전쟁이 일어났다.
My dad always waits for me **until** I come home. 나의 아빠는 내가 집에 들어올 때까지 항상 나를 기다려 주신다.
I**'ve seen** a lot of things **since** I came to Europe. 내가 유럽에 온 이후로 많은 것을 봤다.

04 when, after, before, until 등이 이끄는 시간의 부사절에는 미래를 의미하는 내용이라도 미래시제 will을 쓰지 않는다. **현재시제를 써서 미래를** 나타내고, **미래완료 대신 현재완료를** 쓴다.

Wait here **until** she **comes** back. 그녀가 돌아올 때까지 여기서 기다리세요.
It will not be long **before** he **comes**. 그가 오래지 않아 올 것이다.
I'll tell you **when** I**'ve finished** lunch. 점심 식사가 끝나면 말해 줄게.

서술형 기초다지기

정답 p. 13

Challenge 1 다음 빈칸에 when, until, since, as soon as 중 알맞은 것을 써 넣으세요.

01. 나는 어렸을 때 비행기 조종사가 되고 싶었다.

= _____ I was young, I wanted to be a pilot.

02. 내가 버스 정류장에 도착하자마자 버스가 떠나 버렸다.

= _____ I arrived at the bus stop, the bus left.

03. 내가 다이어트를 시작한 이후로 10킬로그램 이상을 감량했다.

= I've lost over 10 kilograms _____ I started my diet.

04. 너는 네 숙제를 끝낼 때까지 교실에 있어야 한다.

= You must stay in class _____ you finish your homework.

Challenge 2 다음 괄호 안의 단어 중에서 알맞은 것을 고르세요.

01. When she came home, it (begins / began) to snow.

02. Somebody broke into the house while they (were sleeping / slept).

03. Three years (passed / have passed) since I came here.

04. Would you please think of an idea before she (will come / comes) back?

05. Make sure to turn off the TV before you (go / went) to bed.

06. As soon as she (will arrive / arrives), she will put on light clothes and walk in the sun.

Memo

원인과 결과를 나타내는 접속사

Because I was really tired, my wife drove the car instead.
내가 몹시 피곤했기 때문에 아내가 대신 차를 운전했다.

= I was really tired, so my wife drove the car instead.
내가 몹시 피곤해서 내 아내가 대신 차를 운전했다.

01 because, as, since는 '~때문에'라는 의미로 원인을 나타내는 부사절을 이끄는 접속사이다. **as나 since는 이미 알 만한 이유를 나타낼 때 쓰고, because는 듣는 사람이 잘 알지 못하는 이유를 나타낸다.**

As I have never been to Korea, I bought a guidebook. 나는 한국에 가 본 적이 없기 때문에 안내서를 샀다.
Since Jennifer lost her job, she can't afford to buy a car.
Jennifer는 직장을 잃었기 때문에, 그녀는 차를 살 여유가 없다.
I was absent from school yesterday **because** I was sick. 나는 어제 아파서 학교에 결석했다.

02 because는 듣는 사람이 알지 못하는 이유를 말하므로 why에 대한 대답으로 because를 쓴다. 같은 의미의 because of와 due to는 뒤에 명사(구)를 써서 이유를 강조하는 부사구를 만든다. since는 완료시제와 함께 쓰이지 않을 때는 이유를 나타내는 접속사가 된다.

A: **Why** do you look so blue? 왜 우울한 얼굴을 하고 있니?
B: **Because** I broke up with my girlfriend again. 내 여자 친구하고 또 헤어졌기 때문이야.

I like Lucy **because of** her good personality. 나는 Lucy의 좋은 성품 때문에 그녀를 좋아한다.
The baseball game has been cancelled today **due to** rain. 오늘 야구 경기가 비 때문에 취소되었다.

03 결과를 나타내는 접속사
① so: 그래서 (~하다)
   I didn't have an umbrella, **so** I got soaking wet. 나는 우산이 없어서 흠뻑 젖었다.
② 「so + 형용사/부사 + that~」: 매우 ~해서 ~하다.
   The iPhone is **so** expensive **that** I can't buy it. 아이폰이 매우 비싸서 나는 살 수 없다.
③ 「… so that S + V」: ~하기 위해서/~할 수 있도록 (목적을 나타냄)
   I saved my money **so that** I could buy the iPhone. 나는 아이폰을 사기 위해서 돈을 모았다.

서술형 기초다지기

Challenge 1 우리말과 뜻이 같도록 괄호 안의 단어 중에서 알맞은 것을 고르세요.

01. 어떤 차가 갑자기 내 앞에서 멈추어서 깜짝 놀랐다.

I was so surprised (because / because of) a car suddenly stopped in front of me.

02. 우리 아빠는 매우 바빴어. 그래서 내 생일을 잊으셨어.

My dad was very busy, (as / so) he forgot my birthday.

03. 그녀는 책을 가방에 넣고 다니기 위해서 그 가방을 샀다.

She bought a bag so (since / that) she might put her books in it.

04. 너 때문에 모든 것이 잘못됐어.

Everything went wrong (because of / because) you.

Challenge 2 두 문장의 인과관계가 성립하도록 알맞은 것을 골라 빈칸을 완성하세요.

so	because	that

01. We couldn't play tennis. It was raining.

→ We couldn't play tennis _____ it was raining.

→ It was raining _____ much _____ we couldn't play tennis.

02. As he was exhausted, he went to bed early last night.

→ He was exhausted, _____ he went to bed early last night.

→ He was _____ exhausted _____ he went to bed early last night.

Challenge 3 다음 괄호 안의 표현을 이용하여 문장을 다시 쓰세요.

01. I lied. I was afraid. (because)

→ _____

02. We have no classes on weekends. We can go skiing every Saturday. (since)

→ _____

03. My friend lied to me. I don't trust her anymore. (so)

→ _____

If the weather is nice tomorrow, we'll go fishing.
내일 날씨가 좋으면, 우리는 낚시하러 갈 거야.

Although he has got a car, he uses his bicycle in the city.
그는 차가 있는데도 불구하고 도시에서 자전거를 이용한다.

01 If는 조건의 부사절로 쓰인다. **조건의 부사절에서는 현재시제가 미래를 대신**한다. unless는 '~이 아니라면'의 뜻으로 if~not과 같은 의미이다. unless 조건절에는 부정어구를 쓰지 않도록 조심한다.

If I win the Lotto, I'll give the money to poor people. 내가 로또에 당첨된다면, 그 돈을 가난한 사람에게 주겠다.
We will be late **unless** we hurry. 서두르지 않는다면, 우리는 늦을 거야.
= We will be late if we **don't** hurry.

02 **변하지 않는 진리나 사실을 묘사**할 때도 조건의 부사절로 표현한다.

If the temperature falls below zero, water turns to ice. 온도가 0℃ 이하로 떨어지면 물이 언다.
If you water plants, they grow. 네가 식물에 물을 주면, 식물들은 자란다.

03 Although, even though, though, even if는 모두 '~임에도 불구하고, 비록 ~이지만'이라는 의미이다. 단, even if 다음에는 조건이나 가정의 내용이 오고, 나머지는 기정사실의 내용이 온다.

Although she is a math teacher, she speaks English fluently.
그녀는 수학선생님인데도 불구하고 영어를 유창하게 말한다. ▶ 수학 선생님인 것은 기정사실
Though they are poor, they help the homeless people in Seoul Station.
비록 그들도 가난하지만, 그들은 서울역에 있는 노숙자들을 돕는다. ▶ 그들이 가난한 것은 기정사실
Even if it rains, the festival will be held.
설사 비가 온다 할지라도 축제는 열릴 것이다. ▶ 비가 올지 안 올지 모르는 상황에서 온다는 가정
I'll not sell this car **even if** somebody gives me a million dollars.
누가 백만 달러를 준다고 해도 나는 이 차를 팔지 않겠다. ▶ 백만 달러를 준다는 것을 가정

04 In spite of, despite는 '~임에도 불구하고'라는 의미로 (al)though와 같은 뜻이지만, **이 둘은 전치사로 뒤에 명사 또는 명사구가 와야** 한다.

In spite of the heavy traffic, we arrived on time. 심한 교통 체증에도 불구하고, 우리는 시간에 맞춰 도착했다.
Despite his illness, he went to work. 그는 아픈데도 불구하고 일하러 갔다.

서술형 기초다지기

Challenge 1 although, in spite of, because, because of를 이용하여 다음 문장을 완성하세요.

01. _____ she wants to succeed in business, she works day and night.

02. The traffic accidents happened _____ bad weather conditions.

03. _____ the fact, he denied he had done it.

04. _____ Tom apologized, Sunny is still angry with him.

Challenge 2 다음 문장의 if는 unless로, unless는 if로 바꾸어 다시 쓰세요.

01. If you don't have a passport, you can't travel abroad.
    → _____, you can't travel abroad.

02. Let's see a movie unless you are busy.
    → Let's see a movie _____.

03. If you don't take your medicine, you won't feel better.
    → _____, you won't feel better.

04. Unless you exercise regularly, you won't lose weight.
    → _____, you won't lose weight.

05. We won't pass the exam if we don't work hard.
    → We won't pass the exam _____.

06. If you don't read the book, you can't do your homework.
    → _____, you can't do your homework.

"출제자가 노리는 급소" 이것이 시험에 출제되는 영문법이다!

01 출제 100% - 시간을 나타내는 접속사의 의미를 확실히 알아두자.

 출제자의 눈 시간의 접속사 자체를 묻는 문제나 「as soon as」를 「on + -ing」로 바꾸는 주관식 문제가 자주 출제된다. 조건의 부사절 if를 unless로 바꾸는 영작 문제가 나올 가능성도 높다. 결과를 나타내는 「so + 형용사/부사 + that」 구문에서 that을 물어보거나, so 뒤에 형용사나 부사를 쓸 줄 아는지를 묻는 문제도 출제된다.

Ex 1.

빈칸에 들어갈 알맞은 접속사를 바르게 짝지은 것은?

· He has worked here _____ he graduated.

· Don't drive _____ you're tired.

(a) while - when   (b) when - after   (c) after - when

(d) since - before   (e) because of - when

Ex 2.

조건을 나타내는 접속사 if를 이용하여 다음 문장을 고쳐 쓰시오.

Unless you work hard, you won't succeed.

= _____

02 출제 100% - 시간과 조건의 부사절 안에 있는 시제를 조심하라.

 출제자의 눈 시간(when, after 등), 조건(if)의 부사절 안에서는 미래를 나타내기 위해 will 대신에 현재시제를 쓴다. 난이도 있는 문제에서는 시간이나 조건을 나타내는 접속사가 이끄는 절이 명사절로 사용된 경우를 출제하여 혼동을 주기도 한다. when, if 등이 명사절로 사용될 때에는 명사절 안에 will을 쓸 수 있다는 것을 반드시 알아두자.

Ex 3.

A: Are you going out this afternoon?

B: _____, I will not go.

(a) If it will rain   (b) If it rains   (c) If it will be fine   (d) If it will be raining

Ex 4.

I don't know if _____ a new album again.

(a) he puts out   (b) he will put out

03 출제 100% - because와 because of를 구별하라.

 출제자의 눈 문맥을 파악하여 because 또는 (al)though를 넣거나 고르는 기본적인 문제가 출제된다. 특히 because와 (al)though 뒤에는 「주어+동사」가 오지만, because of, in spite of, despite 뒤에는 명사(구)를 쓴다는 것을 잊어서는 안 된다. 이런 유형의 문제는 내신, 수능, 텝스에서도 자주 출제된다.

Ex 5.

The future will be a lonely place to live _____ computers.
(a) because   (b) in spite of
(c) although   (d) because of

Ex 6.

_____ the nasty weather, they went for a walk.
(a) Due to   (b) In spite of
(c) Although   (d) Even if

04 출제 100% - 부사절에서는 시제 문제를 빼놓을 수 없다.

출제자의 눈 since는 완료시제와 함께 쓰일 경우 '~이래로, 이후로'의 뜻이 되고, 완료시제와 쓰지 않을 때는 이미 알만한 이유(~때문에)를 나타낸다. 문맥상 완료시제와 함께 쓸 줄 아는지를 묻거나, 완료시제와 함께 쓰일 때는 반드시 since절 안에 과거시제를 쓸 줄 아는지를 물어본다. 시간의 부사절을 이끄는 when, while, as가 '~하는 중에'로 쓰일 때는 먼저 진행 중이었던 동작은 부사절 안에 과거진행형으로 쓰고, 도중에 끼어든 비교적 짧은 시간 동안 행해진 다른 일은 과거시제로 표현한다. 이 두 시제를 틀리게 해놓고 고치게 하는 문제가 출제된다.

Ex 7.

When I was studying, the phone _____.
(a) was ringing   (b) rang   (c) rings   (d) will ring

Ex 8.

Steve _____ Korean since he was a student.
(a) have studied   (b) studied   (c) studies   (d) has studied

[1-3] 우리말과 의미가 같도록 빈칸에 알맞은 말을 쓰시오.

1.
> 비록 비가 왔지만, 우리는 계속해서 축구를 했다.
>
> = _____ it rained, we continued to play soccer.

2.
> 너와 나 둘 중의 하나는 이것에 대해 책임을 져야 한다.
>
> = _____ you _____ I must be responsible for this.

3.
> 나는 어제 너무 피곤해서 집에 일찍 갔다.
>
> = I was _____ tired _____ I went home early yesterday.

4. **다음 두 문장의 뜻이 다른 것은?**

❶ I take a shower before I have dinner.
   = I have dinner after I take a shower.
❷ I can speak not only Spanish but also Japanese.
   = I can speak Japanese as well as Spanish.
❸ While you were having a bath, Brian called you twice.
   = As you were having a bath, Brian called you twice.
❹ Unless you water the plants, they die.
   = If you water the plants, they die.
❺ Speak louder, or nobody will hear you.
   = If you don't speak louder, nobody will hear you.

[5-6] 다음 빈칸에 들어갈 말로 알맞은 것을 고르시오.

5.
> We don't have dinner until father _____.

❶ will come   ❷ comes
❸ come   ❹ came
❺ will be coming

6.
> I couldn't go out _____.

❶ if he doesn't start now
❷ as I don't go there
❸ when I come back home
❹ because I had a flu
❺ after it gets very dark

7. **다음 중 밑줄 친 When과 뜻이 다른 것은?**

> When we have problems, she listens to us and gives us some useful advice.

❶ When I'm tired, I always listen to music.
❷ When she first met him, she didn't like him much.
❸ When did you go to the library to study English?
❹ You didn't look pretty when you were born.
❺ When I am late, I go to school by taxi.

8. **다음 빈칸에 들어갈 동사 형태로 알맞은 것은?**

> When Kevin _____ to the history museum, he can travel to the past.

❶ go   ❷ goes
❸ will go   ❹ went
❺ is gone

오답 노트 만들기

★틀린 문제 : _____   ★다시 공부한 날 : _____

(1) 문제를 왜? 틀렸는지 곰곰이 생각하고 그 이유를 적어본다.

(2) 핵심 개념을 적는다.

(3) 자신이 몰랐던 단어와 숙어 표현이 있으면 정리한다.

(4) 해설집에서 필요한 부분을 골라 풀이 해법을 정리한다.

★틀린 문제 : _____   ★다시 공부한 날 : _____

(1) 문제를 왜? 틀렸는지 곰곰이 생각하고 그 이유를 적어본다.

(2) 핵심 개념을 적는다.

(3) 자신이 몰랐던 단어와 숙어 표현이 있으면 정리한다.

(4) 해설집에서 필요한 부분을 골라 풀이 해법을 정리한다.

★틀린 문제 : _____   ★다시 공부한 날 : _____

(1) 문제를 왜? 틀렸는지 곰곰이 생각하고 그 이유를 적어본다.

(2) 핵심 개념을 적는다.

(3) 자신이 몰랐던 단어와 숙어 표현이 있으면 정리한다.

(4) 해설집에서 필요한 부분을 골라 풀이 해법을 정리한다.

★틀린 문제 : _____   ★다시 공부한 날 : _____

(1) 문제를 왜? 틀렸는지 곰곰이 생각하고 그 이유를 적어본다.

(2) 핵심 개념을 적는다.

(3) 자신이 몰랐던 단어와 숙어 표현이 있으면 정리한다.

(4) 해설집에서 필요한 부분을 골라 풀이 해법을 정리한다.

1. 다음 두 문장의 의미가 같도록 빈칸에 들어갈 알맞은 것끼리 짝지은 것은?

> I was late for the class _____ the subway broke down.
> = The subway broke down, _____ I was late for the class.

❶ so − because　　❷ if − because
❸ so − though　　❹ because − so
❺ both − and

2. 다음 중 밑줄 친 단어의 쓰임이 적절하지 <u>않은</u> 것은?

❶ Turn off the light <u>when</u> you go out.
❷ <u>When</u> I go to the shop, I'll buy new clothes.
❸ <u>While</u> you eat food, you should brush your teeth.
❹ You can't watch TV <u>until</u> you finish your work.
❺ She couldn't go out <u>because</u> she had a cold.

[3-4] 다음 빈칸에 들어갈 알맞은 접속사를 고르시오.

3. 나는 그녀의 얼굴을 보자마자 웃음을 터뜨렸다.

> = _____ I saw her face, I burst into laughter.

❶ Since　　❷ As soon as　　❸ While
❹ Until　　❺ If

4. 그녀가 나에게 용서를 구하지 않으면, 나는 그녀를 만나지 않을 것이다.

> = _____ she begs me to forgive her, I won't meet her.

❶ If　　❷ Unless　　❸ When
❹ Though　　❺ As

5. 다음 빈칸에 들어갈 알맞은 시제를 고르시오.

> If it _____ tomorrow, the baseball game will be called off.

❶ rains　　❷ will rain　　❸ rained
❹ has rained　　❺ will be raining

6. 다음 밑줄 친 If의 성격이 나머지 넷과 <u>다른</u> 하나는?

❶ <u>If</u> you want, you may take this.
❷ <u>If</u> I don't report this before midnight, my name will be on the list.
❸ I wonder <u>if</u> my mom is at home.
❹ You will have a hearing problem in the future <u>if</u> you listen to music too loudly.
❺ <u>If</u> people are rude and selfish, they haven't got many friends.

7. 두 문장의 뜻이 같도록 빈칸에 알맞은 말을 쓰시오.

> He was too tired to start the journey again.
> = He was _____ tired _____ he couldn't start the journey again.

오답노트

8. 다음 밑줄 친 that과 쓰임이 같은 것은?

> Make sure that you turn off the lights when you go out of the room.

❶ That is my sister Julie.
❷ I know that he is diligent.
❸ Look at the car that they bought yesterday.
❹ I don't want to eat something that is not healthy.
❺ Some things that can be recycled are glass and paper.

오답노트

9. 다음 빈칸에 들어갈 알맞은 말은?

> Although he was poor, he was happy.
> = He was happy, _____ he was poor.

❶ so   ❷ if   ❸ but
❹ so that   ❺ just as

오답노트

[10-11] 다음 빈칸에 들어갈 알맞은 말을 찾아 쓰시오.

> what   where   when   but   so

10. _____ he was young, he worked as a lawyer.

11. He often couldn't remember _____ he put his cell phone.

오답노트

[12-13] 다음 빈칸에 들어갈 공통된 말은?

12.
> Run to the airport, _____ you won't see him.
> = _____ you run to the airport, you won't see him.

❶ and − If   ❷ or − If
❸ or − Unless   ❹ unless − If
❺ and − Unless

13.
> · I could only eat a salad in the restaurant _____ I am a vegetarian.
> · Credit cards have become preferred method of payment _____ risks involved in handling cash.

❶ because − because
❷ because − because of
❸ because of − of because
❹ because of − because
❺ of because − because

오답노트

14. 빈칸에 들어갈 접속사가 다른 하나는?

❶ I think _____ we should help the poor.

❷ I hope _____ you will win the first prize in a math test.

❸ I am so young _____ I can't go to school.

❹ I believe _____ you are a good friend.

❺ Please send me a post card _____ you get there.

오답노트

[15-16] 두 문장이 같은 뜻이 되도록 「명령문 + and / or」 문장으로 완성해 보시오.

15. If you are not responsible for your acts, nobody will trust you.

= _____ responsible for your acts, _____ nobody will trust you.

16. If you take a shuttle bus, you can save time and energy.

= _____ a shuttle bus, _____ you can save time and energy.

오답노트

17. 다음 빈칸에 들어갈 알맞은 말은?

> She called me. I was washing the dishes.
> → _____ she called me, I was washing the dishes.

❶ When ❷ Which ❸ What
❹ How ❺ Why

오답노트

18. 다음 문장에서 어법상 어색한 것은?

❶ Both Kevin and his wife enjoy tennis.

❷ I'm eating less these days because I want to lose weight.

❸ If she got the job, she will buy a car.

❹ If we leave now, we will get there in time.

❺ Jane can speak not only Korean but also Japanese.

오답노트

19. 다음 문장에서 틀린 부분을 찾아 바르게 고치시오.

> They had to cancel the flight to London because the typhoon.

_____ → _____

오답노트

[20-21] 밑줄 친 단어의 의미가 다른 하나는?

20.
❶ Either you <u>or</u> I am to blame for it.

❷ Some people can't read <u>or</u> write.

❸ Which do you like better, summer <u>or</u> winter?

❹ Wear your helmet, <u>or</u> you could be seriously hurt.

❺ You can go home, <u>or</u> you can stay here.

21.
❶ She stayed at home <u>and</u> watched a movie.

❷ Both his father <u>and</u> mother are doctors.

❸ Jennifer stopped at a cafe <u>and</u> had a cup of coffee.

❹ Now I can speak a little Korean, and I like lots of things about Korea.

❺ Be honest with her, and she'll forgive you.

오답노트

[22-23] 다음 중 어법상 바른 문장을 고르시오.

22. ❶ Both you and she has to take the class again.
❷ We danced and sing songs at the graduation party.
❸ Wait here until she comes back.
❹ As soon as she will arrive, she will put on light clothes and walk in the sun.
❺ Bob's going to study either history nor English.

오답노트

23. ❶ Which are you going to do, mop the floor and do the laundry?
❷ Do you know if he will come back?
❸ If we will miss the last bus, we'll have to walk home.
❹ We go on a picnic if the weather is nice next weekend.
❺ Although the heavy traffic, we arrived on time.

오답노트

24. **다음 빈칸에 공통으로 들어갈 알맞은 말은?**

· _____ I was very tired, I fell asleep right away.
· _____ we were taking a walk, we met a ghost.

오답노트

[25-26] 다음 빈칸에 알맞은 말을 쓰시오.

25. Do your best, or you won't pass the exam.
= _____ _____ _____ do your best, you won't pass the exam.

26. Lucy is not only pretty but also cute.
= Lucy is cute _____ _____ _____ pretty.

오답노트

27. **다음 글의 빈칸에 들어갈 적절한 단어는?**

Once upon a time there was a king who had a very pretty daughter. His daughter was so beautiful that everyone was busy singing about her beauty. But no one asked for her hand in marriage, _____ they were greatly afraid of the king. *ask for one's hand: 청혼하다

오답노트

A. 다음 두 문장을 괄호 안의 접속사를 이용하여 한 문장으로 바꾸시오.

> 보기
> Nancy bought a car. She also bought a bicycle. (not only ~ but also ~)
> → *Nancy bought not only a car but also a bicycle.*

1. Bob is going to go to Africa, or he is going to go to Asia. (either ~ or ~)

→ _____

2. He teaches English. He also teaches French. (not only ~ but also ~)

→ _____

3. My dad doesn't like pizza. He doesn't like spaghetti, either. (neither ~ nor ~)

→ _____

B. 명사절(간접의문문)을 활용하여 다음 문장을 완성하시오.

> 보기
> How old is your father?
> → Please tell me *how old your father is.*

1. Why did dinosaurs become extinct?

→ Do you know _____ ?

2. How did she learn to play the harmonica?

→ I wonder _____ .

3. Can she carry out the plan?

→ I doubt _____ .

C. 다음 문장을 if와 unless를 이용하여 같은 의미의 문장으로 다시 쓰시오.

1. Hurry up, or you will miss the first train.

= _____, you'll miss the first train.

= _____, you'll miss the first train.

2. Have a passport, or you can't travel abroad.

= _____, you can't travel abroad.

= _____, you can't travel abroad.

D. 다음 사진을 보고, 접속사 if나 unless 또는 when을 이용하여 문장을 완성하시오.

보 기	 (ticket / have)

Unless you have a ticket,
you can't enter the music hall.

1.

_____,

we'll go fishing.

(nice / tomorrow /
the weather)

2.

_____ along the road,

she met her friend.

(walk)

실전 서술형 평가문제

출제의도 등위접속사를 이용한 문장 완성
평가내용 상황에 맞는 접속사를 이용하여 문장 완성하기

A. 〈보기〉와 같이 주어진 표현을 이용하여 상황에 맞는 문장을 영작하시오. (and / but / so를 한 번만 사용)

[서술형 유형 : 6점 / 난이도 : 중하]

> **보기** 날씨가 너무 더워서, 그녀는 창문을 열었다. (open)
> It was very hot, *so she opened the window.*

1. 우리는 그 식당에 갔지만 문이 닫혀 있었다. (be closed)

We went to the restaurant, _____ .

2. 형은 집에 머물면서 영화를 보았다. (watch)

My brother stayed at home _____ .

3. 수잔은 배가 고프지 않아서 저녁을 먹지 않았다. (eat)

Susan wasn't hungry, _____ .

출제의도 명사절을 이용하여 문장 완성하기
평가내용 명사절 접속사 that의 이해

B. 〈보기〉와 같이 주어진 문장을 읽고 자신의 생각을 I (don't) believe that ~ 또는 I (don't) think that ~의 문장으로 영작하시오.

[서술형 유형 : 8점 / 난이도 : 중]

> **보기** People can live without water.
> → *I don't believe that people can live without water.*

1. Computers will have emotions.

→ _____

2. It is difficult for some people to focus on work when they are at home.

→ _____

3. People will be happy all the time.

→ _____

4. It is difficult for some people to learn languages.

→ _____

출제의도 시간과 조건의 부사절의 쓰임새를 익힌다.
평가내용 시간과 조건의 부사절 문장 완성하기

C. 〈보기〉와 같이 다음 두 문장을 주어진 접속사를 이용하여 부사절과 주절이 있는 문장으로 영작하시오.

[서술형 유형 : 6점 / 난이도 : 중하]

> **보기**
> I want to get good grades. Then, my parents will be happy. (if)
> → *If I get good grades, my parents will be happy.*

1. Nancy should stop eating sweets. Otherwise, she won't lose any weight. (unless)

→ _____

2. I may see Kevin this afternoon. Then I'll tell him to phone you. (if)

→ _____

3. Sometimes the temperature reaches -15℃. Then, the lake freezes. (when)

→ _____

출제의도 since와 함께 쓰이는 시제
평가내용 부사절과 함께 쓰이는 과거시제와 완료시제 활용하기

D. 〈보기〉와 같이 주어진 표현을 현재완료와 과거시제 그리고 접속사 since를 적절히 사용하여 문장을 완성하시오.

[서술형 유형 : 6점 / 난이도 : 중]

> **보기**
> Jennifer / start working   Jennifer / travel abroad / many times
> → *Jennifer has travelled abroad many times since she started working.*

1. Jane / lose ten kilos   Jane / join a health club

→ _____

2. my dad / buy a new car   my dad / not have any accidents

→ _____

3. Kelly / move to Scotland   I / not see / Kelly

→ _____

실전 서술형 평가문제

정답 p. 15

출제의도 전후를 나타내는 부사절의 쓰임새를 익힌다.
평가내용 부사절 접속사 before, after의 활용

E. 다음 괄호 안의 표현을 이용하여 질문에 알맞은 대답을 완성하시오.　　　[서술형 유형 : 12점 / 난이도 : 중상]

1. (cook dinner)

Q : What did you do before your guests arrived?

A : _____ before _____ .

2. (play soccer)

Q : What did he do with his friends after he ate lunch?

A : After _____ , _____ .

3. (have lunch)

Q : What did they do before they sat on the beach?

A : _____ before _____ .

4. (play tennis)

Q : What are you going to do after you finish your homework?

A : _____ after _____ .

서술형 평가문제	채 점 기 준	배 점	나의 점수
A	표현이 올바르고 문법, 철자가 모두 정확한 경우	2점×3문항=6점	
B		2점×4문항=8점	
C		2점×3문항=6점	
D		2점×3문항=6점	
E		3점×4문항=12점	
공통	문법(접속사 등), 철자가 1개씩 틀린 경우	각 문항당 1점씩 감점	
	내용과 전혀 일치하지 않거나 답을 기재하지 못한 경우	0점	

Chapter 5

관계사 (Relatives)

관계대명사

1-1 주격, 목적격으로 쓰이는 who

I have **a friend**. + **She** wants to be a singer.

I have a friend **who** wants to be a singer.
나는 가수가 되길 원하는 친구가 있다.

---

01 명사를 설명해 주거나 꾸며 주는 말은 형용사와 분사이다. 하지만 **명사를 아주 구체적으로 설명하기 위해서는 관계대명사를 사용**한다.

I like the **handsome** boy. 나는 그 잘생긴 소년을 좋아한다. ▶ 명사의 상태 설명

Look at the boy **sitting on the bench.** 벤치에 앉아 있는 소년을 봐. ▶ 명사의 동작 설명

I like the boy **who gave me flowers.** 나는 내게 꽃을 준 그 소년을 좋아한다. ▶ 동작+시제를 통해 명사를 구체적으로 설명

02 영어는 같은 말의 반복을 피하기 위해 대명사(she, he, it...)를 사용한다. 하지만 대명사는 대명사 역할만 할 뿐 문장과 문장을 연결시킬 수 없다. 따라서 **반복을 피하면서 문장도 연결할 수 있는 who, which, that이 탄생**하게 되었다.

I like <u>the woman</u>. + <u>She</u> lives next to me. ▶ She는 문장을 연결할 수 없다. 대명사 who로 바꾼다.

→ I like the woman **who** lives next to me. 나는 옆집에 사는 그 여자를 좋아한다.

▶ 명사의 반복도 피하고 문장끼리 연결도 가능해진다.

03 **who는 사람을 대신할 때 사용**한다. 따라서 **앞에 있는 선행사도 사람이어야 한다.** 주어인 명사(사람)를 대신하면 주격 관계대명사, 목적어(사람)를 대신하면 목적격 관계대명사라고 한다. 관계대명사 that은 주격과 목적격 관계없이 who 대신 쓸 수 있지만 who를 더 자주 쓴다.

He married <u>a woman</u>. + <u>She</u> was from Vietnam.

→ He married a woman **who** was from Vietnam. 그는 베트남에서 온 여자와 결혼했다.
(주격 관계대명사)

I know <u>the girl</u>. + You met <u>her</u> yesterday.

→ I know the girl **who(m)** you met yesterday. 나는 네가 어제 만난 그 여자를 안다.
(목적격 관계대명사)

※ 대명사도 주격은 she, 목적격은 her를 쓰듯이 관계대명사도 주격은 who, 목적격은 whom으로 모양을 바꾼다. 하지만 현대 영어에서는 whom 대신 who를 더 많이 쓴다.

서술형 기초다지기

Challenge 1 밑줄 친 대명사를 who 또는 who(m)으로 고쳐 한 문장으로 만드세요.

01. I have a boyfriend. I can trust <u>him</u>.

→ _____

02. I met the couples. <u>They</u> have just got married.

→ _____

03. The woman is a doctor. <u>She</u> lives next door.

→ _____

04. Do you know the people? <u>They</u> live in Singapore.

→ _____

05. I know a boy. <u>He</u> plays online games every night.

→ _____

06. I met friends. I've known <u>them</u> since elementary school.

→ _____

07. This is the man. <u>He</u> saved her life.

→ _____

08. The girl is now in the hospital. <u>She</u> was injured in the accident.

→ _____

09. She is the teacher. I really wanted to meet <u>her</u>.

→ _____

10. I like the girl. I met <u>her</u> at the party.

→ _____

1-2 주격, 목적격으로 쓰이는 which, that

An orange is **a fruit**. + **It** has a lot of vitamin C.

An orange is a fruit **which** has a lot of vitamin C.
오렌지는 많은 비타민 C를 함유하고 있는 과일이다.

---

01 which는 **사물이나 동물을 대신할 때 사용**한다. 따라서 앞에 있는 선행사도 사물이나 동물이어야 한다. 주어인 사물/동물 명사를 대신하면 주격, 목적어인 사물/동물 명사를 대신하면 목적격 관계대명사라고 한다. 항상 that으로 바꾸어 쓸 수 있는데, that이 더 많이 쓰이기도 한다.

This is <u>the house</u>. + <u>It</u> has 9 bedrooms.

This is the house **which** has 9 bedrooms. 이곳은 침실이 9개인 집이다.
　　　　　　　(주격 관계대명사)

This is <u>the book</u>. + I have written <u>it</u> recently.

This is the book **which** I have written recently. 이것이 내가 최근에 쓴 책이다.
　　　　　　　(목적격 관계대명사)

---

02 관계대명사 **that은 모든 관계사를 대신해서 쓸 수 있다.** 선행사가 사람, 사물, 동물, 어느 것이든 관계없이 모두 쓸 수 있다. 주격과 목적격의 형태는 모두 that이지만 소유격은 없다.

선행사	주격	목적격	소유격
사람	who	who(m)	whose
사물, 동물	which	which	whose / of which
사람, 사물, 동물	that	that	–

He is <u>the man</u>. + <u>He</u> made this camera.

→ He is the man **that(= who)** made this camera. 그는 이 카메라를 만든 사람이다.

This is <u>the camera</u>. + He made <u>it</u>.

→ This is the camera **that(= which)** he made. 이것이 그가 만든 카메라이다.

This is <u>a book</u>. + <u>It</u> is about history.

→ This is a book **that(= which)** is about history. 이것은 역사에 관한 책이다.

서술형 기초다지기

Challenge 1 | 다음 두 문장을 관계대명사 who 또는 which를 이용하여 한 문장으로 만드세요.

01. This is the iPhone. I bought it yesterday.

→ _____

02. These are the problems. I can't solve them on my own.

→ _____

03. The woman is a dancer. She lives next door.

→ _____

04. Look at the house. It is covered with snow.

→ _____

05. I saw the children. They were playing soccer at the park.

→ _____

Challenge 2 | 〈보기〉와 같이 관계대명사가 쓰인 문장을 두 문장으로 다시 쓰세요.

보기	The books which are on the table are mine. → *The books are mine.* + *They are on the table.*

01. Kathy has some photos that I took.

→ _____ + _____

02. Sunny who lives near the school is my friend.

→ _____ + _____

03. I gave her the book which she wanted.

→ _____ + _____

04. I saw an old castle which stood on the hill.

→ _____ + _____

1-3 소유격 관계대명사

I met a person **whose** job is a journalist.
나는 직업이 기자인 사람을 만났다.

01 my book(나의 책)에서 소유격은 my이다. 이 **소유격을 대신 쓸 수 있는 것이 바로 소유격 관계사 whose**이다. 즉, whose book과 my book은 같다. whose를 쓰는 이유는 문장과 문장을 연결해 주는 역할을 겸하고 있기 때문이다.

The man called the police. | His car | was stolen. ▶ 소유격 His는 문장을 연결할 수 없다.
↓
whose car

→ The man [**whose** car was stolen] called the police. 차를 도난당한 남자는 경찰을 불렀다.

I know a girl. | Her brother | is a movie star. ▶ 소유격 Her는 문장을 연결할 수 없다.
↓
whose brother

→ I know a girl [**whose** brother is a movie star]. 나는 오빠가 영화배우인 소녀를 안다.

02 소유격 whose, of which는 주로 학술지 같은 문어체의 딱딱한 글에서 많이 쓰고 일상 영어에서는 **with를 사용하여 소유를 나타내는 간단한 문장**으로 쓴다.

This is the house **whose** roof is blue. 이것은 지붕이 푸른 집이다.
= This is the house **of which** the roof is blue.

→ This is the house **with** the blue roof.
→ The roof **of** this house is blue.

서술형 기초다지기

Challenge 1 다음 괄호 안의 단어 중 알맞은 것을 고르세요.

01. He is the man (who / which / whose) married Diane.

02. The man (which / whose / that) bicycle was stolen called the police.

03. This is the car (whose / which / who) he bought yesterday.

04. The woman (who / whose / which) you saw yesterday is my mom.

05. Mr. Baker has a daughter (which / that / whose) name is Susan.

Challenge 2 다음 두 문장을 관계대명사 whose를 이용하여 한 문장으로 만드세요.

01. I saw a girl. + Her hair is blonde.

→ _____

02. There is a man. + His car was stolen.

→ _____

03. There is a woman. + Her cat died.

→ _____

04. We have a puppy. Its name is Happy.

→ _____

05. There are many words. + I don't know their meanings.

→ _____

Memo

1-4 목적격 관계대명사의 생략

I lost the cell phone (**which**) my dad bought yesterday.
나는 아빠가 어제 산 휴대전화를 잃어버렸다.

---

01 **목적격으로 쓰인 who(m), which, that은 언제나 생략 가능**하다. 특히 일상 회화에서는 거의 생략한다.

The books were expensive.　+　I bought them.　▶ 목적어 them을 관계대명사로 바꾼다.

→ The books **which** I bought were expensive. 내가 구입한 책들은 비쌌다.

→ The books **that** I bought were expensive.

→ The books I bought were expensive.

Do you know the boy?　+　Jane met him.　▶ 목적어 him을 관계대명사로 바꾼다.

→ Do you know the boy **who(m)** Jane met? 너는 제인이 만난 소년을 아니?

→ Do you know the boy **that** Jane met?

→ Do you know the boy Jane met?

02 **전치사 뒤에 오는 (대)명사가 사람이면 whom, 사물이나 동물인 경우 which를 쓴다.** 전치사를 맨 뒤로 보내고 whom과 which를 생략하는 것이 가장 자연스럽다.

Korea is the country.　+　I want to live in the country.

　▶ 전치사의 목적어인 the country를 관계대명사로 바꾼다.

→ Korea is the country **in which** I want to live. 한국은 내가 살고 싶은 나라이다.　▶ that으로 쓰지 않는다.

→ Korea is the country **which** I want to live **in**.

→ Korea is the country **that** I want to live **in**.　▶ 전치사를 뒤로 보낼 때만 that 사용 가능

→ Korea is the country I want to live **in**.　▶ 전치사를 뒤로 보낼 때 관계대명사 생략 가능

The man is over there.　+　I told you about him.　▶ 전치사의 목적어인 him을 관계대명사로 바꾼다.

→ The man **about whom** I told you is over there. 내가 너에게 말한 그 사람이 저기에 있다.　▶ who를 쓰지 않는다.

→ The man **who(m)** I told you **about** is over there.　▶ 전치사가 뒤로 갈 경우 who 사용 가능

→ The man **that** I told you **about** is over there.　▶ 전치사를 뒤로 보낼 때만 that 사용 가능

→ The man I told you **about** is over there.　▶ 전치사를 뒤로 보낼 때 관계대명사 생략 가능

서술형 기초다지기

Challenge 1 다음 문장에서 생략할 수 있는 관계대명사를 괄호로 묶으세요.

01. The library which Kevin recommended was closed.

02. This is the key which opens the garage.

03. I don't know the man about whom you talked.

04. The flower that he gave to her was really pretty.

05. I hate the cheerleader whom you played with.

Challenge 2 두 문장을 관계대명사를 이용하여 가능한 모든 형태의 한 문장으로 만들어 보세요.

01. She is the woman. + I want to marry her.

→ _____

→ _____

→ _____

02. I never found the book. + I was looking for it.

→ _____

→ _____

→ _____

→ _____

03. The woman was interesting. + I was talking to her.

→ _____

→ _____

→ _____

→ _____

1-5 what과 that / 관계사절의 수일치

The thing which[that] he said made me angry.
= What he said made me angry.
그가 한 말은 나를 화나게 했다.

They were talking about something **that** I didn't know.
그들은 내가 모르는 것에 대해 말하고 있었다.

01 What은 **선행사를 포함한 관계대명사**로 '~한 것'이란 뜻이다. 선행사(the thing)를 포함하고 있으므로 what 앞에 명사는 필요하지 않다.

What you really need is self-confidence. 네가 정말로 필요한 것은 자신감이다.
= **The thing which[that]** you really need is self-confidence.

02 선행사에 다음이 포함되어 있을 경우에는 that을 쓴다.

① 최상급, 서수, every, all, the only, the same, any, some 등이 선행사에 포함되어 있을 때
You can have every toy **that** you like. 네가 좋아하는 모든 장난감을 가질 수 있다.
She is the first woman **that** arrived at the top. 그녀는 정상에 도달한 최초의 여성이다.
He is the only person **that** I can trust. 그는 내가 믿을 수 있는 유일한 사람이다.
This is the same bicycle **that** I lost yesterday. 이것은 내가 어제 잃어버린 것과 같은 자전거이다.
All **that** you read in this book will do you good. 이 책에서 읽는 모든 것은 너에게 이익이 될 것이다.

② 형용사의 최상급
She is the most prettiest woman **that** I've ever seen. 그녀는 지금껏 내가 봤던 가장 예쁜 여자이다.

③ 선행사가 -thing으로 끝나는 명사이거나 사람과 사물이 동시에 나왔을 때
Give me something **that** I can drink. 나에게 마실 수 있는 것을 좀 줘.
He made a speech on the men and customs **that** he went through in Africa.
그는 아프리카에서 경험한 사람들과 풍속들에 관해서 연설을 했다.

※ 현대 영어에서는 선행사 앞에 이러한 단어가 있더라도, 선행사가 사람이면 that보다 who를 주로 쓰고, 사물이면 which보다 that을 주로 쓴다. 위의 문법은 구식 영어에 속하나, 시험에 등장하고 있으므로 설명하였다.

03 관계대명사의 수식을 받아 주어가 길어지는 경우, 동사는 관계대명사절과 관계없이 주어의 수에 일치시켜야 한다.

The girls [who are with Bob] **are** my friends. Bob과 함께 있는 소녀들은 내 친구들이다.
The library [which is in my village] **is** very small. 우리 마을에 있는 도서관은 매우 작다.
The books [which he wrote] **are** very interesting. 그가 쓴 책들은 아주 흥미롭다.

서술형 기초다지기

정답 p. 16

Challenge 1 다음 밑줄 친 부분을 the thing which 또는 what으로 바꿔 다시 쓰세요.

01. This is <u>the thing which</u> I wanted.

→ _____

02. She showed me <u>what</u> she bought yesterday.

→ _____

03. I can't believe <u>what</u> Scott said.

→ _____

04. This is <u>the thing which</u> I want to draw.

→ _____

05. <u>The thing which</u> I really want to be is a nurse.

→ _____

06. I don't believe <u>what</u> Julia told me.

→ _____

Challenge 2 다음 괄호 안의 단어 중에 알맞은 것을 고르세요.

01. The girl who can speak three languages (are / is) my sister.

02. The houses which are in the pictures (was / were) built in 1700.

03. He is the tallest man (which / that / who) I've ever seen.

04. Look at the woman and the dog (who / which / that) are crossing the bridge.

05. Kevin is the only student (that / who / which) heard the news.

06. We saw something (which / who / that) is very shocking.

관계부사

2-1 when, where, why, how

Let me know **the day**. + You'll visit me **on the day**.

Let me know the day **when** you'll visit me.
네가 나를 방문할 날을 알려줘.

01 명사를 대신하는 것이 관계대명사이면, **부사(구)를 대신하고 문장과 문장을 연결할 수 있는 것이 바로 관계부사**이다. 관계대명사와 마찬가지로 앞에 있는 명사(선행사)를 꾸며 주며 '~하는, ~했던, ~할'로 해석한다.

관계부사 (= 전치사 + which)	선행사
when (= in/on/at + which)	**시간**: the time, the day, the week 등 Do you remember <u>the day</u>? + We first met <u>then</u>. → Do you remember the day **when** we first met? 　우리가 처음으로 만난 날을 기억하니? → Do you remember the day **on which** we first met?
where (= in/on/at + which)	**장소**: the place, the city, the house 등 That is <u>the library</u>. + We used to study <u>there</u>. → That is the library **where** we used to study. 저기가 우리가 공부했던 도서관이다. → That is the library **in which** we used to study.
why (= for which)	**이유**: the reason I don't know <u>the reason</u>. She isn't here <u>for that reason</u>. → I don't know the reason **why** she isn't here. 　나는 그녀가 여기에 없는 이유를 모르겠다. → I don't know the reason **for which** she isn't here.
how (= in which)	**방법**: the way ※ 관계부사 how는 the way와 함께 쓸 수 없으므로 둘 중 하나는 반드시 생략한다. This is <u>the way</u>. I study Japanese <u>in that way</u>. → This is **how** I study Japanese. 이것이 내가 일본어를 공부하는 방법이다. → This is **the way** I study Japanese.

서술형 기초다지기

정답 p. 16

Challenge 1　다음 괄호 안의 단어 중에 알맞은 것을 고르세요.

01. This is the place (when / where) only the disabled can park.

02. The clerk explained (why / how) the DVD works.

03. What's the name of the restaurant (where / why) we had dinner last night?

04. Do you know the reason (why / when) she was absent?

05. 2002 was the year (where / when) the Korea-Japan World Cup was held.

Challenge 2　다음 두 문장이 같은 뜻이 되도록 빈칸에 알맞은 말을 쓰세요.

01. Do you know the reason why she moved to Egypt?

    = Do you know the reason _____ _____ she moved to Egypt?

02. This is the house in which I was brought up.

    = This is the house _____ I was brought up.

03. She told me the way she escaped from the bus.

    = She told me _____ she escaped from the bus.

Challenge 3　다음 두 문장을 관계부사를 이용하여 한 문장으로 연결하세요.

01. I went back to the village.　+　I was born there.

    → _____

02. Tell me the reason.　+　You didn't call me for the reason.

    → _____

03. That is the way. I solve the problem in that way.

    → _____

2-2 관계부사절의 독특한 특징

Do you know **the reason** Brian is quitting his job?
= Do you know **why** Brian is quitting his job?
= Do you know the reason **that** Brian is quitting his job?
너는 Brian이 직장을 그만둔 이유를 아니?

01 관계부사는 **선행사인 명사(시간, 이유, 방법, 장소)를 생략**해서 쓰기도 하고, **관계부사 자체를 생략**해서 쓰기도 한다. 관계부사가 생략이 되면 '명사+명사'가 연이어 나오므로 목적격 관계대명사의 생략과 혼동해서는 안 된다.

I'll never forget the day **when** I first met you. 나는 처음으로 너를 만난 그 날을 결코 잊지 않을 것이다.

= I'll never forget **when** I first met you. ▶ 선행사 the day 생략

= I'll never forget **the day** I first met you. ▶ 관계부사 when 생략

02 목적격 관계대명사 생략과 관계부사의 생략을 구별하는 것은 간단하다. **관계대명사는** 문장의 목적어인 (대)명사를 대신했으므로 관계사절에 **타동사의 목적어 또는 전치사의 목적어가 빠져** 있다. 반면, 관계부사가 이끄는 절은 「주어＋자동사」, 「주어 + 타동사 + 목적어」, 「전치사 + 목적어」가 완전하게 존재한다.

This is the cell phone I bought yesterday. 이것은 내가 어제 산 휴대전화이다.
▶ 타동사 bought의 목적어가 없다. → 목적격 관계대명사(that) 생략

That's the reason she was angry with me. 그것이 그녀가 내게 화를 낸 이유이다.
▶ 「자동사＋전치사＋목적어」가 온전한 문장 → 관계부사(why) 생략

03 **모든 관계대명사와 관계부사 대신 that을 사용**할 수 있다. 하지만 관계부사절에서 **선행사가 생략된 경우에는 that을 쓸 수 없다.** 선행사가 있을 때에만 that을 쓸 수 있다.

I can't remember the place **where** we met last night. 나는 지난밤에 만났던 장소를 기억해 낼 수 없다.

= I can't remember the place **that** we met last night.

I can't remember <u>**that**</u> we met last night. (×) ▶ 선행사가 생략됐으므로 where를 써야 한다.
    → where

This is the way **that** Michael avoided the accident. 이것이 마이클이 그 사고를 피한 방법이다.

This is <u>**that**</u> Michael avoided the accident. (×) ▶ 선행사가 생략했으므로 how를 써야 한다.
  → how

서술형 기초다지기

정답 p. 16

Challenge 1 다음 빈칸에 알맞은 관계대명사 또는 관계부사를 쓰세요. (단, that은 제외)

01. Saturday is the day _____ she is busy.

02. I love the woman _____ I met at the party.

03. I can't understand the reason _____ I got fired.

04. The movie _____ we saw last night was moving.

05. Have you found the keys _____ you lost?

06. 1998 was the year _____ the Seoul Olympic Games were held.

07. She is the person _____ I don't trust.

08. Tell me the resort _____ you and your wife stayed.

Challenge 2 다음 관계부사 문장을 〈보기〉와 같이 3가지 형태로 다시 써 보세요.

> **보기**
> That is the reason why Kathy left him.
> = That is *why* Kathy left him.
> = That is *the reason* Kathy left him.
> = That is *the reason* *that* Kathy left him.

01. This is the room where I used to live.

= This is _____ I used to live.

= This is _____ _____ I used to live.

= This is _____ _____ _____ I used to live.

02. Monday is the time when I have a lot of work to do.

= Monday is _____ I have a lot of work to do.

= Monday is _____ _____ I have a lot of work to do.

= Monday is _____ _____ _____ I have a lot of work to do.

01 출제 100% - 선행사를 찾아라.

 출제자의 눈 관계대명사와 관계부사를 고르는 문제가 자주 출제되는데 이때는 선행사를 보고 결정한다. 두 개의 문장을 주고 공통으로 들어갈 관계사를 고르거나 that의 용법을 묻는 문제 역시 자주 출제되는데 이는 가장 기본적인 출제 영역들이다.

Ex 1.

I have a friend _____ is a famous movie star.

(a) when   (b) which   (c) who   (d) whose

Ex 2.

밑줄 친 that과 쓰임이 같은 것은?

· The dress <u>that</u> she is wearing is new.

(a) I know <u>that</u> the man is honest.
(b) This is a book and <u>that</u> is an album.
(c) Do you know the boy <u>that</u> Joan met?
(d) This is the dog <u>that</u> likes apples.

02 출제 100% - 관계대명사의 격은 관계대명사가 이끄는 절에서 결정된다.

 출제자의 눈 관계대명사는 명사를 대신하는 대명사의 역할을 하므로 관계사절이 완전하지 못하다. 그러나 관계부사는 부사(구)를 대신하므로 관계부사절은 온전한 하나의 절을 이루고 있다. 관계대명사의 격은 주어가 빠져 있으면 주격 who(사람) 또는 which(사물)를 쓰고, 타동사 또는 전치사 뒤에 오는 목적어가 빠져 있을 때는 목적격을 쓴다. 소유격은 관계대명사 바로 뒤에 명사 또는 「명사 + be동사」가 오면서 완전한 문장을 이룰 때 쓴다.

Ex 3.

The person _____ I told you about is standing over there.

(a) which   (b) whose   (c) who   (d) about whom

Ex 4.

I met the man _____ name is the same as mine.

(a) who   (b) which   (c) why   (d) whose

03 출제 100% - 관계사를 이용하여 영작 연습을 해두자.

 출제자의 눈 관계사를 이용한 영작 문제는 단답형 주관식 또는 서술형으로 출제된다. 자주 출제되는 영역이므로 관계대명사의 격, 관계부사의 쓰임과 용법을 반드시 익혀 두어야 한다. 또한 the thing which와 what을 서로 바꿔 쓸 줄 아는지 묻는 문제가 출제된다.

Ex 5.

다음 두 문장을 연결할 때 빈칸에 알맞은 말을 쓰시오.
Show me the iPhone. + You bought it yesterday.
→ Show me the iPhone _____.

Ex 6.

다음 두 문장을 what과 which를 이용하여 각각 한 문장씩 완성하시오.
This is the thing. + I wanted it.
→ ① _____
→ ② _____

04 출제 100% - 주어가 길어질 때를 조심하라.

 출제자의 눈 관계사절이 주어를 수식할 경우 주어와 동사가 멀리 떨어지게 된다. 때문에 동사의 수 일치를 묻는 문제가 많이 출제된다. 관계사절의 수식을 받을 경우 두 번째 나오는 동사를 주어와 일치시켜 준다. what은 선행사 없이 단독으로 쓰이고, 관계부사 how는 선행사 the way와 함께 쓰지 않고 둘 중 하나만 쓴다는 것도 꼭 기억하자.

Ex 7.

다음 문장에서 어법상 <u>어색한</u> 부분을 찾아 바르게 고치시오.
The people who work in the office is very friendly.
_____ → _____

Ex 8.

다음 문장 중 어법상 <u>어색한</u> 것은?
(a) Seattle is the city where I studied English.
(b) I don't know the way how the thief broke into my house.
(c) She wants to know how Koreans make Gimchi.

1. 다음 두 문장을 관계대명사를 사용하여 한 문장으로 만드시오.

> Jennifer is my friend. Her hair is black.
> → Jennifer _____
> _____.

2. 다음 두 문장을 관계부사를 사용하여 하나의 문장으로 완성하시오.

> This is the house.
> I lived in the house.
> → _____

[3-7] 다음 문장에 이어질 알맞은 관계사절을 아래에서 골라 쓰시오.

> · whose job is a journalist
> · which I really like to play
> · where there is a lot of fresh air
> · why she cried
> · whose color is red

3. I'd like to live in a country _____
_____.

4. This is the car _____.

5. This is the game _____.

6. I met a person _____.

7. Do you know the reason _____?

8. 다음 밑줄 친 곳에 공통으로 들어갈 알맞은 말은?

> · I know girls _____ are good at French.
> · There are no chairs _____ we can sit on.

❶ who 　　❷ which 　　❸ that
❹ whose 　　❺ what

9. 다음 중 어법상 옳은 것은?

❶ He has a daughter that she is a teacher.
❷ He has a daughter who she is a teacher.
❸ He has a daughter who is a teacher.
❹ She has a daughter which she is a teacher.
❺ He has a daughter which is a teacher.

10. 다음 우리말을 영어로 옮길 때 빈칸에 알맞은 말을 넣으시오.

> 저기가 자동차 사고가 일어났던 장소이다.
> → That is _____ _____ _____
> the car accident took place.

11. 다음 중 어법상 어색한 것은?

❶ The apples which grow in my garden is sweet.
❷ We helped a woman whose car had broken down.
❸ The men that she's talking with are doctors.
❹ The pictures which she drew are very interesting.
❺ The picture that is on the wall is so nice.

오답 노트 만들기

★틀린 문제 : _____   ★다시 공부한 날 : _____

(1) 문제를 왜? 틀렸는지 곰곰이 생각하고 그 이유를 적어본다.

(2) 핵심 개념을 적는다.

(3) 자신이 몰랐던 단어와 숙어 표현이 있으면 정리한다.

(4) 해설집에서 필요한 부분을 골라 풀이 해법을 정리한다.

★틀린 문제 : _____   ★다시 공부한 날 : _____

(1) 문제를 왜? 틀렸는지 곰곰이 생각하고 그 이유를 적어본다.

(2) 핵심 개념을 적는다.

(3) 자신이 몰랐던 단어와 숙어 표현이 있으면 정리한다.

(4) 해설집에서 필요한 부분을 골라 풀이 해법을 정리한다.

★틀린 문제 : _____   ★다시 공부한 날 : _____

(1) 문제를 왜? 틀렸는지 곰곰이 생각하고 그 이유를 적어본다.

(2) 핵심 개념을 적는다.

(3) 자신이 몰랐던 단어와 숙어 표현이 있으면 정리한다.

(4) 해설집에서 필요한 부분을 골라 풀이 해법을 정리한다.

★틀린 문제 : _____   ★다시 공부한 날 : _____

(1) 문제를 왜? 틀렸는지 곰곰이 생각하고 그 이유를 적어본다.

(2) 핵심 개념을 적는다.

(3) 자신이 몰랐던 단어와 숙어 표현이 있으면 정리한다.

(4) 해설집에서 필요한 부분을 골라 풀이 해법을 정리한다.

[1-3] 다음 문장의 빈칸에 들어갈 알맞은 말을 아래에서 골라 쓰시오.

who	whose	that

1. Kevin is a person _____ really loves puppies.

2. I have a girlfriend _____ hair is black.

3. Look at the boy and the dog _____ are walking in the park.

오답노트

4. 다음 밑줄 친 부분을 생략할 수 <u>없는</u> 것은?

❶ I like the T-shirt <u>that</u> you are wearing.
❷ Have you found the bag <u>that</u> you lost?
❸ The woman <u>that</u> lives next door is a dentist.
❹ The woman <u>that</u> I saw is my new English teacher.
❺ The people <u>that</u> I met were very friendly.

오답노트

5. 다음 밑줄 친 곳에 들어갈 관계사가 알맞게 짝지어진 것은?

> · I am also your home _____ you live.
> · I'm the source of life, and that's _____ you call me Mother Earth.
> (＊I＝the earth)

❶ where − why ❷ which − why
❸ how − when ❹ when − which
❺ why − which

오답노트

6. I remember the house where I was born.
 = I remember the house _____ _____ I was born.

7. This is the time when the sun rises.
 = This is the time _____ _____ the sun rises.

8. I don't know the reason why she isn't here.
 = I don't know the reason _____ _____ she isn't here.

오답노트

[6-8] 다음 두 문장이 같은 뜻이 되도록 빈칸에 알맞은 말을 쓰시오.

9. 다음 중 어법상 <u>어색한</u> 것은?

❶ Mr. Tailor is the man who wife is a teacher.
❷ He gave me the necklace he bought yesterday.
❸ These are the letters that were sent to her.
❹ My brother has some friends who do strange things.
❺ It rescues people who are in danger.

오답노트

10. 다음 두 문장을 연결하여 하나로 만들 때 밑줄 친 곳에 알맞은 것은?

> I met a boy. His sister is a famous movie star.
> → I met a boy _____ sister is a famous movie star.

❶ which　　❷ whom　　❸ whose
❹ who　　❺ that

오답노트

11. 다음 우리말과 같은 뜻이 되도록 주어진 단어를 바르게 배열하시오.

> 내 동생은 내가 그에게 말한 것을 하려고 하지 않았다.
> = My brother would't do _____
> _____.
> 　　　　(I / him / what / told)

오답노트

12. 다음 밑줄 친 부분과 바꿔 쓸 수 있는 것은?

> Do you know the girl that helped you?

❶ who　　❷ which　　❸ whom
❹ whose　　❺ of which

오답노트

13. 다음 문장의 밑줄 친 부분 중 생략할 수 있는 것은?

❶ I have a friend who sings very well.
❷ This is the house which was built in 1900.
❸ That is the letter which I wrote last night.
❹ The dog that is coming is Happy.
❺ He has two cats which are very cute.

오답노트

14. 다음 문장의 빈칸에 공통으로 들어갈 말을 쓰시오.

> · My students don't listen to _____ I say.
> · I don't know _____ to do next.

오답노트

15. 다음 두 문장을 관계대명사를 이용하여 한 문장으로 만드시오. (단, that은 제외)

> Is this the book? You were looking for it the other day.
> → _____
> _____

오답노트

16. 다음 빈칸에 공통으로 들어갈 알맞은 말을 쓰시오.

오답노트

> · I think _____ the movie is very boring.
> · He is the first man _____ came here.

[17-18] 다음 빈칸에 들어갈 알맞은 한 단어를 쓰시오.

17.

> The hotel _____ we stayed at was very small.
> 우리가 머물렀던 호텔은 아주 작았다.

18.

> I have a friend _____ mother is a famous painter.
> 나는 어머니가 유명한 화가인 친구가 한 명 있다.

오답노트

19. 다음 두 문장을 한 문장으로 바꿀 때 잘못된 것은?

> Korea is the country. + I want to live in the country.

❶ Korea is the country which I want to live in.
❷ Korea is the country in which I want to live.
❸ Korea is the country I want to live in.
❹ Korea is the country that I want to live in.
❺ Korea is the country in that I want to live.

오답노트

[20-21] 다음 빈칸에 알맞은 말을 아래에서 골라 쓰시오. (필요하면 두 번 쓸 것)

> which   when   why   in   for

20. 2010 was the year. + The South Africa World Cup was held in the year.
→ 2010 was the year _____ _____ the South Africa World cup was held.
→ 2010 was the year _____ the South Africa World Cup was held.

21. Do you know the reason? + He invented this machine for the reason.
→ Do you know the reason _____ _____ he invented this machine?
→ Do you know the reason _____ he invented this machine?

오답노트

[22-23] 우리말과 뜻이 같도록 주어진 단어를 배열하시오.

22. 오늘 학교에 지각한 학생은 Susie였다.
→ The student _____
_____.
(who, was late, was Susie, for school today)

23. 그녀는 많은 사람들이 좋아하는 여배우이다.

→ She is _____

_____.

(who, many people like, an actress)

오답노트

24. 다음 빈칸에 들어갈 알맞은 말은?

Korea is the country whose history is very long.

= Korea is the country _____ the history is very long.

❶ in which   ❷ of which   ❸ in that
❹ of that   ❺ that

오답노트

25. 다음 두 문장을 관계사를 이용하여 한 문장으로 쓰시오.

The children loved the beach. They went to the beach last summer.

→ _____

_____

오답노트

26. 다음 밑줄 친 부분의 쓰임이 나머지와 다른 것은?

❶ I know who stole the money.
❷ I know a boy who plays online games every night.
❸ I know the man who can speak English well.
❹ I know the teacher who teaches math.
❺ I like the woman who I met at the party last night.

오답노트

27. 우리말에 맞도록 단어를 배열하여 문장을 완성하시오.

이곳이 내가 자라난 집이다.
This is _____.

(I, grew up, the house, where)

오답노트

A. 다음 빈칸에 들어갈 알맞은 어구를 아래에서 찾아 who와 which 중 하나를 이용하여 완성하시오.

· acts in a play   · you eat with
· takes care of your teeth   · tells the time
· looks after the flight's safety procedures and passenger comfort
---

1. A dentist is a person _____.

2. An actress is a person _____.

3. A flight attendant is a person _____

_____.

4. Chopsticks are a pair of sticks _____.

5. A clock is a thing _____.

B. 다음 중 알맞은 표현을 골라 관계부사를 이용하여 빈칸을 완성하시오.

· You sold your car at a good price.
· We first met.
· We were all excited about the World Cup.
· Kathy left him three years ago.

보기	Do you remember the day *when we first met*?

1. Tell me _____.

2. That is the reason _____.

3. 2002 was the year _____.

4. How could I forget the cafe _____?

C. 관계대명사 which 또는 whose를 이용하여 다음 두 문장을 한 문장으로 연결하시오.

1. Edison invented machines. They do wonderful things.

→ _____

2. This is the room. Its wall is white.

→ _____

3. I met a woman. Her daughter is a movie star.

→ _____

4. There is a river. It flows in front of my house.

→ _____

D. 〈보기〉와 같이 관계대명사를 생략하여 한 문장으로 연결하시오.

보기	The MP3 player is very expensive. She bought it. → The MP3 player *she bought is very expensive.*

1. The computer has already crashed several times. I bought it recently.

→ The computer _____.

2. The trees have doubled in size. We planted them last year.

→ The trees _____.

3. The plane arrived on time. I took it to Korea.

→ The plane _____.

4. Anthropology is the study of people and society. I'm interested in it.

→ Anthropology _____.

실전 서술형 평가문제

출제의도 관계대명사
평가내용 관계대명사를 활용하여 문장 완성하기

A. Group A와 B에서 각각 하나의 표현을 골라 관계대명사와 함께 그림을 설명하는 문장을 완성하시오.

[서술형 유형 : 8점 / 난이도 : 중]

• Group A •	pictures / people's lives / what time it is / you find your way

• Group B •	help / show / draw / save

1.

A painter is someone

_____ .

2.

A map is something

_____

when you're lost.

3.

A firefighter is a person

_____ .

4.

A clock is something

_____ .

출제의도 관계대명사의 격
평가내용 주격, 소유격 관계대명사를 활용하여 문장 완성하기

B. 〈도전골든벨〉의 마지막 남은 학생에게 문제를 출제하려고 한다. 괄호 안의 단어와 관계대명사 who, which, whose 중 하나를 이용하여 문장을 완성하시오.   [서술형 유형 : 10점 / 난이도 : 중]

보 기	전구를 발명한 사람은 누구입니까? (invent / the light bulb) → Who was the person *who invented the light bulb*?

1. 아프리카에 있는 긴 강의 이름은 무엇입니까? (Africa)

→ What is the name of the long river _____?

2. 가장 유명한 그림이 모나리자인 화가의 이름은 무엇입니까? (the Mona Lisa / painting)

→ What is the name of the painter _____?

3. 햄릿을 쓴 작가의 이름은 무엇입니까? (write / Hamlet)

→ What is the name of the writer _____?

4. 수도가 부에노스 아이레스인 나라의 이름은 무엇입니까? (Buenos Aires / capital)

→ What is the name of the country _____?

5. 인도에서 가난한 사람들과 병든 사람들을 도운 여자의 이름은 무엇입니까? (the poor and ill / in India)

→ What is the name of the woman _____?

출제의도 　관계부사
평가내용 　관계부사를 이용하여 문장 완성하기

C. 그림을 참고하여 다음 문장을 자신의 글로 완성하되, 반드시 관계부사가 이끄는 절을 이용하시오.

[서술형 유형 : 6점 / 난이도 : 중하]

보기

(first met)

I'll always remember the day
when I first met you.

1.

(hold / the Korea-Japan World Cup)

2002 was the year _____

_____ .

2.

(they / be getting married)

That's the church _____

_____ .

3.

(dislike)

I don't have a good reason _____

_____ .

서술형 평가문제	채 점 기 준	배 점	나의 점수
A	표현이 올바르고 문법, 철자가 모두 정확한 경우	2점×4문항=8점	
B		2점×5문항=10점	
C		2점×3문항=6점	
공통	문법, 철자가 1개씩 틀린 경우	각 문항당 1점씩 감점	
	내용과 전혀 일치하지 않거나 답을 기재하지 못한 경우	0점	

Chapter 6

문장의 형식과 종류
(Forms and Types of Sentences)

Unit 01 문장의 형식

1-1 1형식/2형식 동사

Is there a gas station near here?
이 근처에 주유소가 있나요?

She **looks** happy.
그녀는 행복해 보인다.

01 **1형식 문장**은 「**주어＋동사**」로 이루어진 문장이다. 특히 there be 구문은 '~가 있다'를 뜻하는 대표적인 1형식 문장으로 be동사 뒤에 주어가 나온다. 주어에 따라 be동사의 단/복수가 결정된다. there be 구문의 there를 '거기에'라고 해석하지 않는다.

She **walked**. 그녀는 걸었다.
She **walked** to school. 그녀는 학교로 걸어갔다. ▶ 「주어＋동사」 뒤에는 부사나 전치사구와 같은 수식어가 올 수 있다.

There is a fly on the wall. 벽에 파리 한 마리가 있다. ▶ 주어는 a fly(단수)
There are two flies on the wall. 벽에 파리 두 마리가 있다. ▶ 주어는 two flies(복수)

02 **2형식 문장**은 「**주어 + 동사 + (주격)보어**」로 이루어진 문장이다. be동사 뒤에 부사나 전치사구가 오면 1형식 동사로 '~이 있다'의 뜻이 되고, be동사 뒤에 명사나 형용사가 오면 2형식 동사로 '~이다'의 뜻이 된다. 주어를 좀 더 구체적으로 설명해 주기 위해 사용하는 **감각동사** 뒤에는 반드시 **보어로 형용사**가 온다.

형용사를 보어로 취하는 감각동사			
look/seem ~처럼 보이다 smell ~의 냄새가 나다 taste ~의 맛이 나다 sound ~하게 들리다 feel ~하게 느껴지다	become ~ 되다 get ~ 되다 turn ~ 되다 grow ~ 되다 go ~ 되다(부정적인 의미)	turn out ~로 판명되다 come out ~로 밝혀지다	remain 계속 ~이다 keep 계속 ~인 채로 있다 stay 계속 ~인 채로 있다

※ 「look like + 명사(~처럼 보이다)」처럼 명사를 쓰려면 전치사 like가 있어야 한다.

She **is** under the tree. 그녀는 나무 아래에 있다. (1형식)
She **is** a doctor. 그녀는 의사이다. (2형식)

In autumn the leaves **turn** yellow. 가을에 나뭇잎은 노랗게 된다.
She **looks** serious. 그녀는 심각해 보인다.
The milk will **go** bad in two days. 우유는 이틀이 지나면 상하게 될 것이다.
His story **sounds** strange. 그의 이야기는 이상하게 들린다.
The report **came out** true the next morning. 그 보고서는 다음 날 아침에 사실로 밝혀졌다.
The weather will **stay** fine. 날씨는 계속 맑을 것이다.

서술형 기초다지기

정답 p. 19

Challenge 1 다음 괄호 안의 단어 중에서 알맞은 것을 고르세요.

01. There (is / are) a banana on the table.

02. There (is / are) thirty-five students in my class.

03. There is (a cat / cats) on the sofa.

04. There are (a ball / three balls) in the box.

05. There is some (sugar / sugars) in the jar.

06. There is a lot of (snow / snows) at the top of the mountain.

Challenge 2 다음 문장에서 밑줄 친 be동사의 뜻을 '이다' 또는 '있다'로 구별하여 쓰세요.

01. You <u>are</u> very sad.　　　　　→ _____

02. My teacher <u>is</u> in the classroom.　　→ _____

03. The lake <u>is</u> very deep.　　　　→ _____

04. My brother <u>is</u> at home.　　　　→ _____

Challenge 3 다음 괄호 안의 단어 중에서 알맞은 것을 고르세요.

01. Her story sounds (strangely / strange).

02. The fried chicken smelled very (badly / bad).

03. The girl looks (happy / happily).

04. This sweater feels (softly / soft).

05. Her voice sounds (beautiful / beautifully).

06. My dad looked really (angry / angrily).

1-2 3형식/4형식 동사

She **eats** an apple every morning.
그녀는 매일 아침 사과를 먹는다.

I **gave** her the gold ring.
나는 그녀에게 금반지를 주었다.

01 3형식은 「주어+동사+목적어」로 이루어진 문장이며, '~을(를)'이라는 의미이다. 목적어에는 (대)명사, 부정사, 동명사, 명사절 등이 올 수 있다.

I **love** her very much. 나는 그녀를 매우 많이 사랑한다.
Tom **likes** to play computer games. Tom은 컴퓨터 게임 하는 것을 좋아한다.

02 4형식은 동사의 동작이 미치는 대상인 목적어가 두 개 필요한 문장이며, **간접목적어 자리에는 사람**(~에게)이 오고, **직접목적어 자리에는 사물**(~을/를)이 온다.

She **bought** a jacket. 그녀는 재킷을 샀다. (3형식)
　　　　　 (직접목적어)

She **bought** me a jacket. 그녀는 나에게 재킷을 사주었다. (4형식)
　　　　　 (간접목적어) (직접목적어)

03 4형식을 3형식으로 바꿀 때는 **직접목적어인 사물이 동사 바로 뒤에 와서** 「동사 + 직접목적어 + 전치사 + 간접목적어」의 순서가 된다. 이때 전치사는 동사의 성격에 따라 to, for, of를 쓴다.

① 동사가 '방향'을 나타낼 때는 전치사 to 사용: give, send, tell, teach, show, read
　 Please tell **me** a funny story. 내게 재미있는 얘기 하나 해 줘.

　 → Pleas tell a funny story **to me**. (3형식)

② 동사가 '~을 위하여'라는 의미를 나타낼 때는 전치사 for 사용: buy, make, get, cook, find
　 My dad bought **me** the iPhone. 아빠가 나에게 아이폰을 사주셨다.

　 → My dad bought the iPhone **for me**. (3형식)

③ 동사가 '질문하다'라는 의미를 나타낼 때는 전치사 of 사용: ask, beg, inquire
　 She asked **us** many questions. 그녀는 우리에게 많은 질문을 했다.

　 → She asked many questions **of us**. (3형식)

서술형 기초다지기

Challenge 1 다음 문장이 몇 형식인지 쓰세요.

01. I have a bicycle. → _____형식

02. My sister is a famous pianist. → _____형식

03. There is a book on the table. → _____형식

04. My dad will make me a kite. → _____형식

05. My dad will make a kite for me. → _____형식

Challenge 2 다음 두 문장의 의미가 같도록 빈칸에 알맞은 전치사를 쓰세요.

01. I made her a cake.

= I made a cake _____ her.

02. Can I ask you something?

= Can I ask something _____ you?

03. I gave him some books.

= I gave some books _____ him.

04. The boss got him a new job at the shopping mall.

= The boss got a new job _____ him at the shopping mall.

Challenge 3 우리말과 같은 뜻이 되도록 괄호 안의 말을 이용하여 문장을 완성하세요.

01. 제니퍼가 우리에게 저녁을 해주었다. (dinner / made / us)

= Jennifer _____.

02. 좀 더 싼 것을 보여주세요. (a cheaper one / me / to / show)

= Please _____.

1-3 5형식 동사

We **kept** our village **clean**.
우리는 마을을 깨끗하게 유지했다.

The doctor **advised** me **to exercise** every day.
그 의사는 나에게 매일 운동하라고 충고했다.

01 「주어＋동사＋목적어」만으로는 문장의 의미가 완전하지 못할 때, 목적어를 보충 설명하기 위해 목적격 보어가 오는데 이런 문장을 5형식이라고 한다. **목적격 보어는 목적어의 성질이나 상태를 설명하는 말로 '명사나 형용사'**를 쓴다.

My dad <u>made</u> me **a famous figure skater**. 우리 아빠는 나를 유명한 피겨 스케이터로 만들었다.
Every teacher <u>thinks</u> Kathy **smart**. 모든 선생님들은 Kathy가 영리하다고 생각한다.

02 **목적어의 행위나 동작을 보충 설명할 때 목적격 보어에 to부정사**를 쓴다. 주로 want, ask, expect, tell, allow, advise 등의 충고나 명령과 관련된 동사와 함께 쓴다.

I <u>want</u> you **to keep** your promise. 나는 네가 약속을 지키기를 원한다.
He <u>ordered</u> the bodyguards **to protect** the president. 그는 경호원들에게 대통령을 보호하라고 명령했다.
Bob <u>told</u> his brother **to stay** home. Bob은 남동생에게 집에 있으라고 말했다.
My dad <u>allowed</u> me **to go** to the party. 아빠는 내가 파티에 가도록 허락하셨다.

03 **사역동사**(make, have, let), **감각동사**(see, watch, hear, feel)는 **목적어의 동작을 표현할 때 목적격 보어 자리에 to없이 동사원형**만 쓴다.

I <u>saw</u> you **go** to the library. 나는 네가 도서관에 가는 걸 봤다.
My mom didn't <u>let</u> me **read** comic books. 엄마는 내가 만화책 읽는 걸 허락하지 않으셨다.
My mom <u>made</u> me **wash** the dishes. 엄마는 나에게 설거지를 시키셨다.

04 **말하는 순간 진행 중인 동작은 목적격 보어에 현재분사**(V-ing)를 쓰고 목적어가 행위를 하는 주체가 아닌 **행동을 받는(당하는) 대상인 경우 과거분사**(V-ed)를 쓴다.

I **felt** the ground **shaking**. 나는 땅이 흔들리고 있는 것을 느꼈다.
We **heard** Sunny **playing** the violin. 우리는 Sunny가 바이올린을 켜고 있는 것을 들었다.

I **had** Scott **repair** the bicycle. 나는 Scott이 자전거를 수리하도록 시켰다.
→ I **had** the bicycle **repaired** (by Scott). 나는 자전거가 수리되도록 시켰다.

서술형 기초다지기

Challenge 1 다음 문장에서 어법상 어색한 부분을 찾아 고쳐 쓰세요.

01. I saw a strange woman to sing a song.　　　_____ → _____

02. I will make them to clean the house.　　　_____ → _____

03. Pleas let me gone home now.　　　_____ → _____

04. She asked me help her.　　　_____ → _____

05. Please tell him calling me.　　　_____ → _____

06. The doctor advised me eat more vegetables.　　　_____ → _____

07. I had my car repair by him.　　　_____ → _____

Challenge 2 다음 우리말과 같도록 빈칸에 알맞은 말을 쓰세요.

01. 규칙적으로 운동하는 것은 너를 계속 건강하게 해 줄 것이다. (you / keep / healthy)

= Exercising regularly will _____.

02. 나는 여동생에게 TV를 꺼달라고 요청했다. (turn off / asked / my little sister)

= I _____ the TV.

03. 나는 그가 내 집을 짓게 했다. (had / build / my house)

= I _____ by him.

Challenge 3 다음 두 문장을 하나의 5형식 문장으로 완성하세요.

01. I saw Nancy. She was playing the piano.

→ I saw Nancy _____.

02. I heard the alarm. It was ringing loudly.

→ I heard the alarm _____.

03. Jane smelled something. It was burning in the oven.

→ Jane smelled something _____.

Unit 02 문장의 종류

2-1 의문사가 있는 의문문

Who is playing the cello?
첼로를 연주하는 사람이 누구니?

Why does Alice like him?
Alice는 왜 그를 좋아하니?

01 의문문의 맨 앞에 의문사를 써서 궁금한 것을 물어 볼 수 있는데 이렇게 **의문사로 시작하는 의문문은 Yes나 No로 대답하지 못한다.**

who (누가)	whom (누구를)	what (무엇)	where (어디서)
when (언제)	why (왜)	how (어떻게)	

02 be동사가 있는 경우 「**의문사 + be동사 + 주어 ~?**」의 어순으로 만든다.

What is your name? 네 이름이 뭐니?　　　　　　– My name is Kevin. 내 이름은 Kevin이야.
Who is the man? 저 사람은 누구니?　　　　　　– He is my father. 우리 아빠야.
When is your birthday? 생일이 언제니?　　　　– It's on July 25. 7월 25일이야.
Why were you so late? 넌 왜 그렇게 늦었니?　　– (Because) I got up late. 늦게 일어났기 때문이야.

※ why의 의문문에 대답할 때는 보통 because로 답하는데, because는 생략할 수 있다.

03 일반동사가 있는 경우 「**의문사 + do/does/did + 주어 + 동사원형 ~?**」의 어순으로 만든다.

What do you want? 넌 무엇을 원하니?　　　　– I want the iPhone. 난 그 아이폰을 원해.
Where do you live? 넌 어디에 사니?　　　　　– I live in Seoul. 난 서울에 살아.

04 조동사가 있는 경우 「**의문사 + 조동사 + 주어 + 동사원형 ~?**」의 어순으로 만든다. **의문사가 문장의 주어일 경우에는 「의문사 + 동사 ~?」의 어순으로 쓴다.**

A: **How** can I get there? 거기에 어떻게 가나요?
B: You can go there by bus. 버스로 갈 수 있어요.

When will Susan wash the dishes? Susan은 언제 설거지를 할 거니?

Who will you invite to the party? 파티에 누구를 초대할 거야?

Who broke the window? 누가 유리창을 깼니?
(의문사 주어) (동사)

※ Who did the window break? (X)

168

Challenge 1   다음 괄호 안의 의문사를 이용하여 의문사가 있는 의문문으로 바꿔 써 보세요.

01. You wrote a letter to Bob. (Why)

→ _____

02. Tom plays soccer after school. (Where)

→ _____

03. You can make a cake. (When)

→ _____

04. The airplane leaves for New York. (When)

→ _____

Challenge 2   다음 A-B 대화에서 B의 답변을 참고하여 A의 의문사가 있는 의문문을 완성하세요.

보기	A: *Where is* the box? B: It's on the desk.

01. A: _____ that man?

B: He's my uncle.

02. A: _____ you live?

B: I live in Busan.

03. A: _____ your favorite soccer player?

B: My favorite soccer player is Lee Chung-yong.

04. A: _____ you visit your grandparents?

B: I visited them last weekend.

05. A: _____ the soccer game?

B: It was great.

06. A: _____ you like that movie?

B: Because I love the actress.

07. A: _____ you go after school?

B: I went to the bookstore.

2-2 부가의문문 / 선택의문문

They **are** high school students, **aren't they**?
그들은 고등학생이야, 그렇지 않니?

Which is your favorite sport, soccer **or** baseball?
축구나 야구 중 어느 것이 네가 좋아하는 운동이니?

---

01 부가의문문이란 **상대방에게 어떤 사실을 확인하거나 동의를** 구할 때 평서문 뒤에 '그렇지?'하고 덧붙여 확인하는 의문문이다.

① 앞 문장이 **긍정이면 부정**으로, 앞 문장이 **부정이면 긍정**으로 쓴다.(단, 부정형은 축약) 앞 문장의 명사를 인칭대명사로 바꿔 쓴다.

You are tired, **aren't you**? 너 피곤하지, 그렇지 않니?

Karen doesn't like Tom, **does she**? Karen은 Tom을 좋아하지 않아, 그렇지?

They like music, **don't they**? 그들은 음악을 좋아해, 그렇지 않니?

② **조동사는 그대로 사용**하고, **일반동사는** 주어의 인칭과 수, 시제에 따라 **do, does, did를 사용**한다.

Nancy can't drive a car, **can she**? Nancy는 차를 운전할 수 없어, 그렇지?

You didn't love him, **did you**? 너는 그를 사랑하지 않았어, 그렇지?

③ 제안문 Let's의 부가의문문은 **shall we?**를 쓰고, **명령문은 will you?**를 쓴다.

Let's start it now, **shall we**? 지금 그것을 시작하자, 어때?

Don't be late again, **will you**? 다시는 늦지 마라, 알겠니?

02 선택의문문은 **2가지 이상의 선택 범위가 정해져 있는 것들 중에서 어느 하나를 선택하는 의문문**이다. or를 사용하고, 둘 중 하나를 선택해서 대답해야 하므로 Yes나 No로 대답하지 않는다.

① 의문사가 없는 선택의문문

Is your sister in Seoul **or** in Busan? 네 여동생은 서울에 있니? 아니면 부산에 있니?

Did you buy a book **or** a magazine? 너는 책을 샀니? 아니면 잡지를 샀니?

② 의문사가 있는 선택의문문

Which do you want, tea **or** coffee? 차와 커피 중에서 어떤 것을 마실래?

Which is bigger, Canada **or** China? 캐나다와 중국 중 어느 나라가 더 크니?

서술형 기초다지기

Challenge 1 다음 빈칸에 알맞은 부가의문문을 쓰세요.

01. Your house is very big, _____?

02. You can speak Japanese, _____?

03. She doesn't like hamburgers, _____?

04. Lucy doesn't drink coffee, _____?

05. It was a good movie, _____?

06. Peter doesn't like Lisa, _____?

07. Pass me the salt, _____?

08. Let's go to the park, _____?

09. They aren't studying for the exam, _____?

10. Yesterday was the last day of school, _____?

Challenge 2 다음 괄호 안의 지시대로 문장을 바꿔 보세요.

01. Steve likes the soccer player. (부가의문문)

   → _____

02. Would you like coffee? Would you like green tea? (선택의문문)

   → _____

03. Will you go to Lotteria? Will you go to McDonald's? (선택의문문)

   → _____

04. You were late for school again. (부가의문문)

   → _____

감탄문 / 제안문

What a fast swimmer! 정말 빠른 수영선수구나!
How fast he is! 그는 정말 빠르구나!

It's one o'clock. **Let's go** to have lunch.
1시다. 점심 먹으러 가자.

---

01 명사를 강조하기 위해 **what**을 이용한 감탄문을 만들 수 있는데, 이때 명사가 단수면 부정관사(a/an)가 오고, 복수면 관사를 붙이지 않는다. 「What + (a/an) + 형용사 + 명사 + 주어 + 동사!」의 어순으로 쓴다.

He is **a brave man**. (명사 발견 → what 감탄문으로)　→ What a brave man he is!
그는 용감한 사람이다.　　　　　　　　　　　　　　　그는 정말 용감한 사람이구나!

It is **a** very **interesting book**. (명사 발견 → what 감탄문으로) → What an interesting book it is!
그것은 매우 재미있는 책이다.　　　　　　　　　　　　굉장히 재미있는 책이구나!

They are **smart students**. (명사 발견 → what 감탄문으로)　→ What smart students they are!
그들은 똑똑한 학생들이다.　　　　　　　　　　　　　　그들은 정말 똑똑한 학생들이구나!

---

02 **How**로 시작하는 감탄문은 형용사/부사를 강조하는 감탄문으로 명사가 없을 때는 「How+ 형용사/부사 + 주어 + 동사!」로 쓴다. 감탄문 뒤에 오는 주어와 동사는 생략할 수 있다.

The doctor is very **kind**. (명사가 없다 → how 감탄문으로)　→ How kind the doctor is!
그 의사는 매우 친절하다.　　　　　　　　　　　　　　　정말 친절한 의사네!

You are very **creative**. (명사가 없다 → how 감탄문으로)　→ How creative you are!
너는 매우 창의적이다.　　　　　　　　　　　　　　　　너는 정말 창의적이구나!

---

03 제안문 「**Let's** + 동사원형」의 형태는 '(우리 함께) ~하자'의 뜻으로 말하는 사람을 포함해 상대방과 주변 사람들에게 제안을 하는 말이다. Let's는 Let us의 줄임말이다. 반대말(~하지 말자)은 「Let's + not + 동사원형」을 쓴다.

Let's order pizza for dinner. 저녁으로 피자를 시키자.

Let's not rush it. 너무 성급하게 하지 말자.

Let's not go shopping. 쇼핑하러 가지 말자.

Let's go to Kevin's birthday party. Kevin의 생일 파티에 가자.

(= Shall we go to Kevin's birthday party?)

서술형 기초다지기

정답 p. 19

Challenge 1   다음 문장을 감탄문으로 바꿔 쓰세요.

01. She sings very beautifully. → _____

02. They are very interesting books. → _____

03. This cake is very delicious. → _____

04. It was a very boring film. → _____

05. She has beautiful eyes. → _____

Challenge 2   다음 감탄문을 평서문으로 바꿔 쓰세요.

01. What a good singer he is! → _____

02. How sad the movie is! → _____

03. What fresh fruits those are! → _____

04. How expensive this ring is! → _____

Challenge 3   다음 문장을 지시대로 바꾸세요.

01. We go to the movie theater. (제안문)

   → _____

02. We go to the library. (부정 제안문)

   → _____

03. We have fish for dinner tonight. (부정 제안문)

   → _____

04. We paint the door. (제안문)

   → _____

간접의문문

Do you know? + How do airplanes fly?

→ Do you know **how** airplanes fly?
비행기가 어떻게 하늘을 나는지 아니?

---

01 의문사가 이끄는 절이 다른 문장의 일부(주어, 목적어, 보어)가 되어 간접적인 의문문의 형식을 취하는 것을 간접의문문이라고 한다. **반드시 「의문사 + 주어 + 동사」의 어순으로 순서를 바꿔 사용**한다.

① 의문사가 있는 경우: 「의문사 + 주어 + 동사」

단, 의문사가 주어인 경우는 「의문사 + 동사」가 된다.

I don't know. + Where is Paul?

→ I don't know **where** Paul is. 나는 Paul이 어디에 있는지 모른다.

Please tell me. + Who is coming to the party?

→ Please tell me **who is coming** to the party. 누가 파티에 오는지 알려 줘.

② 의문사가 없는 경우: 「if / whether + 주어 + 동사」

I wonder. + Did Lucy go to Seattle?

→ I wonder **if [whether]** Lucy went to Seattle. 나는 Lucy가 시애틀에 갔는지 안 갔는지가 궁금하다.

Can you tell me? + Is Kate in her office?

→ Can you tell me **if [whether]** Kate is in her office? Kate가 그녀의 사무실에 있는지 없는지 말해 줄래요?

---

02 **생각이나 추측을 나타내는 동사**(think, believe, guess, imagine, suppose 등)가 있을 때는 **의문사가 문장의 맨 앞에 위치**한다.

Do you guess? + What does it mean?

→ **What** do you guess it means? (O) 너는 그것이 의미하는 게 무엇이라고 추측하니?

→ Do you guess **what it** means? (X) ▶ what을 문장 맨 앞으로 보냄

Do you think? + What is he doing now?

→ **What** do you think he is doing now? (O) 너는 그가 지금 무엇을 하고 있다고 생각하니?

→ Do you think **what** he is doing now? (X) ▶ what을 문장 맨 앞으로 보냄

서술형 기초다지기

Challenge 1 다음 직접의문문을 간접의문문으로 바꾸어 쓰세요.

01. Who is Tom?

→ Do you know _____?

02. Is she married?

→ I don't know _____.

03. Does she like Paul?

→ I asked him _____.

04. Where does Susan work?

→ I don't know _____.

05. Is your mother at home?

→ Can you tell me _____?

06. Why did he leave here?

→ Please tell me _____.

Challenge 2 간접의문문을 이용하여 다음 두 문장을 한 문장으로 쓰세요.

01. Do you think? + How did he solve the problem?

→ _____

02. Do you think? + Where did he go yesterday?

→ _____

03. Do you believe? + Who did it?

→ _____

04. Do you think? + Who will win the game?

→ _____

01 출제 100% - 1형식 / 2형식 동사를 조심하라.

 출제자의 눈 1형식은 there be 구문을 이용한 문제로, 주어에 따라 be동사의 수일치를 묻거나 is와 are를 주고 주어의 단/복수를 결정하는 문제가 출제된다. 2형식에서는 감각동사 (look, seem, taste, sound, feel 등) 뒤에 형용사가 아닌 부사를 주고 틀린 것을 고르는 문제가 출제된다. 부사처럼 해석되어도 감각동사는 be동사에서 나온 것이므로 보어에는 형용사를 써야 한다는 점을 명심해야 한다.

Ex 1.

There _____ a lot of snow on the roof.

(a) are   (b) is   (c) were   (d) comes

Ex 2.

Kathy got a good grade in the English test. She looked _____.

(a) happy   (b) happily   (c) angry   (d) angrily

02 출제 100% - 4형식은 3형식으로, 5형식은 목적격 보어가 핵심이다.

 출제자의 눈 4형식을 3형식으로 고칠 줄 아는지를 묻는 주관식이 출제된다. 3형식으로 문장 전환할 때 동사의 특성에 따라 전치사 'to, for, of'를 고르는 문제는 객관식으로 반드시 나온다. 5형식 동사는 목적격 보어 자리에 동작을 표현할 때 to부정사와 동사원형, 현재분사와 과거분사를 구별하여 사용할 줄 아는지를 집중적으로 물어본다. 사역동사와 지각동사의 정확한 내용을 다시 한번 숙지하고 언제 to부정사를 쓰는지, 언제 동사원형을 쓰는지를 확실히 익혀두어야 한다.

Ex 3.

The girl gave him apples.

= The girl gave _____ to _____.

Ex 4.

빈칸에 들어갈 말로 바르게 짝지어진 것은?

I _____ the computer _____ by Tom.

(a) told − to repair   (b) wanted − repair

(c) had − repaired   (d) saw − to repair

03 출제 100% - 감탄문은 주관식으로, 부가의문문/선택의문문/제안문은 형태를 물어본다.

 출제자의 눈 평서문을 What이나 How로 시작하는 감탄문으로 바꾸는 주관식 문제가 출제된다. 또는 감탄문 안에서 명사와 형용사를 적절히 사용할 줄 아는지를 묻기도 한다. 선택의문문은 올바른 의문사를 고르거나 접속사 or이 제대로 쓰였는지, 선택의문문에 대한 대답이 적절한지 확인하는 문제가 출제되기도 한다. 제안문은 let's 뒤에 동사원형을 쓰고 부정문을 만들 때는 let's 뒤에 not을 붙인다는 것도 기억하자.

Ex 5.

밑줄 친 우리말에 해당하는 표현은?

A: You have a toothache, <u>그렇지 않니</u>?　　B: Yes, I do.

(a) doesn't I　　　(b) doesn't you　　　(c) don't I　　　(d) don't you

Ex 6.

주어진 문장을 감탄문으로 고치시오.

They are very nice people. → _____

04 출제 100% - 간접의문문은 주관식으로 자주 묻는다.

 출제자의 눈 간접의문문 어순을 반드시 기억하라. 의문문일 때 「의문사 + 동사 + 주어」였던 어순이 「의문사 + 주어 + 동사」로 바뀐다. 주어진 의문사가 없으면 if 또는 whether를 이용한다. 특히 동사가 생각이나 추측에 관련된 think, believe, guess, imagine일 때 의문사를 문장 맨 앞으로 보내야 한다는 것도 반드시 기억하자.

Ex 7.

두 문장을 하나로 만들 때 바른 것은?

Do you know?　+　Why did he run?

(a) Do you know why he did run?　　　(b) Do you know why he ran?

Ex 8.

두 문장을 한 문장으로 쓰시오.

Do you think?　+　How can he solve the problem?

→ _____

1. 다음 두 문장이 같은 의미가 되도록 빈칸에 들어갈 전치사로 바르게 짝지어진 것은?

> · She teaches us English.
> = She teaches English _____ us.
> · My mom cooked us a great dinner.
> = My mom cooked a great dinner
> _____ us.
> · May I ask you a question?
> = May I ask a question _____ you?

❶ to – to – for   ❷ for – to – of
❸ to – of – for   ❹ of – for – to
❺ to – for – of

2. 다음 두 문장의 의미가 같도록 빈칸에 들어갈 알맞은 말은?

> Her fan club has many members.
> = _____ _____ many members
> in her fan club.

3. 다음 문장과 형식이 다른 것은?

> We found the movie interesting.

❶ My mom made me study English.
❷ My parents want me to be a teacher.
❸ My dad made me a kite.
❹ My mom made me a pro-golfer.
❺ We elected him the captain of our team.

4. 다음 문장의 빈칸에 알맞지 <u>않은</u> 것은? (2개)

> My parents _____ me to study hard.

❶ made   ❷ got   ❸ told
❹ advised   ❺ let

5. 다음 대화의 빈칸에 들어갈 가장 알맞은 말은?

> A : _____.
> B : John is taller.

❶ Who is taller, Bob or John?
❷ Do you think John is tall?
❸ Are you taller than John?
❹ Is John tall?
❺ Which is taller, John or Bob?

6. 다음 밑줄 친 곳에 들어갈 알맞은 말은?

> A : This book has many interesting
> stories.
> B : Please tell me one, _____?

❶ do you   ❷ will you
❸ don't you   ❹ really
❺ how about you

7. 다음 빈칸에 들어갈 말로 가장 알맞은 것은?

> Mi-na: _____ do you like better,
> basketball or baseball?
> John : I like baseball better. How about
> you?
> Mi-na: So do I.

❶ What   ❷ Where   ❸ Which
❹ How   ❺ When

8. 다음 두 문장을 한 문장으로 연결하시오.

> · I saw Jane.
> · Jane was playing soccer with her friends.

→ I saw Jane _____.

오답 노트 만들기

★틀린 문제 : _____ ★다시 공부한 날 : _____

(1) 문제를 왜? 틀렸는지 곰곰이 생각하고 그 이유를 적어본다.

(2) 핵심 개념을 적는다.

(3) 자신이 몰랐던 단어와 숙어 표현이 있으면 정리한다.

(4) 해설집에서 필요한 부분을 골라 풀이 해법을 정리한다.

★틀린 문제 : _____ ★다시 공부한 날 : _____

(1) 문제를 왜? 틀렸는지 곰곰이 생각하고 그 이유를 적어본다.

(2) 핵심 개념을 적는다.

(3) 자신이 몰랐던 단어와 숙어 표현이 있으면 정리한다.

(4) 해설집에서 필요한 부분을 골라 풀이 해법을 정리한다.

★틀린 문제 : _____ ★다시 공부한 날 : _____

(1) 문제를 왜? 틀렸는지 곰곰이 생각하고 그 이유를 적어본다.

(2) 핵심 개념을 적는다.

(3) 자신이 몰랐던 단어와 숙어 표현이 있으면 정리한다.

(4) 해설집에서 필요한 부분을 골라 풀이 해법을 정리한다.

★틀린 문제 : _____ ★다시 공부한 날 : _____

(1) 문제를 왜? 틀렸는지 곰곰이 생각하고 그 이유를 적어본다.

(2) 핵심 개념을 적는다.

(3) 자신이 몰랐던 단어와 숙어 표현이 있으면 정리한다.

(4) 해설집에서 필요한 부분을 골라 풀이 해법을 정리한다.

[1-2] 다음 밑줄 친 부분 중 잘못된 것을 고르시오.

1. ❶ Mom had me <u>cleaned</u> my room.
❷ He had his digital camera <u>repaired</u>.
❸ I had my tooth <u>pulled out</u>.
❹ She'll have her hair <u>cut</u>.
❺ I had my picture <u>taken</u>.

오답노트

2. ❶ I had them <u>cleaning</u> the classroom.
❷ She felt the ants <u>crawl up</u> her leg.
❸ My mother wants me <u>to be</u> a doctor.
❹ I heard my name <u>called</u> by someone.
❺ He finished <u>writing</u> a letter to his mother.

오답노트

3. **다음 두 문장의 내용이 같지 <u>않은</u> 것을 고르시오.**
❶ He let me go first.
= He allowed me to go first.
❷ I will make them start tonight.
= I will force them to start tonight.
❸ She had her secretary type the letter.
= She encouraged her secretary to type the letter.
❹ I had him paint the house.
= I got the house painted by him.
❺ They helped me recover soon.
= They helped me to recover soon.

오답노트

4. **다음 대화의 빈칸에 들어갈 말로 알맞은 것은?**

> A : I met you somewhere before. You look _____.
> B : Oh, aren't you Brian? We met at the park. I'm Lisa!
> A : Oh, Yes, I remember now.

❶ kind   ❷ strange   ❸ sad
❹ familiar   ❺ happy

오답노트

5. **다음 밑줄 친 빈칸에 들어갈 말로 알맞은 것은?**

> I asked. + What does Kelly want?
> → I asked _____.

❶ what did Kelly want
❷ what Kelly did want
❸ what Kelly wanted
❹ Kelly wants what
❺ what wanted Kelly

오답노트

[6-7] 다음 빈칸에 들어갈 말로 알맞지 <u>않은</u> 것은?

6.
> Sunny looks _____ this morning.

❶ sadly   ❷ excited   ❸ lovely
❹ beautiful   ❺ angry

오답노트

7.

| My dad _____ me wash his car. |

❶ had   ❷ made   ❸ helped
❹ ordered   ❺ let

오답노트

8. 다음 빈칸에 들어갈 말이 알맞게 짝지어진 것은?

| · My dad doesn't want me _____ TV.
· He never let me _____ computer games. |

❶ watch − play   ❷ watch − to play
❸ to watch − to play   ❹ to watch − play
❺ studying − to play

오답노트

9. 다음 중 4형식 문장을 3형식으로 바르게 전환하지 못한 것은?

❶ He sent her a letter every day.
→ He sent a letter to her every day.
❷ She often makes me a delicious cake.
→ She often makes a delicious cake for me.
❸ May I ask you a favor?
→ May I ask a favor of you?
❹ We gave Kevin a big hand.
→ We gave a big hand for Kevin.
❺ He bought me a model airplane.
→ He bought a model airplane for me.

오답노트

[10-12] 다음 문장을 감탄문으로 바꿀 때 빈칸에 알맞은 말을 쓰시오.

10. It was a very boring movie.
→ _____ _____ _____ movie it was!

11. The iPhone is very expensive.
→ _____ _____ the iPhone is!

12. Jennifer has beautiful eyes.
→ _____ _____ _____ Jennifer has!

오답노트

13. 다음 대화의 빈칸에 들어갈 알맞은 대답은?

| A : Which city is warmer, Seoul or Busan?
B : _____ |

❶ Not at all.
❷ Yes, Seoul is.
❸ Busan is warmer.
❹ Yes, I like Seoul better.
❺ No, I like Busan better.

오답노트

14. 우리말과 같은 뜻이 되도록 빈칸을 채우시오.

| 녹차와 오렌지 주스 중에 어떤 것이 더 좋으니?
→ _____ do you like better, green tea _____ orange juice? |

오답노트

[15-16] 우리말을 영어로 바르게 옮긴 것을 고르시오.

15.

우리는 건물이 흔들리고 있는 것을 느꼈다.

❶ We felt shaking the building.
❷ We felt the building shaking.
❸ We felt the building to shake.
❹ We felt to shake the building.
❺ We shook the building felt.

오답노트

16.

그녀는 버스에서 지갑을 도난당했다.

❶ She had her purse to steal in a bus.
❷ She had to steal in a bus her purse.
❸ She had her purse stolen in a bus.
❹ She had stolen her purse in a bus.
❺ She had her purse stealing in a bus.

오답노트

17. 다음 중 A의 질문으로 가장 적절한 것은?

A : _____
B : Because he told a lie.

❶ What do you want?
❷ Where do you go on Friday?
❸ Who told a lie?
❹ Why did you fight with him?
❺ How did you fight with her?

오답노트

18. 다음 질문에 대한 알맞은 대답을 happy를 포함한 세 단어로 쓰시오.

Q : How does Kevin look today?
A : _____
(그는 행복해 보인다.)

오답노트

19. 다음 빈칸에 들어갈 알맞은 말을 쓰시오.

We gave Seo-yoon a big hand.
= We gave a big hand _____ Seo-yoon.

오답노트

20. 다음 빈칸에 공통으로 들어갈 알맞은 말을 쓰시오.

· The news _____ me happy.
· I _____ her a pretty doll yesterday.
· Mom _____ me brush my teeth.

오답노트

21. 다음 우리말과 같은 뜻이 되도록 빈칸을 채우시오.

너는 그녀가 왜 여기에 있는지 아니?
= Do you know _____ _____ _____ here?

오답노트

22. 다음 두 문장을 한 문장으로 연결할 때 빈칸에 들어갈 알맞은 말을 쓰시오.

> Can you tell me? + Is the flight on time?
> → Can you tell me _____ the flight is on time?

오답노트

23. 다음 우리말과 같은 뜻이 되도록 빈칸을 채우시오.

> 치즈와 버터 중에 너는 어느 것을 원하니?
> → _____ do you _____, cheese _____ butter?

오답노트

24. 다음 괄호 안에 들어갈 말로 알맞은 것은?

> A : How does Nancy look today?
> B : She looks (   ).
> A : Do you know why?

❶ tired ❷ happily ❸ beauty
❹ angrily ❺ sadly

오답노트

25. 다음 문장의 밑줄 친 부분 중 어색한 것은?

> When we ❶ have problems, he ❷ listens to us and ❸ gives ❹ to us some useful ❺ advice.

오답노트

26. 밑줄 친 부가의문문의 쓰임이 옳은 것은?

❶ You work at the hospital, <u>does you</u>?
❷ Jack found his MP3 player, <u>did him</u>?
❸ Laura came to the party, <u>didn't she</u>?
❹ They aren't close friends, <u>aren't they</u>?
❺ Sunny doesn't drink coffee, <u>doesn't she</u>?

오답노트

[27-28] 다음 표를 보고 아래와 같이 문장을 완성하시오.

6:00 a.m.	get up and exercise
7:30 a.m.	have breakfast
8:00 a.m.	take the school bus

> (6:00 a.m.)
> Mom wanted me *to get up and exercise*.

27. (7:30 a.m.)
Mom told me _____.

28. (8:00 a.m.)
Dad had me _____.

오답노트

A. 〈보기〉와 같이 괄호 안의 단어를 이용하여 간접의문문의 문장을 완성하시오.

> 보 Have your friends gone home? (where)
> 기 → I don't know *where they've gone*.

1. Is Kathy in her office? (if)

→ Do you know _____?

2. Is the building very old? (how old)

→ I don't know _____.

3. Will Paul be here soon? (when)

→ I don't know _____.

4. Was she angry because I was late? (why)

→ I don't know _____.

5. Has Mary lived here a long time? (how long)

→ I don't know _____.

B. 우리말과 뜻이 같도록 괄호 안의 말을 이용하여 문장을 완성하시오.

1. 개그 콘서트는 나를 웃게 했다. (make / laugh)

= The Gag Concert _____.

2. 나는 네가 그녀와 함께 춤추는 것을 보았다. (see / with her / dance)

= I _____.

3. Tom은 나에게 전기코드를 만지지 말라고 경고했다. (touch / not)

= Tom warned _____ the electrical outlet.

C. 다음 괄호 안의 표현을 이용하여 주어진 상황에 맞게 빈칸을 채우시오.

1.

(play / tennis)

A : _____ , don't they?

B : Yes, they do. Every Sunday.

2.

(can / swim)

A : _____ , can he?

B : No, he can't.

3.

(sleep / at 12:00)

A : _____ , wasn't she?

B : Yes, she was sleeping.

4.

(snow / in the mountain)

A : _____ , isn't it?

B : Yes, it's snowing.

D. 다음 사진을 보고 괄호 안의 단어를 배열하여 감탄문을 쓰시오.

1.

(What / buildings / tall / are / they)

→ _____

2.

(What / they / are / watermelons / sweet)

→ _____

3.

(her / is / long / hair / how)

→ _____

실전 서술형 평가문제

출제의도 5형식/사역/지각동사
평가내용 5형식 동사를 이용하여 문장 만들기

A. 〈보기〉와 같이 5형식 문장으로 영작하시오. [서술형 유형 : 6점 / 난이도 : 중]

보기

My English teacher said, "Memorize English words every day."
A : What did your English teacher have you do?
B : *My English teacher[She] had[made] me memorize English*
words every day.

1.

The doctor said, "You should go on a diet."

A : What did the doctor advise you to do?

B : _____

2.

Her father said, "Wash the car."

A : What did your father have you do?

B : _____

3.

Miranda's friend said, "Don't drive so fast, Miranda!"

A : What did Miranda's friend tell her?

B : _____

출제의도 간접의문문에 대한 이해
평가내용 사진을 보고 간접의문문 완성하기

B. 〈보기〉와 같이 다음 문장을 간접의문문으로 다시 쓰시오.　　　　　[서술형 유형 : 9점 / 난이도 : 중상]

| 보기 |  | What time does the film start, George?
→ Lucy asked *George what time the film started.* |

1.

When are you flying back to Rome, Sophia?

→ Wilson asked _____.

2.

Must I cook dinner tonight, Jim?

→ Vicky asked _____ that night.

3.

What will you do on Saturday if you don't go to the concert, Peter?

→ Tina asked _____

_____.

실전 서술형 평가문제

 출제의도 부가의문문의 이해 및 쓰임
평가내용 실생활에서 부가의문문 활용하기

C. 주어진 상황과 단어를 참고하여 부가의문문과 함께 문장을 완성하시오. [서술형 유형 : 6점 / 난이도 : 중하]

보기	 (a beautiful day)	You look out of the windows. The sky is blue and the sun is shining. What do you say to your friend? **I say**: It *is a beautiful day*, *isn't it*?

1.
(has a beautiful voice)

Tom and Kevin are listening to a woman singing. Tom likes her voice very much. What does Tom say to Kevin?

Tom says: She _____, _____?

2.
(not look very good)

You are trying on a jacket. You look in the mirror and you don't like what you see. What do you say to your friend?

I say: It _____, _____?

3.
(expensive)

You and your friend are at the shopping mall. You're looking at the price tag, which is very high. What do you say?

I say: It _____, _____?

서술형 평가문제	채 점 기 준	배 점	나의 점수
A	표현이 올바르고 문법, 철자가 모두 정확한 경우	2점 × 3문항 = 6점	
B		3점 × 3문항 = 9점	
C		2점 × 3문항 = 6점	
공통	문법(부가의문문과 시제 등), 철자가 1개씩 틀린 경우	각 문항당 1점씩 감점	
	내용과 전혀 일치하지 않거나 답을 기재하지 못한 경우	0점	

Chapter 7

전치사 (Prepositions)

Unit 01 전치사 Ⅰ

1-1 장소와 방향을 나타내는 전치사 1

People are standing **at** the bus stop.
사람들이 버스 정류장에 서 있다.

Who is that woman **on** the bicycle?
자전거에 타고 있는 저 여자는 누구니?

---

01 **in**: 건물이나 구체적인 공간 안에 있는 것, 비교적 넓은 장소(도시, 나라 등)에 사용한다.

She has lived **in** Korea for 15 years. 그녀는 한국에 15년 동안 살았다.
The cell phone is **in** her pocket. 휴대폰은 그녀의 주머니에 있다.

02 **at**: 장소의 한 지점, 건물의 목적이 분명한 장소(정거장, 공항, 영화관 등), 단체 행동이 이루어지는 장소(콘서트, 회의, 파티 등) 앞에 사용한다.

The car is waiting **at** the traffic light. 그 차는 신호등에서 기다리고 있다. ▶ 한 지점
I will pick you up **at** the airport tomorrow. 내가 내일 공항으로 너를 태우러 갈게. ▶ 목적이 분명한 장소
We had a good time **at** the party. 우리는 파티에서 즐거운 시간을 보냈다. ▶ 단체 행동이 이루어지는 장소

03 **on**: 어떤 표면에 접촉해 있는 상태나 버스, 기차, 비행기, 자전거, 말, 오토바이를 타고 있을 때 사용한다.
대신 자동차를 타고 있을 때는 in a car / in a taxi로 쓴다.

We live **on** the third floor of this apartment. 우리는 이 아파트 3층에 산다.
Don't sit **on** the grass. 잔디 위에 앉지 마라.
Nancy is **on** the bus. Nancy는 버스에 타고 있다.
It's important to buckle up when you're **in** a car. 차에 타고 있을 때는 안전벨트를 매는 것이 중요하다.

04 **on the way to**는 '~로 가는 길에'라는 뜻이다. on my[your, her, his, their] way to로 쓸 수 있다.

I met Lucy **on the way to** school. 나는 학교 가는 길에 Lucy를 만났다.
Would you mind mailing this letter **on your way to** the office? 사무실 가는 길에 이 편지 좀 부쳐 줄래요?

서술형 기초다지기

Challenge 1 다음 빈칸에 전치사 at, in, on 중 알맞은 것을 넣어 문장을 완성하세요.

01. There is a clock _____ the wall.

02. They are _____ a meeting now.

03. Karen arrived _____ the airport.

04. Don't sit _____ this chair.

05. My uncle lives _____ Chicago.

06. There is a carpet _____ the floor.

07. The restaurant is _____ the second floor.

Challenge 2 다음 주어진 단어를 활용하여 B의 대답을 「전치사 + 명사」로만 써 보세요.

보기	A: Where is the clock? B: *On the wall.* (the wall)

01. A: Where is she standing?

　　B: _____ (the balcony)

02. A: Where's the Eiffel Tower?

　　B: _____ (Paris)

03. A: Where is the woman?

　　B: _____ (the airport)

1-2 장소와 방향을 나타내는 전치사 2

She is running **up** the hill.
그녀는 언덕 위로 달리고 있다.

They are running **into** the water.
그들은 물 속으로 뛰어 들어가고 있다.

01 전치사의 종류

up / down	~위로 / ~아래로	Tom's walking **up** the stairs. Tom은 계단을 오르고 있다. Jane's walking **down** the stairs. Jane은 계단을 내려가고 있다.
along	~을 따라서	He jogs **along** the river. 그는 강을 따라 조깅을 한다.
across / across from	~을 가로질러 / ~맞은편	Kevin's swimming **across** the river. Kevin은 강을 가로질러 수영하고 있다.
through	~을 관통하여	They walked **through** the forest. 그들은 숲 속을 통과하여 걸었다.
in front of / behind	~앞에 / ~뒤에	Sunny is **in front of** the door. Sunny는 문 앞에 있다. Peter is **behind** the door. Peter는 문 뒤에 있다.
over / under / beneath	~위에 / ~아래에 / ~바로 아래에	There's a bridge **over** the river. 강 위에 다리가 있다. The river flows **under** the bridge. 그 강은 다리 아래로 흐른다.
between / among	(둘) 사이에 / (셋 이상의) 사이에	Korea is **between** Japan and China. 한국은 일본과 중국 사이에 있다. I found Steve **among** the people. 나는 사람들 사이에서 Steve를 발견했다.
by(= beside, next to)	~옆에(서)	Susan is standing **by** the mirror. Susan은 거울 옆에 서 있다.
out of / into	~밖으로 / ~안으로	He took his PDA **out of** his backpack and put it **into** his pocket. 그는 배낭에서 PDA를 꺼내어 호주머니 안에 집어넣었다.
around	~주위에	They are sitting **around** the fire. 그들은 불 주위에 앉아 있다.
from ~ to	~로부터 ~까지	She walked **from** her house **to** the library. 그녀는 집에서 도서관까지 걸어갔다.
past	~을 지나서	We walked **past** the police station. 우리는 경찰서를 지나서 걸었다.

02

to, toward, for는 '~로의 접근'을 의미하고, away from, off, out of는 '~로부터의 이탈'을 의미한다.

He goes **to** Seoul every Sunday. 그는 일요일마다 서울에 간다.

She left **for** Beijing yesterday. 그녀는 어제 베이징으로 떠났다.

Can I take the Post-it **off** the wall? 포스트잇을 벽에서 떼어도 될까요?

Get **away from** the tiger. 그 호랑이에게서 떨어져라.

She got **off** the train and ran **toward** her father. 그녀는 기차에서 내려 아빠를 향해 달려갔다.

서술형 기초다지기

Challenge 1 다음 빈칸에 알맞은 전치사를 써서 문장을 완성하세요.

01. 새 한 마리가 나무 위로 날아갔다.
= A bird flew _____ the tree.

02. 이상한 여자가 나무 뒤에 서 있다.
= A strange woman is standing _____ the tree.

03. 우리는 해변을 따라 걸었다.
= We walked _____ the beach.

04. 그 도로는 사막을 관통하여 지나간다.
= The road runs _____ the desert.

05. 그 배는 두 섬 사이를 항해한다.
= The ship sails _____ the two islands.

06. 제과점 앞에 버스 정류장이 있다.
= There is a bus stop _____ _____ _____ the bakery.

07. 그 소년들은 풀장 안으로 뛰어들고 있다.
= The boys are jumping _____ the swimming pool.

08. Sunny는 Kevin 맞은편에 앉아 있다.
= Sunny is sitting _____ _____ Kevin.

Challenge 2 다음 빈칸에 by, over, behind, around 중 알맞은 전치사를 골라 넣으세요.

01.

Look at the bridge _____ the river!

02.
The girls walked _____ the tree.

03.
She is standing _____ the window.

04.

He is standing _____ his wife.

Unit 02 전치사 Ⅱ

2-1 시간을 나타내는 전치사 1

We go to school **at** 8 o'clock.
우리는 8시에 학교에 간다.

The Korean War broke out **in** 1950.
한국전쟁은 1950년에 발발했다.

---

01 **at** : **구체적인 시각**이나 **어느 정확한 시점**을 나타낼 때 사용한다.

I will see you **at** 9 o'clock tomorrow. 내일 9시에 볼게. ▶ 시각
I'm going to visit you **at** lunchtime. 내가 점심시간에 방문할게. ▶ 시점
Bill watches TV **at** night. Bill은 밤에 TV를 본다. ▶ at night에는 the를 쓰지 않는다

02 **in** : **하루의 일부분**을 말할 때나 **월, 계절, 연도** 등 at보다 비교적 긴 기간을 나타낼 때 사용한다.

We always watch TV **in** the evening. 우리는 항상 저녁에 TV를 본다. ▶ 하루의 일부분
In summer, many people like to swim in the sea. 여름에는 많은 사람들이 바다에서 수영하길 좋아한다. ▶ 계절
The Brazil World Cup will be held **in** 2014. 브라질 월드컵이 2014년에 개최된다. ▶ 연도

03 **on** : **요일이나 날짜 앞, 특정 요일의 아침/오후/저녁**에 쓴다.

I have violin lessons <u>**on** Wednesdays</u>. 수요일마다 바이올린 수업이 있어. ▶ 요일
  = every Wednesday
The concert is **on** November 22. 그 공연은 11월 22일에 있다. ▶ 날짜
See you **on** Sunday morning. 일요일 아침에 만나자. ▶ 특정 요일의 아침

04 **before**(~전에), **after**(~후에) : **현재를 기준으로 '지금부터 ~후에'**라는 뜻의 in은 미래시제와 함께 사용되고, 이 경우에는 after를 쓰지 않는다.

Let's have lunch **before** the meeting. 회의 전에 점심을 먹자.
Watch TV **after** dinner. 저녁 식사 후에 TV를 봐라.
Don't go anywhere. I'll be back **in** ten minutes. 아무 데도 가지 마라. 10분 후에 돌아올 거야.

※ next, last, this, that, every, all 등이 시간 앞에 올 경우에는 전치사(at, in, on)를 쓰지 않는다.

| next year | last month | every Friday |
| this morning | that evening | all day |

서술형 기초다지기

Challenge 1 다음 빈칸에 알맞은 전치사를 쓰세요.

01. 아침에 _____ the morning

02. 밤에 _____ night

03. 1998년에 _____ 1998

04. 봄에 _____ spring

05. 토요일에 _____ Saturday

06. 8시 전에 _____ 8 o'clock

07. 아침 식사 후에 _____ breakfast

08. 저녁에 _____ the evening

09. 회의 후에 _____ the meeting

10. 겨울에 _____ winter

11. 2012년에 _____ 2012

12. 지금부터 2시간 후에 _____ two hours

Challenge 2 다음 빈칸을 알맞은 형태의 동사와 알맞은 전치사로 채워 보세요.

01. The students _____ (do) their homework _____ the afternoon.

02. Steve _____ (visit) his grandparents _____ weekends.

03. Brian _____ (wake) up _____ 6:00 _____ the morning.

Challenge 3 다음 빈칸에 알맞은 전치사를 쓰세요.

01. 그 영화는 한 시간 후에 끝날 것이다.

= The movie will end _____ an hour.

02. 2차 세계대전 후에 사람들은 평화를 지키려고 노력했다.

= _____ World War II, people tried to keep the peace.

03. 그녀는 토요일마다 요가 수업에 간다.

= She goes to a yoga class _____ Saturdays.

04. 금요일 저녁에 영화 보러 가는 게 어때?

= Why don't you go to the movies _____ Friday evening?

2-2 시간을 나타내는 전치사 2

You must finish your homework **by** tomorrow.
너는 내일까지 숙제를 끝내야 한다.

She has been sick **since** last Friday.
그녀는 지난 금요일 이후로 계속 아프다.

01 by vs. until[till] : 둘 다 '~까지'라는 뜻이지만 by는 **'늦지 않게 ~까지'의 완료의 의미**를 나타내고 until은 **특정 시점까지 어떤 상태나 상황이 계속됨**을 나타낸다.

I'll finish my homework **by** 9 o'clock. 나는 9시까지 숙제를 끝낼 것이다.
I'm waiting for you **until** 11 o'clock. 11시까지 너를 기다리고 있을게.

02 from vs. since : from은 '~부터'의 뜻으로 어떤 동작이나 상태가 시작한 시점만 나타내고 지금은 알 수 없다. since는 '~ 이래로'의 뜻으로 완료시제와 함께 쓰이며 '과거 이래로 계속'이라는 뜻을 담고 있어 현재에도 영향을 끼치고 있음을 나타낸다.

I'll study Japanese **from** March. 나는 3월부터 일본어를 공부할 거야.
I have studied Japanese **since** 2009. 나는 2009년 이래로 일본어를 공부해 왔다.

03 for vs. during : 둘 다 '~동안'의 뜻이지만 for 뒤에는 **구체적인 기간의 길이**를 표시하는 말이 오고, during은 정확한 시간의 길이를 언급하지 않은 **'기간'**을 나타낸다.

She will stay here **for** three days. 그녀는 여기에 3일 동안 머무를 것이다.
He swims every day **during** the summer. 그는 여름 동안 매일 수영을 한다.

04 그 외에 시간을 나타내는 전치사 : about / around(~쯤에, ~ 경에), over(~동안에, ~의 사이에), through (~동안 줄곧, ~내내) 등이 있다.

She likes to take a walk **around** sunrise. 그녀는 일출 무렵에 산책하길 좋아한다.
We're going to go fishing **over** the weekend. 우리는 주말 동안에 낚시를 갈 것이다.
I tossed and turned all **through** the night. 나는 밤새도록 뒤척였다.

Challenge 1 〈보기〉와 같이 주어진 시간 표현을 이용하여 문장을 완성하세요.

> **보기**
> A: Did Bob watch TV for three hours last night? (two hours)
> B: No, *he didn't*. *He watched TV for two hours*.

01. A: Can you wait for me until 5:30? (5:00)

    B: No, _____. _____

02. A: Did Alex live in Singapore from 2000 to 2008? (2005 to 2008)

    B: No, _____. _____

03. A: Can you finish your project by tomorrow? (next week)

    B: No, _____. _____

Challenge 2 다음 빈칸에 for와 during 중 알맞은 것을 쓰세요.

01. It rained _____ three days without stopping.

02. I fell asleep _____ the movie.

03. I waited for you _____ half an hour.

04. Jack stayed in Miami _____ the summer vacation.

05. I'll come and see you _____ a few minutes.

Challenge 3 다음 빈칸에 from과 since 중 알맞은 것을 쓰세요.

01. Lucy has played the drum _____ 2005.

02. We have lived in France _____ 1999.

03. We lived in London _____ 1999 to 2005.

04. I will learn Japanese _____ next week.

3-1 기타 알아두어야 할 전치사

Susan goes to school **by** bus.
Susan은 버스를 타고 학교에 다닌다.

They fought bravely **for** their country.
그들은 자신들의 나라를 위해 용감하게 싸웠다.

01

전치사	의미	예문
for/ from	때문에(원인) / ~을 위하여(목적) / ~로 인해(이유)	We wept **for** joy. 우리는 기뻐서 울었다. He will do anything **for** money. 그는 돈을 위해서라면 뭐든지 할 거다. She cried **from** fear. 그녀는 두려워서 소리를 질렀다.
with	with+사람(~와 함께) with+사물(~을 가지고)	Do you live **with** your parents? 너는 부모님과 함께 사니? Please sign your name **with** a pen. 펜으로 사인을 해주세요.
like	~ 와 같은 ~ 처럼	I love Korean food **like** Gimchi. 나는 김치와 같은 한국 음식을 좋아한다.
in	~을 입고, 신고, 끼고(wearing) / in+언어(~나라 말로)	A woman **in** white came to see you. 흰옷을 입은 여인이 당신을 찾아왔다. She spoke **in** English during the meeting. 그녀는 회의 동안 영어로 말했다.
for/ against	~에 찬성하는 / ~에 반대하는	Are you **for** or **against** it? 너는 그것에 찬성이니 아니면 반대니?
by	~을 타고 ~로(방법) ~에 의해	Do you like traveling **by** train? 기차로 여행하는 것을 좋아하니? ▶ by 뒤에 교통수단이 올 때는 관사를 쓰지 않는다. ※ 단 '걸어서, 도보로'의 뜻은 on foot을 쓴다. I usually go to school **on foot**. We will keep in touch **by** e-mail. 우리는 이메일로 연락할 거야. I'm looking at art work **by** Rodin. 나는 로뎅의 예술 작품을 보고 있다.
at	나이, 온도, 속도	You can get a driver's license **at** 18. 18살에 운전면허를 딸 수 있다. Water boils **at** 100 degrees Celsius. 물은 100도에서 끓는다. ▶ 온도 He was driving **at** 150km an hour. ▶ 속도 그는 시속 150킬로미터로 운전하고 있었다.
about/ on	~에 대하여(일반적) / ~에 대하여(전문적)	I don't know much **about** cars. 나는 자동차에 대해 잘 모른다. She wrote a book **on** Korean history. 그녀는 한국 역사에 관한 책을 썼다.
of/from	~로 만들어지다(재료)	The box is made **of** paper. 그 상자는 종이로 만들어진다. ▶ 재료 본래의 성질이 남아 있을 때 Cheese is made **from** milk. 치즈는 우유로 만들어진다. ▶ 재료 본래의 성질이 사라지고 없을 때

서술형 기초다지기

Challenge 1   다음 괄호 안의 단어 중에서 알맞은 것을 고르세요.

01. Thank you (for / of) coming to my party.

02. I was in bed (with / from) a bad cold for a week.

03. Will you pay (by / with) credit card?

04. I cut the paper (by / with) a pair of scissors.

05. I go to school (in / by) bus, but sometimes I go to school on foot.

06. The desk is made (of / from) wood.

Challenge 2   다음 빈칸에 공통으로 들어갈 말을 by, on, for 중에 골라 쓰세요.

01. This novel was written _____ her.

     Send it _____ e-mail, please.

02. Do you go to school _____ foot?

     He gives us the information _____ Korean history.

03. Are you _____ or against the death penalty?

     I'm sorry _____ coming late.

Memo

3-2 형용사와 함께 잘나가는 표현들

He is afraid of dogs.
그는 개를 무서워한다.

The city was crowded with tourists.
그 도시는 관광객들로 붐볐다.

01

be good at ~을 잘하다	Sunny **is good at** playing the violin. Sunny는 바이올린 연주를 잘한다.
be poor at ~에 서투르다	He **is poor at** swimming. 그는 수영이 서툴다.
be crowded with ~로 붐비다, 가득 차다	The roads in Korea **are crowded with** cars. 한국의 도로는 차들로 가득하다.
be full of ~로 가득하다	The room **was full of** furniture. 그 방은 가구로 가득 찼다.
be different from ~와 다르다	The movie **was different from** what I'd expected. 그 영화는 내가 기대했던 것과는 달랐다.
be interested in ~에 흥미가 있다, 관심이 있다	**Are** you **interested in** art? 너는 예술에 관심이 있니?
be afraid[frightened / scared] of ~을 두려워하다	**Are** you **afraid of** snakes? 너는 뱀을 무서워하니?
be proud[fond / ashamed / jealous / envious] of ~을 자랑스러워[좋아/부끄러워/질투/시기]하다	Why **are** you always so **jealous of** other people? 너는 왜 항상 다른 사람들을 그렇게 질투하니?
be similar to ~와 비슷하다	Your opinion **is similar to** mine. 너의 견해는 내 견해와 비슷하다.
be dependent on ~에 의존하다	I don't want to **be dependent on** anybody. 나는 누구에게도 의존하고 싶지 않다.
be famous for ~로 유명하다	What **is** Korea **famous for**? 한국은 무엇으로 유명한가요?
be responsible for ~에 대해 책임이 있다	Once I **was responsible for** an Olympic team. 한때는 내가 올림픽 팀의 책임을 맡았었다.

서술형 기초다지기

Challenge 1 다음 괄호 안의 단어 중에서 알맞은 것을 고르세요.

01. Kathy is good (in / at) playing the guitar.

02. The letter I wrote was full (of / for) mistakes.

03. Your writing is similar (from / to) mine.

04. Who was responsible (for / of) all that noise last night?

05. I don't like climbing ladders. I'm afraid (of / about) heights.

06. I'm not ashamed (for / of) what I did.

07. France is famous (in / for) its food.

Challenge 2 다음 빈칸에 알맞은 전치사를 쓰세요.

01. There were lots of tourists in the city. The city was crowded _____ tourists.

02. I'm not a very good tennis player. I'm not good _____ tennis.

03. I don't like sports very much. I'm not very fond _____ sports.

04. My problem isn't the same as yours. My problem is different _____ yours.

05. Don't worry. I'll take care of you. There's nothing to be afraid _____ .

06. I never watch the news on TV. I'm not interested _____ it.

07. We've got plenty to eat. The fridge is full _____ food.

08. Our house is similar _____ yours. Perhaps yours is a little larger.

09. Kevin has no money of his own. He's totally dependent _____ his parents.

3-3 동사와 함께 잘나가는 표현들

Jane **listens to** music.
Jane은 음악을 듣는다.

She is **waiting for** the subway for 20 minutes.
그녀는 20분 동안 지하철을 기다리고 있다.

01

listen to ~를 듣다	My hobby is **listening to** music. 내 취미는 음악을 듣는 것이다.
wait for ~을 기다리다	She is **waiting for** me in the car. 그녀는 차 안에서 나를 기다리고 있다.
look for ~을 찾다 look at ~을 보다 look after ~을 돌보다	The beggar is **looking for** a place in which to sleep. 그 거지는 잠을 잘 곳을 찾고 있다. Why are you **looking at** me like that? 너는 왜 그렇게 나를 보고 있니? I need someone to **look after** my dog while I'm away. 내가 없는 동안 애완견을 봐줄 누군가가 필요하다.
laugh at ~을 보고 웃다/비웃다 smile at ~을 보고 웃다	Everybody will **laugh at** you. 모든 사람들이 너를 보고 비웃을 거다.
consist of ~로 구성되어 있다	The test **consists of** writing and speaking. 그 시험은 쓰기와 말하기로 구성되어 있다.
belong to ~에 속하다, ~의 소유물이다	Does this iPhone **belong to** you? 이 아이폰이 네 것이니?
die of ~로 죽다(주로 질병, 부상 등)	She **died of** cancer last year. 그녀는 작년에 암으로 죽었다.
care about ~에 신경 쓰다, 관심을 가지다 care for ~을 좋아하다(= like), ~을 돌보다(= take care of)	Nancy is selfish. She doesn't **care about** other people. Nancy는 이기적이다. 그녀는 다른 사람들에 대해 관심을 갖지 않는다. I don't **care for** cold weather. 나는 추운 날씨를 좋아하지 않는다. Who **cares for** this babies? 누가 이 아기들을 돌보니?
apply for ~에 지원하다	Are you going to **apply for** the company? 너는 그 회사에 지원할 거니?
complain(to someone) about ~에 대해 불평하다	She **complains about** everything. 그녀는 사사건건 불평해
depend[rely] on ~에 의지하다, 달려 있다	It **depends on** the weather. 그건 날씨에 달려 있다.

서술형 기초다지기

Challenge 1 다음 빈칸에 알맞은 전치사를 쓰세요.

01. We had an enormous meal. It consisted _____ eight courses.

02. She doesn't have a job. She depends _____ her parents for money.

03. Look _____ these flowers. Aren't they pretty?

04. Don't listen _____ what he says.

05. Does this bag belong _____ you?

06. Water consists _____ oxygen and hydrogen.

07. Bob died _____ a heart attack.

08. We spent the evening listening _____ music.

09. Would you care _____ a cup of coffee?

10. I think you'd be good at this job. Why don't you apply _____ it?

11. I've lost my keys. Can you help me look _____ them?

12. You can have a pet dog if you promise to look _____ it.

13. Some people are dying _____ hunger.

Memo

01 출제 100% - 전치사의 기본 의미에 충실하자.

출제자의 눈 시간이나 위치를 나타내는 기본적인 전치사 문제가 가장 많이 출제된다. 가장 기본이 되는 in, on, at이 나타내는 시간이나 위치의 뜻을 정확하게 이해하고 있어야 한다.

Ex 1.

빈칸에 전치사 in이 들어갈 수 <u>없는</u> 것은?

(a) I started working here _____ 1995.

(b) I wake up at 6 o'clock _____ the morning.

(c) Our teacher will be back _____ an hour.

(d) She often works _____ night.

(e) We have a lot of snow _____ winter.

02 출제 100% - 비슷한 의미를 가진 전치사를 구별하라.

출제자의 눈 for와 during, by와 until, from과 since를 구별하는 문제가 자주 출제된다. 우리말로는 비슷한 의미인 것 같지만 쓰임새를 구별하여 암기해 두어야 한다.

Ex 2.

We will stay in London _____ the Olympic Games.

(a) during   (b) for   (c) by   (d) at

Ex 3.

You have to submit the report _____ Friday.

(a) for   (b) during   (c) since   (d) by

03 출제 100 % - 방향을 나타내는 전치사는 시험에 단골손님으로 등장한다.

 출제자의 눈 간단한 그림을 주고 그림의 위치를 파악하여 방향의 전치사(next to, across from 등)를 쓰게 한다든가, 우리말에 맞는 표현의 전치사를 고르라는 문제가 자주 출제된다.

Ex 4.

다음 빈칸에 알맞은 것은?

The bank is _____ the gas station and the bookstore.

(은행은 주유소와 서점 사이에 있다.)

(a) across   (b) behind   (c) by   (d) between

04 출제 100 % - 「형용사 / 동사 + 전치사」 표현은 숙어처럼 암기해 두자!

출제자의 눈 형용사 또는 동사와 함께 만나 여러가지 의미를 나타내는 전치사는 반드시 암기해 두어야 한다. '~로 가득찬'의 full of에서 of를 with로 바꿔 틀리게 하거나 알맞은 전치사를 함께 고르는 문제들이 출제된다.

Ex 5.

다음 빈칸에 공통으로 들어갈 말은?

· Could you help me look _____ my cell phone?

· She is waiting _____ the bus for 10 minutes.

(a) at   (b) for   (c) on   (d) after

Ex 6.

Are you interested _____ Picasso's paintings?

(a) on   (b) for   (c) in   (d) against

1. 다음 빈칸에 공통으로 들어갈 단어는?

· I was surprised ____ the news.
· They will have a meeting ____ 7 o'clock.

❶ on ❷ in ❸ with ❹ at ❺ by

2. 다음 빈칸에 들어갈 알맞은 말은?

· We watched TV _____ two hours.
· My wedding anniversary is _____ May 26th.
· Kelly is standing _____ the window.

❶ for − on − by ❷ on − by − for
❸ by − for − on ❹ in − at − for
❺ in − until − next to

3. 다음 우리말을 영어로 바르게 옮긴 것은?

우루과이는 1950년 이래로 월드컵에서 계속 우승을 하지 못했다.

❶ Uruguay didn't win the World Cup since 1950.
❷ Uruguay hasn't won the World Cup by 1950.
❸ Uruguay didn't win the World Cup until 1950.
❹ Uruguay has not won the World Cup since 1950.
❺ Uruguay didn't win the World Cup in 1950.

4. 두 문장이 일치하도록 할 때 빈칸에 알맞은 말은?

The train left and then we got to the station.
→ We got to the station ____ the train left.

❶ if ❷ after ❸ before
❹ for ❺ until

5. 다음 빈칸에 공통으로 들어갈 알맞은 말은?

· We arrived at Muju _____ 1 p.m.
(우리는 1시쯤에 무주에 도착했다.)
· Everybody got together _____ the campfire.
(모든 사람이 모닥불 주위에 모였다.)

❶ for ❷ until ❸ around
❹ before ❺ about

6. 우리말과 일치하도록 빈칸에 알맞은 말을 쓰시오.

시골을 통과하여 오랫동안 버스를 타고 갔다.
→ It was a long bus ride _____ the countryside.

7. 다음 중 어법상 옳지 않은 것은?

❶ She got out of the car and walked to me.
❷ You had better wear a suit for a job interview.
❸ Please let me off at the next bus stop.
❹ I saw lots of students in uniform on my way to the school.
❺ My grandfather died with a heart attack five years ago.

8. 다음 중 밑줄 친 like의 뜻이 나머지 넷과 다른 것을 고르시오.

❶ He likes sports, like baseball or soccer.
❷ What music do you like best?
❸ He often eats fast food, like burgers or french fries.
❹ She collected old but useful things, like toys or books.
❺ I want to have a pet, like dogs or cats.

오답 노트 만들기

★틀린 문제 : _____   ★다시 공부한 날 : _____

(1) 문제를 왜? 틀렸는지 곰곰이 생각하고 그 이유를 적어본다.

(2) 핵심 개념을 적는다.

(3) 자신이 몰랐던 단어와 숙어 표현이 있으면 정리한다.

(4) 해설집에서 필요한 부분을 골라 풀이 해법을 정리한다.

★틀린 문제 : _____   ★다시 공부한 날 : _____

(1) 문제를 왜? 틀렸는지 곰곰이 생각하고 그 이유를 적어본다.

(2) 핵심 개념을 적는다.

(3) 자신이 몰랐던 단어와 숙어 표현이 있으면 정리한다.

(4) 해설집에서 필요한 부분을 골라 풀이 해법을 정리한다.

★틀린 문제 : _____   ★다시 공부한 날 : _____

(1) 문제를 왜? 틀렸는지 곰곰이 생각하고 그 이유를 적어본다.

(2) 핵심 개념을 적는다.

(3) 자신이 몰랐던 단어와 숙어 표현이 있으면 정리한다.

(4) 해설집에서 필요한 부분을 골라 풀이 해법을 정리한다.

★틀린 문제 : _____   ★다시 공부한 날 : _____

(1) 문제를 왜? 틀렸는지 곰곰이 생각하고 그 이유를 적어본다.

(2) 핵심 개념을 적는다.

(3) 자신이 몰랐던 단어와 숙어 표현이 있으면 정리한다.

(4) 해설집에서 필요한 부분을 골라 풀이 해법을 정리한다.

[1-3] 다음 빈칸에 알맞은 전치사를 골라 쓰시오.

from	by	during

1. She traveled to Seattle _____ train.

2. We visited Hawaii _____ the summer vacation.

3. The bank is open _____ nine to four thirty.

오답노트

[4-5] 다음 중 밑줄 친 표현이 바르지 <u>않은</u> 것은?

4. ❶ The war continued <u>during</u> seven years.
  ❷ He slept <u>during</u> the meeting.
  ❸ I have studied English and French <u>for</u> six years.
  ❹ <u>During</u> her visit, she went to the Hong Kong Disneyland.
  ❺ I went there twice <u>during</u> the vacation.

5. ❶ I have been ill <u>since</u> last Sunday.
  ❷ Be sure to come back <u>by</u> 5 o'clock in the afternoon.
  ❸ She worked as a photographer <u>until</u> 2002.
  ❹ You should give it back to me <u>by</u> this Friday.
  ❺ I studied for the examination <u>by</u> 12 o'clock in the evening.

오답노트

6. 다음 밑줄 친 우리말과 같은 뜻이 되도록 빈칸에 알맞은 단어를 쓰시오.

> <u>집에 가는 길에</u>, 그녀는 부모님을 위해 선물을 샀다.
> = _____ _____ _____ _____,
> she bought some gifts for her parents.

오답노트

7. 다음 빈칸에 공통으로 들어갈 알맞은 전치사는?

> · He left for Europe _____ plane to visit several countries.
> · I'll let you know _____ e-mail.

❶ with ❷ for ❸ in
❹ by ❺ at

오답노트

8. 다음 빈칸에 들어갈 말이 알맞게 짝지어진 것은?

> _____ September, I went _____ Korea. It was Chuseok. While I was _____ Korea, I experienced many interesting things.

❶ At – to – in ❷ In – for – at
❸ In – to – in ❹ For – to – in
❺ On – to – at

오답노트

9. 다음 빈칸에 들어갈 알맞은 말을 쓰시오.

> I did my English homework from 8 p.m.
> to 10 p.m.
> = I did my English homework _____
>   two hours.

오답노트

10. 우리말을 영작한 것으로 바르지 <u>않은</u> 것은?

❶ 서윤이는 2008년 5월 15일에 태어났다.
  = Seo-yoon was born on May 15th, 2008.
❷ Lisa는 화요일마다 드럼을 연주한다.
  = Lisa plays the drum on Tuesdays.
❸ 그 남자는 강당 안을 통과하여 뛰기 시작했다.
  = The man began running through the hall.
❹ 우리는 막 체육관에 들어가는 중이다.
  = We are just going out of the gym.
❺ Jason은 저 핑크색 코트를 입은 소녀를 좋아해.
  = Jason likes the girl in the pink coat.

오답노트

[11-13] 우리말과 같은 뜻이 되도록 주어진 단어를 이용하여 문장을 완성하시오.

11. 원숭이 한 마리가 나무 위로 올라가고 있다.

→ _____

  (up, the tree, a monkey, is climbing)

12. 그녀는 문 앞에서 책을 읽고 있다.

→ _____

  (in front of, is reading, the door, she)

13. 버스 정류장에서 만나자.

→ _____

  (Let's, at, meet, the bus stop)

오답노트

14. 다음 빈칸에 들어갈 말이 알맞게 짝지어진 것은?

> · I'm going to play soccer _____ Saturday.
> · I entered high school _____ 2004.

❶ on – in   ❷ in – in
❸ at – on   ❹ on – on
❺ in – on

오답노트

15. 다음 두 문장의 뜻이 같도록 빈칸에 들어갈 알맞은 단어를 고르시오.

> Koreans take pride in their unique cultural heritage and history.
> = Koreans are proud _____ their unique cultural heritage and history.

❶ at   ❷ on   ❸ of
❹ with   ❺ in

오답노트

실전 서술형 평가문제

 출제의도 장소에 맞는 전치사
평가내용 전치사를 이용하여 사물의 위치 표현하기

A. 아래는 Helen의 방이다. 방 안의 사물들을 이용하여 〈보기〉와 같이 영작하시오. [서술형 유형 : 12점 / 난이도 : 중]

보기	*Helen's bag is on the table.* (bag)

1. _____ (toy)

2. _____ (shoe)

3. _____ (cat's basket)

4. _____ (cat)

5. _____ (painting)

6. _____ (book)

출제의도　장소의 전치사
평가내용　실생활에서 장소의 전치사 활용하기

B. 다음 질문에 대한 답을 완전한 문장으로 영작하시오.　　　　　[서술형 유형 : 10점 / 난이도 : 중]

| 보기 |  | Q : Where is the fish?
A : *It is in the fishbowl.* |

1.

Q : Where is the girl?
A : _____ .

2.

Q : Where are the children?
A : _____ .

3.

Q : Where is the man?
A : _____ .

4.

Q : Where is she sitting?
A : _____ .

5.

Q : Where are they?
A : _____ .

실전 서술형 평가문제

출제의도 시간의 전치사 이해
평가내용 시간을 나타내는 전치사를 이해하고 실생활에 적용하기

C. 〈보기〉와 같이 from ~ to / for / until / since를 이용한 문장으로 완성하시오. [서술형 유형 : 8점 / 난이도 : 중하]

Peter
· I live in Korea now.
· I lived in Canada. (1999~2002)
· I came to Korea in 2002.

Lucy
· I live in Australia now.
· I lived in Korea. (2002~2010)
· I came to Australia in 2010.

Cindy
· I work in a restaurant now.
· I worked in a hotel. (1999~2005)
· I started work in the restaurant in 2005.

보 기	Peter *lived in Canada from 1999 to 2002*. (1999~2002) Peter *lived in Canada for three years*. Peter *lived in Canada until 2002*. Peter *has lived in Korea since 2002*.

1. Lucy _____. (2002~2010)

Lucy _____.

Lucy _____.

Lucy _____.

2. Cindy _____. (1999~2005)

Cindy _____.

Cindy _____.

Cindy _____.

서술형 평가문제	채 점 기 준	배 점	나의 점수
A	표현이 올바르고 문법, 철자가 모두 정확한 경우	2점 × 6문항 = 12점	
B		2점 × 5문항 = 10점	
C		4점 × 2문항 = 8점	
공통	문법, 철자가 1개씩 틀린 경우	각 문항당 1점씩 감점	
	내용과 전혀 일치하지 않거나 답을 기재하지 못한 경우	0점	

Chapter 8

가정법 (Conditionals)

Unit 01 가정문

1-1 현재와 미래를 나타내는 1차 가정문

If it **is** fine tomorrow, I **will go** fishing.
내일 날씨가 좋으면, 나는 낚시하러 갈 거야.

01 **1차 가정문은 현재나 미래에 발생할 가능성이 있는 일을 표현**하는 문장이다. 실제 현재의 가능성이 있는 일을 예상하며 말할 때는 **if절에 현재시제를 쓰고, 주절에도 현재시제를 쓴다.**

If you **are** late, **don't forget** to call. 네가 늦게 되면, 전화하는 거 잊지 마.
　　　　현재시제　　　　현재시제

02 **미래의 가능성 있는 일을 추측할 때는 if절 안에 현재시제를 쓰고**(미래를 나타내는 조건의 부사절임), **주절에는 미래시제를 쓴다.** will말고도 미래를 나타내는 어떤 형태의 동사든 쓸 수 있다.

If Sunny **doesn't come** late, we**'ll go** out for dinner. Sunny가 늦게 오지 않으면 우리는 저녁 먹으러 나갈 거야.
If I **finish** my homework soon, I **can go to** bed. 숙제를 곧 끝내면 자러 갈 수 있다.
If my sister **visits** me, we**'re going to** go to the park. 누나가 나를 방문하면 공원에 갈 거야.

03 **일반적인 사실, 일상적으로 일어나는 일이나 정해진 상황을 가정할 때 if절과 주절에 현재시제를 쓴다.**

① 일반적 사실(General facts)

If the temperature **doesn't fall** below 0℃, water **doesn't freeze**.
　　　　　　　　　현재시제　　　　　　　　　　　현재시제
온도가 섭씨 0도 이하로 내려가지 않으면 물은 얼지 않는다.

If you **mix** oil and water, the oil **stays** on top. 기름과 물을 섞으면 기름은 물에 뜬다.

② 일상적인 일(Everyday things)

If I **go** to work by car, it **takes** thirty-five minutes. 내가 차를 타고 일하러 가면 35분이 걸린다.
I always **walk** to school if it **doesn't rain**. 비가 오지 않으면 나는 항상 학교에 걸어간다.

③ 정해진 일(Definite things)

If I **have** a big lunch, it **makes** me sleepy. 점심을 많이 먹으면 졸음이 올 거야.
If she **hears** his name, she **gets** angry. 그녀가 그의 이름을 들으면 화를 낼 거야.

※ 지금까지 우리나라 영문법에서는 가정법 현재라는 말로 현재나 미래에 대한 의심, 불확실 등을 나타내고, 조건절에 직설법 현재동사를 사용할 수 있다고 설명하고 있어 가정법과 조건의 부사절을 이해하는 데 굉장한 어려움이 있었다. 현대 영어에서는 모두 다 조건의 부사절이고 시제나 상황에 따라 가능성을 나타내는 것으로, 말하는 사람의 태도나 확신의 정도, 가능성에 전적으로 달려 있다.

서술형 기초다지기

정답 p. 24

Challenge 1 다음 괄호 안의 단어를 알맞은 형태로 바꾸어 문장을 완성하세요.

01. If Scott _____ (help) me with the work, I _____ (finish) earlier.

02. If you _____ (eat) too much, you _____ (put on) weight.

03. If people _____ (sneeze), they _____ (close) their eyes.

04. If we _____ (go) to London, we _____ (see) Buckingham Palace.

05. You _____ (die) if you _____ (not / get) oxygen.

06. If you _____ (go) without a coat, you _____ (catch) cold.

07. If you _____ (break) a nail, it _____ (grow) back again.

Challenge 2 다음 문장을 괄호 안의 접속사를 이용하여 다시 써 보세요.

> **보기**
> I want to get good marks. Then, my parents will be happy. (if)
> → *If I get good marks, my parents will be happy.*

01. Sometimes the temperature reaches -15℃. Then, the lake freezes. (when)

→ _____

02. Jane should stop eating sweets. Otherwise, she won't lose any weight. (unless)

→ _____

03. Babies are often hungry. Then, they cry. (when)

→ _____

04. I may see Tom this afternoon. I'll tell him to phone you. (if)

→ _____

1-2 가능성이 거의 없는 2차 가정문 Ⅰ

If I **had** enough money, I **would buy** a new car.
내게 돈이 충분하면 새 차를 살 텐데.

---

01 우리나라 영문법에서는 가정법 과거라는 표현을 쓰면서 현재 사실과 반대되는 것을 가정한다고 하지만 이는 시제로 설명하기 위한 어색한 표현이다. 실제 가정법 과거는 현재 사실에 대해 가능성이 현저히 떨어지는 상황을 설명하는 것으로, 가능성이 희박하지만 일단 한번 말해 보는 것이다.

If절(부사절)	주절
If + 과거시제	would could + 동사원형 might

※ 현실의 가능성과 멀리 떨어지게 하기 위해 과거시제와 과거조동사를 쓰기로 정했다. If절 안에 쓰이는 과거시제는 과거가 아니라 가능성이 적은 현재나 미래를 나타낸다.

---

02 가정문에 쓰이는 현재시제는 현재나 미래에 발생할 가능성이 있는 일, **과거시제는 현재 가능성이 전혀 없진 않지만 10~20% 정도의 가능성**을 염두에 두고 말하는 분위기(mood)일 때 쓴다.

If Lucy **comes** tomorrow, we **will go** to the movies. Lucy가 내일 오면 우리는 영화 보러 갈 거야.
▶ 화자는 Lucy가 내일 올 것을 알고 있고, 가능성이 높기 때문에 If절에는 현재, 주절에는 미래시제를 쓴 것이다.

If you **saw** someone breaking into your house, what **would** you do?
누군가 너의 집에 침입하는 것을 보면 어떻게 하겠니?
▶ 화자는 희박한 가능성의 일을 가정하는 것이다. 가능성이 희박할 뿐 현재나 미래에 발생하지 않는다는 보장은 없다.

---

03 If 조건절에서는 **주어의 인칭과 수에 관계없이 be동사의 과거는 were**를 쓴다. 주로 견해를 밝히거나 충고를 할 때 쓴다. 일상 영어에서는 was를 쓰기도 하지만 주로 충고할 때는 If I were you(내가 만약 너라면)처럼 were가 더 자연스럽게 쓰인다. 이것 역시 현재 또는 미래에 가능성이 현저히 떨어지기 때문에 과거시제를 쓴다.

If I **were[was]** a doctor, I **could help** sick children in Africa.
내가 의사라면 아프리카에 있는 아픈 어린이들을 도울 수 있을 텐데.

If I **were** you, I **wouldn't buy** that cell phone. 내가 너라면 저 휴대폰을 사지 않을 텐데.

If Lisa **were[was]** here, she **would help** me. Lisa가 여기에 있다면 그녀는 나를 도와 줄 텐데.

Challenge 1 〈보기〉와 같이 가정법 문장을 완성하세요.

> **보기** I don't know the answer. If I _knew_ the answer, I'd tell you.

01. I'm not rich. If I _____ rich, I would spend all my time travelling.

02. I have a car. I couldn't travel much if I _____ a car.

03. I don't have a camera. If I _____ a camera, I would attend the photo contest.

04. I'm not hungry. I would have something to eat if I _____ hungry.

Challenge 2 〈보기〉와 같이 괄호 안의 말을 이용하여 가정법 과거 문장을 완성하세요.

> **보기** A: Should we take the 10:00 train?
> B: No. _If we took the 10:00 train, we'd arrive too early._
>   (arrive / too early)

01. A: Why don't we stay in a hotel?

　　 B: No. _____

　　　　　　　　　　　　　(it / cost / too much money)

02. A: Let's tell them the truth.

　　 B: No. _____

　　　　　　　　　　　　　(not believe / us)

If I **knew** your address, I **could write** you a letter.
네 주소를 안다면 편지를 썼을 텐데.

= As I **don't know** your address, I **can't write** you a letter.
네 주소를 모르기 때문에 나는 네게 편지를 쓸 수 없다.

---

01 분명히 knew는 과거시제이다. 하지만 **가정법 문장에서는 knew를 과거를 나타내는 시제로 착각해선 안 된다. 가능성이 현저히 떨어지는 현재(미래)를 나타내는 시제**이다. 조건의 부사절에서 현재시제로 미래를 나타내듯이, 조건의 부사절에서 과거가 현재와 미래를 나타낼 수도 있다. 이를 직설법으로 고치면 과거가 아닌 현재시제를 써야 한다는 것이 분명해진다.

※ 직설법 현재로의 문장 전환

시제 :	과거 → 현재	동사 :	긍정 → 부정 ,	부정 → 긍정

If I **were** rich, I **could buy** a yacht. 내가 부자라면 요트를 살 수 있을 텐데.

= As I'**m not** rich, I **can't buy** a yacht. 내가 부자가 아니라서 요트를 살 수 없다.

If she **spoke** English well, we **would** hire her. 그녀가 영어를 잘한다면 우리는 그녀를 고용할 텐데.

= As she **doesn't speak** English well, we **won't hire** her.
그녀가 영어를 잘 못하기 때문에 우리는 그녀를 고용하지 않을 것이다.

02 가정법 미래를 나타내는 should, were to

① **should : 실현 가능성은 있지만 일어날 것 같지 않다고 생각되는 경우**에 쓴다. 주절에는 조동사의 현재형 또는 과거형을 모두 사용할 수 있다.

If he **should** die, what **would/will** become of his family? 만일 그가 죽는다면, 그의 가족은 어떻게 될까?

② **were to : should보다 가능성이 더 적어서 불가능하다고 생각되는 경우**에 쓴다. 주절에는 조동사의 과거형만 쓸 수 있다.

If the sun **were to** rise in the west, I **would** never change my mind.
만일 해가 서쪽에서 뜬다 할지라도 나는 내 마음을 바꾸지 않을 것이다.

※ 실제 가정법 미래는 잘 사용하지 않는다. 현대 영어에 접어들면서 내용에 따라 과거형 또는 현재형으로 그 뜻을 명확히 전달할 수 있기 때문이다. 그러나 아직 시험에 등장하므로 소개해 본다.

If anyone <u>should call</u> me, please take a message.
→ If anyone <u>calls</u> me, please take a message.

서술형 기초다지기

정답 p. 24

Challenge 1 다음 문장을 가정법 과거로 바꾸세요.

01. As he doesn't have a car, he isn't happy.

    → _____, he would be happy.

02. As I am not a millionaire, I don't have an airplane.

    → _____, I would have an airplane.

03. As she doesn't study hard, she can't pass the exam.

    → _____, she could pass the exam.

04. As I am not tall, I can't play basketball well.

    → _____, I could play basketball well.

05. As I don't know her phone number, I can't call her up.

    → _____, I could call her up.

Challenge 2 다음 문장을 직설법은 가정법으로, 가정법은 직설법으로 바꾸세요.

01. As Michael is sick, he may not come to see us.

    → _____

02. If we had a car, we could go on a vacation.

    → _____

03. As I don't know her well, I can't invite her to the party.

    → _____

04. If my brother was hungry, he would go out for dinner.

    → _____

가능성이 0%인 3차 가정문

If I **had heard** the weather report, I **would have brought** my umbrella.
일기예보를 들었다면 나는 우산을 가져왔을 텐데.

01 우리나라 영문법에서는 가정법 과거완료라는 표현을 쓰면서 과거 사실에 대한 정반대를 가정하거나 소망할 때 사용한다고 설명하지만 이는 어색한 설명이다. 실제 **가정법 과거완료는 현재 가능성이 없는(가능성 0%) 상황을 설명**한다. 가능성이 전혀 없지만 일단 한번 말해 보는 것이다.

If절(부사절)	주절
If + had + 과거분사(p.p.)	would, could might, should + have + 과거분사(p.p.)

※ 현재와 아무런 관련이 없다는 것을 나타내기 위해 특별한 시제를 쓴다.

02 과거에 이미 끝났으므로 현재와는 아무런 관련이 없고 따라서 **현재나 미래에 그 일이 일어날 가능성은 단 1%도 없는 것**이다. 이를 직설법으로 고치면 과거시제를 써야 하는 것이 분명해진다.

If I **had checked** the e-mail, I **would have attended** the meeting. ▶ 이메일을 확인했을 가능성 0%
내가 이메일을 확인했다면, 회의에 참석했을 텐데.

→ As I **didn't check** the e-mail, I **didn't attend** the meeting.
내가 이메일을 확인하지 않았기 때문에 회의에 참석하지 못했다.
  ▶ 과거에 이미 끝나서 돌이킬 수 없는 사실로, 이메일을 확인하고 미팅에 참석할 가능성 0%

If it **hadn't snowed**, we **might not have had** the accident. ▶ 눈이 이미 내렸고 눈이 오지 않을 가능성은 0%
눈이 오지 않았다면, 우리는 사고가 나지 않았을지도 모른다.

→ As it **snowed**, we **had** the accident. ▶ 과거에 이미 끝나서 돌이킬 수 없는 사실로 사고가 나지 않을 가능성은 0%
눈이 왔기 때문에 사고가 났다.

If I **had had** a car, I **could have driven** you to the airport. ▶ 차가 있을 가능성 0%
내게 차가 있었다면, 널 공항까지 데려다 줄 수 있었을 텐데.

→ I **couldn't drive** you to the airport because I **didn't have** a car.
내가 차가 없기 때문에 너를 공항까지 데려다 줄 수 없었다.
  ▶ 차를 갖고 있지 않아서 공항까지 데려다 주지 않았음

서술형 기초다지기

Challenge 1   다음 괄호 안의 단어 중에서 알맞은 것을 고르세요.

01. If he hadn't broken the window, he wouldn't (be / have been) punished yesterday.

02. If I (had worked / worked) harder, I would have passed the exam.

03. If I had known you were coming, I (would bake / would have baked) a cake.

04. Jessica (were / would have been) surprised if she had opened the box.

Challenge 2   다음 문장을 읽고 괄호 안의 단어를 이용하여 빈칸을 채우세요.

01. I didn't know you were in the library. If I had known, I _____
to see you. (go / would)

02. I didn't go out last night. I would have gone out if I _____
so tired. (not / be)

03. The view was wonderful. If I had had a digital camera, I _____
some pictures. (take / would)

Challenge 3   다음 각 문장을 가정법을 이용하여 바꿔 쓸 때 빈칸에 알맞은 말을 쓰세요.

01. I wasn't hungry, so I didn't eat anything.
→ If I _____ _____ hungry, I _____ _____ _____ something.

02. The player was sick, so he didn't join in the game.
→ If the player _____ _____ _____ sick, he _____ _____ _____
in the game.

03. As we didn't get free time, we couldn't go to the movies.
→ If we _____ _____ free time, we _____ _____ _____ to the movies.

Unit 02 Wish 가정법

2-1 현재 또는 미래에 대한 소망(wish+과거시제)

I **wish** I **knew** Paul's phone number.
Paul의 전화번호를 알면 좋겠는데.
(= I don't know it and I regret this.)

---

01 **현재나 미래에 대한 소망을 wish로 표현**한다. that절에 과거동사(조동사도 과거)를 쓰는데, 마찬가지로 단순 과거로 보면 안 된다. **가능성이 현저히 떨어지기 때문에 과거를 쓰는 것**이다. that은 생략할 수 있다.

Tiffany **wishes** (that) she **had** a good job. Tiffany는 좋은 직장을 갖길 원한다.
(→ Tiffany doesn't have a job.)

I **wish** I **could speak** Japanese. 일본어를 말할 수 있으면 좋겠는데.
(→ I can't speak Japanese.)

02 2차 가정문과 똑같이 **주어의 인칭과 관계없이 be동사는 were를 쓴다**. 일상 영어에서는 was를 쓰기도 한다.

We **wish** (that) she **weren't[wasn't]** ill now. 우리는 그녀가 아프지 않으면 좋겠다.
(→ She is ill now.)

I **wish** I **were[was]** on the beach now. 내가 지금 해변에 있으면 좋겠다.
(→ I'm not on the beach now.)

03 **미래에 일어날 일에 대한 소망은 will 대신 would, be going to 대신 were[was] going to를 쓴다.**

I **wish** Lucy **would come** to see me. Lucy가 날 보러 온다면 좋을 텐데.
(→ I want Lucy to come to see me.)

I **wish** he **were[was] going to** take a shower. 나는 그가 샤워를 했으면 좋겠다.
(→ I want him to take a shower.)

04 I wish I would ~는 쓰지 않는다. 하지만 **다른 사람이 미래에 해주길 바라는 소망을 공손하게 부탁**할 때, I wish you would/wouldn't ~로 쓸 수 있다.

The phone has been ringing for five minutes. I wish somebody **would** answer it.
전화기가 5분 동안 울리고 있다. 누군가 전화를 받으면 좋겠다.

I wish you **wouldn't** keep interrupting me. 네가 날 계속 방해하지 않았으면 좋겠어.

서술형 기초다지기

Challenge 1 다음 문장의 어색한 부분을 올바른 형태(가정법 과거)로 바꾸어 다시 쓰세요.

01. I wish that he is a pilot. → _____

02. I wish that I have a puppy. → _____

03. I wish I am a university student. → _____

04. I wish Jessica knows my phone number. → _____

05. I wish I can speak Chinese. → _____

Challenge 2 다음 문장을 wish를 이용한 가정문으로 바꾸어 쓰세요.

01. I don't have a job.

 → _____

02. I can't speak English.

 → _____

03. I don't know how to drive.

 → _____

Challenge 3 다음 문장을 I wish you would/wouldn't ~를 이용하여 다시 쓰세요.

01. Don't smoke anymore.

 → _____

02. Don't make the same mistake.

 → _____

03. Buy me a new car.

 → _____

2-2 과거에 대한 소망(wish + 과거완료)

I wish you **had come** to the lake last weekend.
지난 주말에 네가 호수에 왔으면 좋았을 텐데.
(→ You didn't come to the lake last weekend.)

01 **과거의 상황에 대한 유감**이나 **과거의 사실과 다른 소망**은 wish 다음에 오는 that절에 **과거완료(had + p.p.)**를 쓴다.

I **wish** I **had done** the work. 내가 그 일을 했었더라면 좋았을 텐데.
→ I didn't do the work ; now I'm sorry.

I **wish** I **had gone** to college after high school. 고교를 졸업하고 대학에 갔더라면 좋았을 걸.
→ I didn't go to college after high school ; now I'm sorry.

02 3차 가정문에서도 과거완료를 써서 가능성이 전혀 없는(0%) 상황을 말하듯이, **wish절에 과거완료(had + p.p.)를 쓰는 이유도 과거에 이미 끝나 현재와는 아무런 관련이 없기 때문이다. 즉 현재나 미래에 1%의 가능성도 없다는 것을 나타내기 위해서이다.** 단지 과거에 대해 후회하거나 소망하는 일을 푸념하듯 말해 보는 것이다.

I **wish** I **had been** rich then. 그 당시에 부자였더라면 좋았을 텐데. ▶ 부자였을 가능성 0%
→ I'm sorry that I was not rich then.
  ▶ 현재와 아무런 관련이 없는 과거로 부자가 될 가능성은 0%

03 부정의 내용을 쓰려면 「had not + 과거분사」를 쓴다.

I **wish** I **had not gone** there. 내가 거기에 가지 않았더라면 좋았을 텐데.
→ I went there ; now I'm sorry.

Robert **wishes** he **hadn't told** the secret. Robert는 그가 그 비밀을 말하지 않았더라면 하고 바란다.
→ Robert told the secret ; now he's sorry.

서술형 기초다지기

Challenge 1 다음 빈칸에 알맞은 말을 넣어 문장을 완성하세요.

01. 나는 고등학교를 마쳤더라면 좋았을 텐데.

→ I wish I _____ _____ high school.

02. 어젯밤에 너무 많이 먹지 않았으면 좋았을 걸.

→ I wish I _____ _____ too much last night.

03. 내가 학생이었을 때, 더 열심히 공부했으면 좋았을 걸.

→ I wish I _____ _____ harder when I was a student.

Challenge 2 다음 문장을 I wish로 시작하는 가정법 문장으로 바꾸어 쓰세요.

01. I ate too much. I'm sorry about that.

→ _____

02. Bob didn't learn to play a musical instrument. Now he regrets this.

→ _____

03. Brian didn't finish high school and now he regrets it.

→ _____

04. Jennifer was walking in the country. She would like to take some pictures, but she didn't bring her digital camera.

→ _____

Memo

"출제자가 노리는 급소" 이것이 시험에 출제되는 영문법이다!

---

01 출제 100% - 반드시 함께 쓰이는 단짝들이 있다.

 출제자의 눈 1차 가정문에서 if절 안에 현재시제, 주절에는 미래 또는 현재시제를 쓰고, 2차 가정문인 가정법 과거는 if절 안에 과거시제, 주절에는 조동사 과거를 쓴다. 3차 가정문인 가정법 과거완료는 if절 안에 「had + p.p」, 주절에는 「would[could, might] + have + p.p」로 쓰는데 이들 모두 단짝들로 함께 쓰이기 때문에 빈칸을 채우거나 틀린 부분을 찾아 고치는 문제로 출제될 수 있다.

Ex 1.

If I _____ more money, I could have bought a car.

(a) had   (b) had had   (c) have   (d) could have

Ex 2.

If she _____ her homework soon, we're going to go to the movies.

(a) finished   (b) had finished   (c) finishes   (d) will finish

---

02 출제 100% - 직설법으로 고치는 연습을 꾸준히 하라.

 출제자의 눈 우리말 표현을 주고 2차, 3차 가정문을 만드는 부분 영작을 출제하거나, 직설법을 가정법으로 또는 가정법을 다시 직설법으로 고쳐 쓰라는 주관식 문제, 그리고 직설법이나 가정법으로 고쳤을 때 바르게 고친 것을 고르는 객관식 문제를 출제한다. 부분 영작할 때 가정법에서 함께 쓰이는 단짝들을 반드시 기억하고, 가정법 과거에서 be동사는 주어와 관계없이 were을 쓴다는 것도 잊지 말자.

Ex 3.

If Steve _____ sick, he would go to the birthday party.

(a) is   (b) weren't   (c) won't be   (d) were

Ex 4.

If we had a car, we could go on a vacation.

= As we _____, we can't go on a vacation.

(a) don't have a car   (b) have a car

(c) didn't have a car   (d) had a car

226

03 출제 100 % - 직설법을 가정법으로 고치는 주관식 문제는 반드시 출제된다.

 출제자의 눈 직설법을 가정법으로 바꾸는 문제는 주관식으로 가장 자주 출제된다. 그리고 wish 가정법에서 우리말 표현을 주고 과거시제와 과거완료를 구별하는 문제나 직설법 표현을 주고 부분적으로 wish 가정법을 영작하게 하는 문제가 출제된다.

Ex 5.

As I didn't check the e-mail, I didn't attend the meeting.

= If _____ .

Ex 6.

그 여자가 즉시 구조되었더라면 좋았을 텐데.

= I wish the woman _____ _____ _____ at once. (save)

Memo

1. 두 문장의 의미가 같도록 빈칸에 알맞은 말을 쓰시오.

> I'm sorry he doesn't love me.
> = I wish he _____ me.

2. 짝지어진 두 문장의 의미가 같지 <u>않은</u> 것은?

❶ As he does not work hard, he cannot be rich.
  = If he worked hard, he could be rich.
❷ Since I had a bad cold, I didn't attend the meeting.
  = If I had not had a bad cold, I would have attended the meeting.
❸ As my father is not rich enough, he can't buy a car.
  = If my father were rich enough, he could have bought a car.
❹ Because I don't know his address, I can't write to him.
  = If I knew his address, I could write to him.
❺ I am sorry I wasted my time when I was young.
  = I wish I had not wasted my time when I was young.

[3-4] 다음 빈칸에 들어갈 말로 알맞은 것은?

3.
> If it _____ raining, we could go to the park.

❶ isn't ❷ aren't ❸ was
❹ were ❺ weren't

4.
> It's raining. I wish it _____ raining.

❶ would stop ❷ had stopped ❸ will stop
❹ stops ❺ were stopping

5. 다음 빈칸에 들어갈 알맞은 말은?

> Listen carefully, or you won't understand it.
> = If you _____ carefully, you won't understand it.

6. 다음 빈칸에 들어갈 말이 바르게 짝지어진 것은?

> As I don't know her number, I can't call her.
> = If I _____ her number, I _____ call her.

❶ know – can ❷ knew – could
❸ had known – could ❹ knew – will
❺ had known – will

7. 다음 가정법 구문을 직설법으로 고칠 때 빈칸에 알맞은 말을 쓰시오.

> If he had not helped me, I could not have finished it.
> = As he helped me, I _____.

8. 다음 문장을 가정법으로 바꿀 때 옳은 것은?

> It snowed yesterday, so we didn't climb the mountain.

❶ If it snowed yesterday, we could not climb the mountain.
❷ If it have snowed yesterday, we could not climb the mountain.
❸ If it didn't snow yesterday, we could have climb the mountain.
❹ If it had snowed yesterday, we could climb the mountain.
❺ If it had not snowed yesterday, we could have climbed the mountain.

오답 노트 만들기

★틀린 문제 : _____   ★다시 공부한 날 : _____

(1) 문제를 왜? 틀렸는지 곰곰이 생각하고 그 이유를 적어본다.

(2) 핵심 개념을 적는다.

(3) 자신이 몰랐던 단어와 숙어 표현이 있으면 정리한다.

(4) 해설집에서 필요한 부분을 골라 풀이 해법을 정리한다.

★틀린 문제 : _____   ★다시 공부한 날 : _____

(1) 문제를 왜? 틀렸는지 곰곰이 생각하고 그 이유를 적어본다.

(2) 핵심 개념을 적는다.

(3) 자신이 몰랐던 단어와 숙어 표현이 있으면 정리한다.

(4) 해설집에서 필요한 부분을 골라 풀이 해법을 정리한다.

★틀린 문제 : _____   ★다시 공부한 날 : _____

(1) 문제를 왜? 틀렸는지 곰곰이 생각하고 그 이유를 적어본다.

(2) 핵심 개념을 적는다.

(3) 자신이 몰랐던 단어와 숙어 표현이 있으면 정리한다.

(4) 해설집에서 필요한 부분을 골라 풀이 해법을 정리한다.

★틀린 문제 : _____   ★다시 공부한 날 : _____

(1) 문제를 왜? 틀렸는지 곰곰이 생각하고 그 이유를 적어본다.

(2) 핵심 개념을 적는다.

(3) 자신이 몰랐던 단어와 숙어 표현이 있으면 정리한다.

(4) 해설집에서 필요한 부분을 골라 풀이 해법을 정리한다.

[1-3] 다음 빈칸에 들어갈 알맞은 것을 고르시오.

1.

I'm not hungry. I would have something to eat if I _____ hungry.

❶ were
❷ will be
❸ won't be
❹ would be
❺ am

오답노트

2.

I don't know the answer. If I _____ the answer, I could tell you.

❶ know
❷ had known
❸ knew
❹ could know
❺ don't know

오답노트

3.

If I _____ the train, I could not have met her.

❶ took
❷ takes
❸ have taken
❹ had taken
❺ could have taken

오답노트

4. **두 문장의 뜻이 같도록 빈칸에 들어갈 알맞은 것은?**

As she fastened a seat belt, she wasn't injured in the crash.

= _____, she would have been injured in the crash.

❶ If she had fastened a seat belt
❷ If she hadn't fastened a seat belt
❸ As she had fastened a seat belt
❹ When she had fastened a seat belt
❺ Though she had fastened a seat belt

오답노트

[5-6] 다음 문장을 가정법으로 고쳐 쓸 때 빈칸에 들어 갈 알맞은 말을 쓰시오.

5.

I am sorry I don't know her phone number.
→ I wish I _____ her phone number.

오답노트

6.

I am sorry you didn't attend the meeting.
→ I wish you _____ _____ the meeting.

오답노트

7. 다음 빈칸에 알맞은 말을 쓰시오.

> A : Can you help me with my work, Susan?
> B : Oh, I'm sorry, Kevin. I'm very busy now.

→ If Susan _____ busy, she would _____ Kevin.

오답노트

8. 다음 밑줄 친 부분이 어법상 틀린 것은?

❶ If I <u>were</u> you, I would tell her the truth.
❷ If he had exercised, he <u>would have been</u> healthy.
❸ I wish I <u>learned</u> how to drive when I was young.
❹ If I <u>had set</u> my alarm clock, I wouldn't have been late for the meeting.
❺ If I weren't busy, I <u>could go</u> to the concert with you.

오답노트

[9-10] 다음 문장을 가정법으로 바꿔 쓰시오.

9. I don't have million dollars, so I can't buy you a car.

→ _____

_____

오답노트

10. As we didn't get free time, we couldn't go to the movies.

→ _____

_____.

오답노트

11. 다음 문장과 의미가 같은 것을 고르시오.

> I wish I didn't live in a big city.

❶ I'm sorry I don't live in a big city.
❷ I'm sorry I live in a big city.
❸ I'm sorry I didn't live in a big city.
❹ I'm sorry I lived in a big city.
❺ I'm sorry I had lived in a big city.

오답노트

12. 다음 문장을 아래와 같이 바꿀 때 밑줄 친 곳에 들어갈 공통된 단어를 쓰시오.

> · I don't have a computer.
>   → I wish I _____ a computer.
> · Mary doesn't have a car.
>   → Mary wishes she _____ a car.

→ _____

오답노트

A. 우리말과 같은 뜻이 되도록 빈칸에 알맞은 말을 쓰시오.

1. 만일 내가 좀 더 생각이 깊었더라면, 그를 이해할 수 있었을 텐데.

→ If I _____ _____ more thoughtful, I could have understood him.

2. 네가 병원에 있는 걸 알았다면, 너를 방문했을 텐데.

→ If I'd known you were in hospital, I might_____ _____ you.

3. 만일 내가 너의 비밀을 알고 있다면, 너는 어떻게 할래?

→ If I _____ your secret, what _____ you _____?

4. 네가 어제 약속을 지켰으면 좋았을 텐데.

→ I wish you _____ _____ your promise yesterday.

B. 다음 문장을 가정법 문장으로 고쳐 쓰시오.

1. As I'm not rich, I can't buy a digital camera.

→ _____

2. As I don't have time, I can't help you.

→ _____

3. As she works at a restaurant, she doesn't have time to relax.

→ _____

4. As the weather isn't fine, we can't go on a picnic.

→ _____

중학교 2학년 영문법

2-B

한국에서 유일한 중학영문법

알짜 3000제

BOOK 정답 및 해설

I am books

중학교 2학년 영문법

2-B

한국에서 유일한

중학영문법

알짜 3000제

정답 및 해설

I am books

Chapter 01 형용사

1-1 형용사의 역할
p. 11

Challenge 1

01 She was a guest on a live TV show.
02 Nancy is a famous dentist.
03 Look at the small car over there.
04 We watched an exciting movie yesterday.

Challenge 2

01 asleep   02 main   03 drunken
04 sleeping   05 alike   06 alive
07 scared

1-2 -thing[-one, -body]+형용사 / the+형용사
p. 13

Challenge 1

01 nothing interesting   02 something cold to drink
03 something hot to drink
04 have nothing new   05 something fun

Challenge 2

01 The / the   02 The   03 the

Challenge 3

01 are   02 have

2-1 many, much, a lot of, lots of
p. 15

Challenge 1

01 many   02 much   03 much
04 much   05 many   06 much

Challenge 2

01 Bob has many problems.
02 People in the office waste much paper.
03 We usually have much homework.
04 Are there many roses in the vase?
05 My mom uses much salt for cooking.
06 We didn't take many pictures when we were on vacation last winter.
07 You can get much information on how to stay healthy in magazines.

2-2 some, any, no, none
p. 17

Challenge 1

01 some   02 any   03 some / any
04 any   05 some   06 some
07 any

Challenge 2

01 Does your brother like any cheese?
My brother doesn't like any cheese.
02 Are there any flowers in the garden?
There aren't any flowers in the garden.

Challenge 3

01 There are no students in the library.
02 We saw nobody.
03 She had no pencils to write with.

2-3 (a) few, (a) little
p. 19

Challenge 1

01 a little   02 a few   03 a few
04 a little   05 a few   06 a little

Challenge 2

01 few   02 little   03 little
04 few

Challenge 3

01 a little / a few   02 little / a few
03 A few / little

3-1 분사의 형용사 역할
p. 21

Challenge 1

01 boring / bored   02 shocking / shocked
03 moving / moved   04 exciting / excited

Challenge 2

01 The book written in English is mine.
02 They threw stones at a moving bus.
03 There is a man breaking into the house.
04 The injured woman was put into an ambula

Ex1 (b)　　　**Ex2** (a)　　　**Ex3** (c)　　　**Ex4** (d)
Ex5 (b)　　　**Ex6** (d)　　　**Ex7** (b)
Ex8 is → are

| 해설 |

Ex1 「seem＋형용사」를 쓴다. 내용상 형용사 angry가 알맞다.

Ex2 smell의 보어로 형용사 good을 쓴다. better는 비교급, well은 부사이다.

Ex3 권유나 부탁의 의문문에 some을 쓸 수 있다.

Ex4 house는 셀 수 있는 명사이므로 many를 쓰고 복수 명사인 houses를 쓴다.

Ex5 「-thing＋형용사＋to부정사」의 어순이다.

Ex6 셀 수 있는 명사(tourists) 앞에 a few 또는 few를 쓴다. 문맥상 긍정이므로 a few를 쓴다.

Ex7 '외국에서 사는 것'이 흥미나 재미를 주는 것이므로 능동의 의미인 현재분사(exciting)를 쓴다.

Ex8 「the＋형용사」는 복수 명사이므로 be동사는 are로 써야 한다.

기출 응용문제　　p. 24

1 ④　　　　2 ④　　　　3 ④
4 afraid you are wrong
5 ②　　　　6 ①　　　　7 ③

| 해설 |

1 some은 셀 수 있는 명사와 셀 수 없는 명사 앞에 모두 쓴다. 명사 milk는 셀 수 없는 명사이므로 a little을 쓸 수 있지만, 부정의 의미인 little은 문맥상 적절하지 않다.

2 「-thing＋형용사＋to부정사」의 어순(something hot to eat)으로 쓴다.

3 영화가 감정을 주는 주체이므로 exciting과 boring을 쓴다.

4 형용사 afraid를 be동사 다음에 쓰고 그 뒤에 주어와 동사를 이어서 쓴다. 접속사 that이 생략되어 있다.

5 look 뒤에는 형용사를 쓴다. down은 형용사로 '기운 없는, 풀이 죽은'의 뜻이 있다. 문맥상 happy는 쓸 수 없다. many 뒤에는 복수 명사를 쓰므로 mistakes를 쓰는 것이 알맞다.

6 -thing으로 끝나는 대명사는 뒤에 형용사를 써야 한다. 따라서 Nothing special.로 써야 한다.

7 cities는 복수 명사이므로 much로 바꿔 쓸 수 없고, many를 써야 한다.

중간·기말고사 100점 100승　　p. 26

1　These books are not very useful.
2　The nurses are very kind.
3　sleep → asleep　　　　4　⑤　　　　5　③
6　nothing important to see　　　　　　7　②
8　much → a lot of 또는 lots of 또는 many
9　④　　　　10　②
11　have a book to buy 또는 have to buy a book
12　③　　　　13　few → a few
14　many → much / are → is
15　some → any　　　　16　④　　　　17　①
18　④　　　　19　④　　　　20　③　　　　21　④
22　④　　　　23　The rich / the poor
24　disappointing / disappointed
25　exhausting / exhausted
26　depressing / depressed
27　③　　　　28　③　　　　29　②

| 해설 |

1-2 「형용사＋명사」의 형태를 「명사＋be동사＋형용사」로 전환한다.

3 fall sleep에서 fall과 sleep은 모두 동사라서 두 개가 나란히 쓰일 수 없다. 형용사인 asleep을 이용하여 fall asleep(잠이 들다)이 되어야 맞다.

4 ⑤의 days는 셀 수 있는 명사이므로 little을 few로 바꾼다.

5 friends는 셀 수 있는 명사이고 문맥상 부정을 뜻하므로 few를 쓴다.

6 「-thing＋형용사＋to부정사」의 어순으로 쓴다.

7 사람이 감정을 받는 것이므로 surprised를 쓴다.

8 much는 셀 수 없는 명사에 쓰는 수량 형용사로, books처럼 셀 수 있는 명사에는 a few, many, a lot of, lots of를 쓴다. 내용상 '해변에 와서도 책을 읽을 정도로 많은 책을 읽는다'라는 의미가 되어야 하므로 a few는 적합하지 않다.

9 첫 번째 빈칸은 '돈이 좀 있느냐?'는 의미로 의문문에는 any를 쓴다. 두 번째 빈칸은 '돈은 좀 있지만 책을 사야 한다'는 의미로 긍정문에서는 some을 쓴다.

10 I'm broke는 '돈이 하나도 없다'(I have no money)는 뜻이다.

11 명사 뒤에 to부정사를 써서 have a book to buy로 쓰거나 have to를 이용하여 have to buy a book으로 쓸 수 있다.

12 사람이 감정을 받은 상태이므로 surprised를 쓴다.

13 '그의 아이디어는 (이해하기) 어렵지만 몇몇 사람들이 이해했다'는 뜻이므로 few를 a few로 쓴다. few를 쓰면 이해한 사람이 거의 없다는 부정의 뜻이 되기 때문에 어색하다.

14 butter는 셀 수 없는 명사이므로 many를 much로 바꾸고, 셀 수 없는 명사는 단수 취급하므로 be동사(are)를 is로 바꿔야 한다.

15 hardly(거의 ~ 없는)가 쓰인 부정문이므로 any를 사용한다.

16 look 뒤에는 형용사를 쓴다. happily를 happy로 고친다.

17 politely는 부사이므로 명사를 꾸미는 형용사 역할을 할 수 없다.

18 「the+형용사」는 복수 명사가 되므로 are와 think를 쓴다.

19 drunken man은 '술에 취한 사람'을 뜻하고 live는 명사 앞에서 수식하는 '살아있는'의 뜻을 지닌 형용사이다. 반면, alive는 연결동사 뒤에서만 수식하는 서술적 용법의 형용사이다.

20 행위의 주체인 student 앞에는 sleeping을 쓰고, be동사 뒤에 형용사로 alike(닮은)를 쓴다.

21 「-thing+형용사」의 어순으로 쓰되, 의문문이므로 anything 이 알맞다.

22 '화나게 만들었다'라는 뜻의 「make+목적어+목적보어」구 문에서 목적격 보어로는 형용사 angry를 써야 한다.

23 '돈이 많은 사람들'이란 말은 the rich로, '충분한 돈이 없는 사람들'이란 말은 the poor로 쓸 수 있다.

24 영화는 감정을 주는 주체이므로 disappointing을 쓰고, 사람은 감정을 받는 대상이므로 disappointed를 쓴다.

25 직업은 감정을 주는 주체이므로 exhausting을 쓰고, 그녀 는 감정을 받는 대상이므로 exhausted를 쓴다.

26 날씨는 감정을 주는 주체이므로 depressing을 쓰고, 나 는 감정을 받는 대상이므로 depressed를 쓴다.

27 '많은'이란 뜻의 a number of는 셀 수 있는 명사 앞에서 쓰 이는 형용사로, many와 바꿔 쓸 수 있다.

28 '붉은악마'는 사람을 뜻하므로 감정을 받는 대상이 된다. 따 라서 disappointed를 쓴다.

29 사람이 관심을 받는, 즉 감정을 받는 대상이므로 interested 를 쓰고 실험(experiment)은 감정을 주는 주체이므로 interesting을 쓴다.

중간 · 기말고사 평가대비 단답형 주관식   p. 30

A 1 excited   2 exciting

B 1 Please give me a little(=some) orange juice.

   2 There is nothing new in today's newspaper.

   3 I saw something strange there.

C 1 few   2 little   3 a few   4 a little

| 해설 |

A 1 사람들이 감정을 받는 대상이므로 excited를 쓴다. 2 축구 경기는 어떤 감정을 주는 주체이므로 exciting을 쓴다.

B 1 orange juice는 셀 수 없는 명사이므로 a few 대신 a little 또는 some을 쓴다. 2-3 -thing으로 끝나는 대명사 는 형용사를 뒤에 써야 한다.

C 1 '사람들이 거의 없다'라는 뜻이 되어야 하므로 few를 쓴 다. 2 우유가 <u>없어서</u> 사러 가야 한다는 의미이므로 little을 쓴다. 3 셀 수 있는 명사 앞이면서 긍정의 의미인 '몇 개의 강좌'라는 뜻이므로 a few를 쓴다. 4 영어를 <u>조금</u> 알고 있

어 영국인의 말을 이해한다는 긍정의 의미이므로 a little을 쓴다. English는 셀 수 없는 명사이므로 a few가 아니라 a little을 써야 한다.

실전 서술형 평가문제 A   p. 31

모범답안

1 There are some bananas on the table but there isn't any milk.

2 There is some orange juice in the refrigerator but there isn't any yoghurt.

3 There is some bread on the table but there isn't any sugar.

4 There is some coffee in the cupboard but there isn't any rice.

5 There are some tomatoes in the refrigerator but there aren't any carrots.

실전 서술형 평가문제 B   p. 32

모범답안

1 She looks happy.

2 They look angry. / They look upset.

3 They look happy. / They look comfortable.

실전 서술형 평가문제 C   p. 33

모범답안

1 interesting   2 interested

3 exciting   4 excited

5 fascinated   6 fascinating

7 bored / confused   8 boring / confusing

실전 서술형 평가문제 D   p. 34

모범답안

1 Are there many eggs on the table? / there are a few eggs (on the table)

2 Is there much coffee on the table? / there is a little coffee (on the table)

3 Is there much orange juice on the table? / there is a little orange juice (on the table)

4 Is there much cheese on the table? / there isn't any cheese (on the table)

5 Are there many pencils on the table? / there aren't any pencils (on the table)

Chapter **02** 부사

1-1 부사 만들기

p. 37

Challenge 1

01 slowly	02 quickly	03 clearly
04 nicely	05 safely	06 quietly
07 sincerely	08 suddenly	09 angrily
10 easily	11 happily	12 luckily
13 heavily	14 busily	15 simply
16 terribly	17 idly	18 reasonably
19 visibly	20 comfortably	21 truly
22 duly	23 fully	24 dully
25 basically	26 dramatically	

1-2 형용사와 모양이 같은 부사

p. 39

Challenge 1

01 quickly	02 fast	03 well
04 hard	05 late	06 happy

Challenge 2

01 late	02 long	03 good
04 fast	05 high	06 early
07 hard	08 last	

Challenge 3

01 fast / fast	02 last / last
03 high / high	04 hard / hard

1-3 -ly가 붙으면 의미가 달라지는 부사

p. 41

Challenge 1

01 부사 / 매우	02 형용사 / 어려운
03 형용사 / 늦은	04 부사 / 늦게
05 형용사 / 높은	06 부사 / 거의 ~ 않는

Challenge 2

01 hard	02 hardly	03 highly
04 high	05 late	06 lately
07 near	08 nearly	

2-1 부사의 위치

p. 43

Challenge 1

01 The bus was really dirty.
02 He is running very fast.
03 My mother drives her car carefully.

Challenge 2

01 Peter always comes to work on time.
02 She usually doesn't work on Saturday.
03 Jane seldom goes to a rock concert.
04 I'm always happy to be with you.
05 You must often memorize English words.
06 Is she sometimes late for work?
07 Do you often drink tea with dinner?
08 Maria doesn't always watch TV.

2-2 very, much, too, either

p. 45

Challenge 1

01 very	02 too	03 very
04 too		

Challenge 2

01 too	02 too	03 either
04 too	05 either	06 neither

Challenge 3

01 very	02 much	03 very
04 much	05 very	

2-3 already, yet, still / too many, too much

p. 47

Challenge 1

01 already	02 yet	03 still
04 already	05 already	06 still
07 still	08 yet	09 still

Challenge 2

01 too many	02 too much	03 There is
04 too many		

2-4 주의해야 할 부사의 위치
p. 49

Challenge 1

01 pick you up
02 put on the trousers 또는 put the trousers on
03 took it off
04 picked up a coin 또는 picked a coin up
05 turn it on
06 put it out
07 Put on your sweater 또는 Put your sweater on

Challenge 2

01 cool enough
02 enough time
03 old enough
04 enough money
05 big enough
06 enough eggs

2-5 의문부사
p. 51

Challenge 1

01 How does he teach music to his students?
02 Why do Jessica and Scott learn Korean?
03 Where does your mom wash the dishes?
04 When does she take a walk?

Challenge 2

01 How tall are you?
02 How often do you use your car?
03 How old is your father?
04 How far is it from here to the airport?
05 How high is Mt. Everest?

이것이 시험에 출제되는 영문법이다!
p. 52

Ex1 (a) Ex2 (d) Ex3 (b) Ex4 (c)
Ex5 turned off it → turned it off Ex6 (c)
Ex7 (b)

| 해설 |

Ex1 빈도부사 sometimes는 일반동사인 sleep 앞에 써야 한다.
Ex2 부정문에서는 either로 '또한, 역시'란 의미를 나타낸다.
Ex3 긍정문에서는 '역시, 또한'의 의미로 too를 쓴다.
Ex4 부정문에 대해 동의를 할 때 I haven't, either. 또는 줄여서 Me, neither.를 쓴다.
Ex5 「동사+부사」로 이루어진 동사구 표현에서 대명사가 목적어로 등장하면 반드시 동사와 부사 사이에 써야 한다.
Ex6 비교급은 much로 수식한다.
Ex7 원급과 현재분사는 very가 수식할 수 있다.

기출 응용문제
p. 54

1 ③	2 ②	3 ⑤	4 ⑤
5 ④	6 ③	7 ④	

| 해설 |

1 ③은 '예쁜'이란 의미의 형용사로 쓰였고, 나머지는 '꽤, 상당히'란 의미의 부사로 쓰였다.
2 ① either ③ late ④ late ⑤ hardly가 되어야 한다.
3 빈도부사는 be동사 뒤에 위치한다.
4 빈도부사는 일반동사 play 앞에 위치한다.
5 ④를 제외하고 나머지는 내용과 일치하지 않는다.
　①의 seldom을 sometimes로, ②의 often은 sometimes로, ③의 sometimes는 seldom으로, ⑤의 seldom은 often으로 써야 한다.
6 ③의 much는 '많이'의 의미로 쓰였고, 나머지는 모두 비교급 앞에서 '훨씬'의 의미로 쓰였다.
7 부정에 대해 동의를 할 때 Me, neither.(=I can't speak Korean, either.)를 쓴다.

중간·기말고사 100점 100승
p. 56

1 ①	2 ③	3 ④	4 ⑤
5 ②	6 ②		
7 She is always late for the meeting.			8 ③
9 ⑤	10 ⑤	11 ⑤	12 ②
13 well	14 fast	15 carefully	
16 slowly	17 ④	18 I was sick	
19 ②	20 ①	21 ④	
22 too	23 ③		
24 tall enough to reach		25 ②	
26 much			

| 해설 |

1 빈도부사는 일반동사인 eats 앞에 위치한다.
2 부정에 대해 동의할 때 either를 쓴다.
3 hard의 부사는 hard이다. hardly도 부사이긴 하나 그 의미가 다르다.
4 speak 뒤에는 부사를 써야 한다. 형용사 good은 쓸 수 없다.
5 부정에 대한 동의는 either를 쓴다.
6 '얼마나 많은'의 의미로 How much를 쓴다.
7 빈도부사 always를 is 뒤에 쓴다.
8 yet은 부정문에서 '아직'의 의미로 쓰이고 의문문에서는 '벌써'의 의미로 쓰인다.
9 부정에 대해 동의할 때는 either를 쓰고 부사 carefully를 수식할 때는 very를 쓴다.
10 방법을 나타내는 How를 쓴다.
11 very는 비교급을 수식할 수 없다.
12 빈도부사는 조동사 뒤에 위치한다.

13 good의 부사형은 well이다.

14 fast의 부사는 그대로 fast를 쓴다.

15 careful의 부사형은 carefully를 쓴다.

16 slow의 부사형은 slowly이다.

17 빈도, 횟수를 물어보는 표현은 How often ~?이다.

18 시제가 과거이므로 I was sick로 문장을 완성한다.

19 '너무'라는 의미의 too를 쓰고, 긍정에 대해 동의할 때도 too를 쓴다.

20 일반적인 빈도부사는 부정어구 앞에 오지만 always는 부정어구 바로 뒤에 쓴다.

21 동사와 부사에서 대명사는 반드시 그 사이에 둔다.

22 '너무'라는 뜻의 too는 '어떤 문제나 어려움이 있어 할 수 없다'는 의미를 담고 있다.

23 도표에서 나타난 날씨의 빈도를 볼 때 ③의 빈도부사 표현이 가장 적절하다.

24 enough가 형용사를 수식할 때는 뒤에 쓴다.

25 각각 긍정문에 already, 부정문에 yet, 과거시제에 ago, '여전히'의 의미인 still을 쓴다.

26 비교급과 과거분사를 모두 수식할 수 있는 것은 much이다.

중간 · 기말고사 평가대비 단답형 주관식   p. 60

A 1 good / well   2 noisy / noisily
   3 fast / fast   4 happy / happily

B 1 I sometimes get up early in the morning.
   2 I always walk to school.
   3 I often watch TV.
   4 I usually go to bed after doing my homework.

| 해설 |

A 1 명사 앞에 형용사 good, 부사는 well을 쓴다. 2 be동사 뒤에 보어로 noisy, 부사는 noisily를 쓴다. 3 명사 앞에 형용사 fast, 부사도 같은 형태인 fast를 쓴다. 4 명사 앞에 형용사 happy를 쓰고, 부사는 happily를 쓴다.

B 주어진 예문을 그대로 이용하여 빈도부사의 위치가 정확하면 정답 처리하고 다른 문장을 만들었을 때는 빈도부사와 함께 바르게 영작했는지를 확인한다.

실전 서술형 평가문제 A   p. 61

모범답안

1 Nancy[She] usually listens to music.

2 Nancy[She] often goes shopping with her mother.

3 Nancy[She] sometimes meets friends.

4 Nancy[She] seldom eats hamburgers for breakfast.

실전 서술형 평가문제 B   p. 62

모범답안

1 Q : Does she work hard?
   A : Yes, she works hard.

2 Q : How does she usually drive?
   A : She usually drives very carefully.

3 Q : How often does she take a subway?
   A : She sometimes takes a subway.

4 Q : How did she drive yesterday evening?
   A : She drove badly (yesterday evening).

5 Q : Did she have an accident?
   A : No, but she almost had an accident.

실전 서술형 평가문제 C   p. 63

모범답안

1 She can't wear it because it is too big.

2 She can't finish it because she is too sleepy.

3 She can't eat it because it is too hot.

실전 서술형 평가문제 D   p. 64

모범답안

1 She[My mother] never washes clothes by hand.

2 She[Kelly] always drinks milk.

3 They sometimes go shopping on Sunday.

4 She[Susan] usually takes the school bus.

1-1 비교급 만드는 방법   p. 67

Challenge 1

01 younger than	02 longer than
03 taller than	04 larger than
05 warmer than	06 smarter than
07 smaller than	08 faster than
09 fresher than	10 older than

Challenge 2

01 easier than   02 prettier than   03 bigger than
04 busier than   05 hotter than   06 healthier than
07 heavier than   08 thinner than   09 lazier than
10 happier than

Challenge 3

01 more difficult than	02 more quickly than
03 more helpful than	04 more shocking than
05 more beautifully than	06 more boring than
07 more fluently than	08 more slowly than

1-2 최상급 만드는 방법   p. 69

Challenge 1

01 younger – youngest	02 slower – slowest
03 bigger – biggest	04 longer – longest
05 older – oldest	06 happier – happiest
07 hotter – hottest	08 thinner – thinnest
09 smarter – smartest	10 healthier – healthiest
11 earlier – earliest	12 higher – highest
13 heavier – heaviest	14 dirtier – dirtiest

15 more popular – most popular
16 more slowly – most slowly
17 more expensive – most expensive
18 more serious – most serious
19 more excited – most excited
20 more useful – most useful
21 more foolish – most foolish
22 more patient – most patient

1-3 불규칙 변화형   p. 71

Challenge 1

01 better – best   02 older – oldest

03 elder – eldest   04 more – most
05 more – most   06 worse – worst
07 worse – worst   08 less – least
09 latter – last   10 farther – farthest
11 further – furthest   12 later – latest

Challenge 2

01 best   02 more   03 latter
04 fewer   05 latest

2-1 비교급의 쓰임   p. 73

Challenge 1

01 older	02 more beautiful
03 more expensive	04 cheaper
05 earlier	06 funnier

Challenge 2

01 younger than / older than
02 taller than / shorter than
03 bigger than / smaller than

2-2 비교급 강조 / 열등 비교(less＋원급＋than)   p. 75

Challenge 1

01 much older than   02 far faster than
03 a lot stronger than

Challenge 2

01 is still faster than a cat
02 sings even better than anyone else
03 is much longer than that

Challenge 3

01 doesn't drive as carefully as Tim
02 isn't as important as health

2-3 비교구문을 이용한 표현   p. 77

Challenge 1

01 earlier than	02 less thoughtful than
03 fatter / or	04 more and more serious

05 bigger / or
06 The darker / the more scared

Challenge 2

01 The closer / the warmer
02 The higher / the harder
03 The longer / the angrier

3-1 최상급의 활용   p. 79

Challenge 1

01 tallest	02 older
03 most expensive	04 the prettiest

Challenge 2

01 the largest city	02 the longest river
03 the largest country	04 the fastest animal
05 the shortest month	06 the coldest place

3-2 최상급의 다양한 쓰임   p. 81

Challenge 1

01 is one of the most beautiful cities in the world
02 is one of the most famous men in the world
03 is one of the highest mountains in Korea
04 is one of the prettiest parks in St. Louis

Challenge 2

01 The Han River is longer than any other river in Seoul.
02 No other city in the United States is as big as New York.
03 Alex is more handsome than all the other boys in his class.
04 Bill Gates is richer than any other man in the world.

4-1 as+원급+as   p. 83

Challenge 1

01 young	02 smarter	03 hot
04 heavy	05 could	06 possible

Challenge 2

01 is as old as your bicycle
02 got home as late as Jason

03 isn't as[so] big as an ocean

Challenge 3

01 is more expensive than that one
02 is more difficult than history class

4-2 기타 비교 표현   p. 85

Challenge 1

01 twice as heavy as	02 three times as high as
03 twice as much as	

Challenge 2

01 from	02 as	03 from	04 to

Challenge 3

01 similar / to	02 similar
03 same / as	04 different / from

이것이 시험에 출제되는 영문법이다!   p. 86

Ex1 (a)	Ex2 (a)	Ex3 (d)
Ex4 stronger		Ex5 (b)
Ex6 possible		Ex7 taller / other / girl
Ex8 as fast as		

| 해설 |

Ex1 heavy의 비교급은 heavier이다.
Ex2 small의 최상급은 smallest이다.
Ex3 very는 비교급을 수식할 수 없고, 원급을 수식한다.
Ex4 원급 비교의 부정문은 비교급으로 바꾸어 쓸 수 있다. 공통으로 들어갈 단어는 stronger이다.
Ex5 「the+비교급, the+비교급」 구문이다.
Ex6 「as+원급+as possible」 구문이다.
Ex7 최상급은 「비교급+than any other+단수 명사」이다.
Ex8 원급 비교는 as와 as 사이에 형용사 / 부사의 원급(fast)을 쓴다.

기출 응용문제   p. 88

1 ②	2 ①	3 ⑤	4 ⑤
5 twice / as / fast / as		6 she / could	
7 ④	8 The more / the more		9 ③

| 해설 |

1 원급 비교인 as big as a house를 쓴다. 비교 대상은 두 번째 as 뒤에 쓴다.

2 비교급의 의미를 강조할 때 a lot을 쓴다. lots of는 수량 형용사로 명사를 수식한다.

3 Lucy가 Bob보다 성적이 좋다. 따라서 ⑤는 Lucy is smarter than Bob.으로 써야 한다.

4 less 뒤에는 원급이 와서 「less+원급+than」으로 쓰인다.

5 「배수사+as+원급+as」이므로 twice as fast as로 쓴다.

6 「as~as possible」을 「as~as+주어+can[could]」으로 쓴다. 여기서 시제는 과거이므로 can이 아니고 could를 쓴다.

7 「단모음+단자음」으로 된 단어의 비교급 형태는 단모음을 한 번 더 쓰고 -er, -est를 붙인다. thinner, thinnest가 맞다.

8 「the+비교급, the+비교급」은 「~하면 할수록 더 ~할 것이다」라는 의미이다.

9 ③을 제외한 나머지는 모두 최상급 의미이다.

중간·기말고사 100점 100승   p. 90

1 ④	2 ⑤		
3	Who is taller, Jennifer or Susan?		
4	It is getting colder and colder.		
5 the best	6 ⑤	7 ③	8 ⑤
9 ⑤	10 ②	11 ⑤	
12 the	13 more / interesting / than		
14 ①	15 ②	16 ⑤	17 ③
18	Which do you like better		
19	more beautiful than I expected		
20	as[so] long as	21 higher / better	
22	as hard as possible	23 ③	24 ⑤
25 ⑤			

| 해설 |

1 hot – hotter – hottest

2 easily – more easily – most easily

3 「의문사(Which / Who) ~ 비교급, A or B」형태로 쓴다.

4 「점점 더 ~하는」의 의미인 「비교급+and+비교급」을 쓴다.

5 good의 최상급은 the best를 쓴다.

6 「as~as」는 원급 비교이므로 비교급 shorter를 쓸 수 없다.

7 「one of+최상급+복수 명사」를 쓴다. 비교급 better는 어울리지 않는다.

8 sad의 비교급은 sadder를 쓴다.

9 Sally는 Julie보다 키가 작다. 따라서 Sally is shorter than Julie.로 써야 한다.

10 ① Peter는 Juliet보다 어리다. ③ Nancy는 Peter보다 어리다. ④ Nancy가 가장 키가 크다. ⑤ Nancy와 Peter는 서로 나이가 같지 않다.

11 「비교급+than any other+단수 명사」는 최상급과 의미가 같다.

12 「the+비교급, the+비교급」구문과 「the+최상급」에 공통으로 들어갈 단어는 the이다.

13 원급의 부정은 비교급으로 바꾸어 쓸 수 있다. interesting 이 2음절 이상이므로 more interesting than을 쓴다.

14 very는 비교급을 수식하지 않는다.

15 「의문사+비교급」형태에서 정해진 것 중 하나를 고를 때는 의문사 which를 쓴다. 「비교급(warmer)+than」구문과 「as+원급(warm)+as」의 원급 비교 구문으로 비교급 warmer와 원급 warm을 쓴다.

16 메론이 수박보다 크지 않다.

17 Sunny가 Julie보다 춤을 더 잘 추고, Laura는 Julie만큼 춤을 추지 못한다고 하였으므로 Sunny가 셋 중 가장 춤을 잘 추는 사람이다.

18 Which do you like better ~?의 어순으로 쓴다.

19 beautiful 앞에 more을 쓰고 than 뒤에 주어와 동사를 쓴다.

20 비교급은 원급의 부정문(not so[as]~as)으로 바꾸어 쓸 수 있다. not이 나와 있으므로 빈칸에 as[so] long as를 쓰면 된다.

21 「the+비교급, the+비교급」구문이다.

22 「as~as+주어+can」=「as~as possible」

23 순서를 비교할 때 late의 비교급은 latter(후자의)를 쓰고 최상급은 the last(마지막의)를 쓴다.

24 시간을 기준으로 late의 비교급은 later, 최상급은 the latest(최근의)를 쓴다.

25 고기(meat)는 셀 수 없는 명사이므로 little의 비교급 less 를 쓰고, 채소(vegetables)는 셀 수 있는 명사이므로 many 의 비교급인 more를 쓴다.

중간·기말고사 평가대비 단답형 주관식   p. 94

A the / largest[biggest] / animal / in

B ⓐ giraffes ⓑ elephants

C 1 Health is more important than wealth.

   2 This cell phone is less expensive than the iPhone.

   3 The book is more interesting than the movie.

D 1 Linda is not as old as Peter.

   2 Linda is not as tall as Peter.

   3 Linda's hair isn't as short as Peter's hair.

E wiser / any / other

F 1 The blue whale is the biggest (animal) of mammals.

   2 Mt. Everest is the highest (mountain) in the world.

   3 Sunny is the tallest (girl) of the four.

| 해설 |

A 「the+최상급」을 이용하여 the largest[biggest] animal in으로 쓴다. '~에서'라는 말로 전치사 in이 필요하다.

B 표에 따르면 기린이 가장 키가 크고, 코끼리가 가장 무겁다. 따라서 빈칸에 들어갈 동물은 차례대로 기린과 코끼리이다.

C 비교 대상을 than 뒤에 두고 문장을 완성한다.
D 비교급 문장은 원급 비교의 부정문으로 바꾸어 쓸 수 있다.
E 「the＋최상급」=「비교급＋than＋any other＋단수 명사」
F 「the＋최상급」을 만들어 영작한다.

실전 서술형 평가문제 A

모범답안

1 Steve is the tallest
2 Nancy is the shortest
3 Kim's bicycle is the most expensive.
4 Karen's bicycle is the cheapest.
5 Bob is the fastest
6 John is the slowest

실전 서술형 평가문제 B
p. 96

모범답안

1 This book is more expensive than that book.
   That book is cheaper than this book.
2 A mouse is smaller than an elephant.
   An elephant is bigger than a mouse.
3 English class is more difficult than history class.
   History class is easier than English class.

실전 서술형 평가문제 C
p. 97

모범답안

1 Steve is as old as Jennifer. 또는 Jennifer is as old as Steve.
2 Brian sings as well as Jennifer. 또는 Jennifer sings as well as Brian.
3 Steve is more handsome than Brian. 또는 Brian is uglier than Steve.
4 Jennifer is taller than Brian. 또는 Brian is shorter than Jennifer.
5 Steve is the tallest of the three.
6 Brian is the shortest of the three.

실전 서술형 평가문제 D
p. 98

모범답안
주어진 형용사를 이용하여 원급, 비교급 표현을 완성할 경우 정답으로 인정한다.(easier than, worse than, better than, more boring than, more difficult than, more exciting than 등)

Chapter 04 접속사

1-1 and, but, or
p. 101

Challenge 1

01 or   02 and   03 or
04 but   05 but

Challenge 2

01 so   02 yet   03 yet
04 for   05 so

Challenge 3

01 Speak / or   02 Help / and   03 Come / or
04 Be / and

2-1 상관접속사의 종류
p. 103

Challenge 1

01 Both / and   02 either / or   03 neither / nor
04 neither / nor   05 both / and

Challenge 2

01 Either / or   02 Not / only / but / also

Challenge 3

01 not only hot coffee but also iced coffee
02 not fish but mammals

3-1 명사절로 쓰이는 that
p. 105

Challenge 1

01 대명사   02 접속사   03 대명사   04 접속사

Challenge 2

01 It is certain that he will win the game.
02 It is a pity that Tiffany hasn't been able to make any friends.
03 It is true that a cat isn't able to taste sweet things.

Challenge 3

01 I don't believe that people can live without light.
02 I doubt[don't doubt] that there will be peace in the world soon.
03 I think that it is difficult for some people to learn languages.

3-2 의문사로 시작하는 명사절(간접의문문) p. 107

Challenge 1

01 Please tell me how old your father is.
02 Tell me what you bought.
03 Do you know when the Korean War broke out?

Challenge 2

01 why she[Jessica] is laughing
02 how long pengins live
03 where she[Victoria] bought her laptop

Challenge 3

01 why dinosaurs became extinct
02 how deep this lake is

3-3 if / whether로 시작하는 명사절 p. 109

Challenge 1

01 if[whether] she is coming (or not)
02 if[whether] Jane has finished medical school yet
03 if[whether] the flight is on time
04 if[whether] there is enough gas in the car
05 if[whether] Jennifer changed jobs

Challenge 2

01 if Kevin has to come
02 if penguins ever get   03 if I am

이것이 시험에 출제되는 영문법이다! p. 110

Ex1 (d)   **Ex2** (c)   **Ex3** (b)
Ex4 neither soccer nor tennis   **Ex5** (d)
Ex6 If you don't get some sleep / Unless you get some sleep
Ex7 that
Ex8 I wonder if[whether] there is life on other planets.

| 해설 |

Ex1 원인과 결과를 나타내는 접속사는 so를 쓴다.
Ex2 등위접속사 and로 연결되었으므로 앞에 나온 stayed와 같은 과거시제인 watched를 써야 한다.
Ex3 Not only~but (also)를 쓴다. also는 생략 가능하다.
Ex4 양자부정이므로 neither~nor를 쓴다.
Ex5 '~해라, 그러면~'의 뜻에는 「명령문+and」를 쓴다.
Ex6 「명령문+or」은 「If+주어+don't[doesn't]」로 바꾸어 쓸 수 있다. Unless는 자체가 부정의 뜻을 담고 있으므로 동사를 부정으로 만들어서는 안 된다.
Ex7 접속사와 관계사 모두 쓸 수 있는 that이 공통으로 들어간다.
Ex8 의문사가 없는 의문문에서는 if 또는 whether를 이용해서 간접의문문을 만든다. 간접의문문의 어순은 「의문사+주어+동사」이다.

기출 응용문제 p. 112

1 ②   2 or   3 ④
4 bought not only a car but (also) a house
     또는 bought both a car and a house
5 I don't know if she likes Chinese food or not.
6 I want to know whether the bus stops here or not.
7 ⑤   8 ⑤

| 해설 |

1 나머지는 모두 and, ②는 but을 쓴다.
2 '~하라, ~하지 않으면'의 의미이므로 「명령문+or」을 쓴다.
3 명사절로 목적절과 보어절을 이끄는 접속사는 that이 적절하다.
4 「not only~but (also)」 또는 「both A and B」로 연결해서 영작할 수 있다.
5-6 명사절로 쓰인 간접의문문의 어순은 「의문사(if 또는 whether)+주어+동사」이다. 이때 시제에 주의한다.
7 나머지는 모두 that, ⑤는 앞 내용과 서로 상반된 내용이 연결되므로 접속사 but을 쓴다.
8 「not A but B」와 「명령문+and」 구문이다.

4-1 시간을 나타내는 접속사 p. 115

Challenge 1

01 When 02 As soon as
03 since 04 until

Challenge 2

01 began 02 were sleeping
03 have passed 04 comes
05 go 06 arrives

4-2 원인과 결과를 나타내는 접속사 p. 117

Challenge 1

01 because 02 so 03 that
04 because of

Challenge 2

01 because / so / that 02 so / so / that

Challenge 3

01 I lied because I was afraid. 또는 Because I was afraid, I lied.
02 Since we have no classes on weekends, we can go skiing every Saturday. 또는 We can go skiing every Saturday since we have no classes on weekends.
03 My friend lied to me, so I don't trust her anymore.

4-3 조건 / 양보의 부사절 p. 119

Challenge 1

01 Because 02 because of
03 In spite of 04 Although

Challenge 2

01 Unless you have a passport
02 if you aren't busy
03 Unless you take your medicine
04 If you don't exercise regularly
05 unless we work hard
06 Unless you read the book

이것이 시험에 출제되는 영문법이다! p. 120

Ex1 (c)
Ex2 If you don't work hard, you won't succeed.
Ex3 (b) Ex4 (b) Ex5 (d) Ex6 (b)
Ex7 (b) Ex8 (d)

| 해설 |

Ex1 '졸업한 후'에(after he graduated), '피곤할 때'(when you're tired)라는 의미가 되어야 한다.
Ex2 Unless는 부정의 의미를 담고 있으므로 If ~ don't로 문장을 전환한다.
Ex3 조건의 부사절에서는 미래를 표현하더라도 현재(rains)를 써서 미래를 나타낸다.
Ex4 if는 know의 목적어 역할을 하므로 명사절에 해당한다. 명사절에서는 부사절과 달리 미래시제를 그대로 쓴다.
Ex5 빈칸 뒤에 명사만 있으므로 because of를 쓴다. in spite of도 뒤에 명사를 쓰지만 의미가 다르다.
Ex6 명사 the weather가 있으므로 In spite of를 쓴다.
Ex7 앞서 진행 중이었던 동작은 과거진행, 나중에 끼어드는 동작은 과거시제(rang)를 쓴다.
Ex8 주절은 의미상 '~ 이래로'의 의미로 쓰인 since절이 있으므로 완료시제를 써야 한다.

기출 응용문제 p. 122

1 Though 또는 Although 2 Either / or
3 so / that 4 ④ 5 ② 6 ④
7 ③ 8 ②

| 해설 |

1 '~임에 불구하고'의 뜻인 Although 또는 Though를 쓴다.
2 양자택일은 either ~ or을 쓴다.
3 '너무 ~ 해서 ~ 하다'의 뜻인 「so + 형용사 / 부사 + that S + V」구문을 쓴다.
4 Unless는 부정의 의미를 담고 있으므로 If you don't water ~로 써야 한다. 참고로, water는 '물을 주다'는 의미의 동사이다.
5 시간의 접속사 안에서는 현재시제(comes)가 미래를 대신한다.
6 '외출할 수 없었다'에 대한 이유가 나와야 하므로 because I had a flu(독감에 걸려서)가 알맞다.
7 ③은 '언제'라는 의미의 의문사이고, 나머지는 모두 '~할 때'라는 의미의 접속사이다.
8 시간의 접속사 when절 안에서는 현재시제(goes)가 미래를 대신한다.

1	④	2	③	3	②	4	②
5	①	6	③	7	so / that	8	②
9	③	10	When	11	where	12	③
13	②	14	⑤	15	Be / or		
16	Take / and			17	①	18	③
19	because → because of			20	④	21	⑤
22	③	23	②	24	As		
25	If / you / don't			26	as / well / as	27	for

| 해설 |

1 앞 문장이 결과이고 뒤 문장이 원인일 때는 because, 앞 문장이 원인이고 뒤 문장이 결과일 때는 so를 쓴다.

2 while은 '~하는 동안'이라는 뜻으로 주로 진행시제와 함께 쓰인다. ③은 While이 아니라 After(~후에)가 나와야 자연스럽다.

3 '~하자마자'에 해당하는 표현은 as soon as이다.

4 '~하지 않으면'은 unless를 쓴다.

5 조건의 부사절 내에서는 현재시제가 미래를 나타낸다.

6 나머지는 모두 조건의 부사절이고 ③의 if절은 wonder의 목적어로 명사절이다.

7 「too~to부정사」=「so~that+주어+can't / couldn't」

8 ①은 지시대명사, ③, ④, ⑤는 명사 뒤에서 수식하는 관계대명사로 쓰였다. ②가 명사절로 쓰임이 같다.

9 '가난했음에도 불구하고 행복했다'의 의미로 가장 가까운 것은 접속사 but이다.

10 시간의 접속사 when이 적절하다.

11 '휴대폰을 어디에 두었는지'라는 뜻이 되기 위해서는 장소를 나타내는 where가 적절하다.

12 「명령문+or」은 unless로 바꾸어 쓸 수 있다.

13 첫 번째 빈칸 뒤 문장(절)이 원인을 나타내므로 because가 적절하고, 두 번째 빈칸 뒤에는 명사 risk가 원인을 나타내므로 because of를 쓴다.

14 나머지는 모두 접속사 that, ⑤는 접속사 when이 들어간다.

15 부정의 의미이므로 「명령문+or」을 쓴다.

16 긍정의 의미이므로 「명령문+and」를 쓴다.

17 '때'를 나타내는 시간의 접속사 when을 쓴다.

18 조건의 부사절에서는 현재시제가 미래를 대신한다. ③get 대신 gets를 쓴다.

19 the typhoon은 명사이므로 because of를 쓴다.

20 나머지는 모두 양자택일의 의미인 or, ④는 「명령문+or」로 '~해라, 그러지 않으면'이란 뜻이다.

21 나머지는 모두 등위접속사 and, ⑤는 「명령문+and」로 '~해라, 그러면~'의 뜻이다.

22 ① 「both A and B」는 복수 주어 취급하므로 have를 쓴다. ② 등위접속사 앞뒤의 시제가 같아야 하므로 과거형(sang)을 쓴다. ④ 시간의 부사절이므로 현재시제(arrives)가 미래를 대신한다. ⑤ either는 or과 연결된다.

23 ① 양자택일을 묻는 것이므로 and를 or로 써야 한다. ③ 조건의 부사절에서는 현재시제(miss)가 미래를 대신한다. ④ 부사절이 아닌 주절에서는 미래시제를 써야 한다. 따라서 We will go on a picnic if~로 써야 한다. ⑤ the heavy traffic은 명사이므로 접속사 Although를 In spite of로 바꿔야 한다.

24 첫 번째 문장에는 이유를 나타내는 As, 두 번째 문장에는 시간을 나타내는 As가 들어간다.

25 「명령문+or」=「If+주어+don't[doesn't]」

26 「not only A but also B」=「B as well A」

27 문장 중간에 쉼표로 분리되었을 때 원인을 나타내는 접속사로 for를 쓴다.

A 1 Bob is going to go to either Africa or (to) Asia. 또는 Bob is going to go either to Africa or (to) Asia.

   2 He teaches not only English but (also) French.

   3 My dad likes neither pizza nor spaghetti.

B 1 why dinosaurs became extinct

   2 how she learned to play the harmonica

   3 if[whether] she can carry out the plan

C 1 If you don't hurry up / Unless you hurry up

   2 If you don't have a passport / Unless you have a passport

D 1 If the weather is nice tomorrow

   2 When she was walking

| 해설 |

A 1 either to Africa or (to) Asia 또는 go to either Africa or (to) Asia로 쓴다. 2 not only English but also French로 쓰는데 이때 also는 생략해도 된다. 3 neither pizza nor spaghetti로 쓴다.

B 1 「의문사+주어+동사」로 쓴다. 시제가 과거이므로 become을 became으로 바꿔 써야 한다. 2 「의문사+ 주어+동사」의 어순으로 쓴다. 시제가 과거이므로 learn을 learned로 고쳐 쓴다. 3 의문사가 없는 의문문에서는 「if / whether+주어+동사」의 어순으로 쓴다.

C 1 if절에는 부정형 동사(don't hurry up / don't have)를, unless는 자체가 부정의 의미를 담고 있으므로 부정어구 (don't)를 함께 쓰지 않는다.

D 1 조건의 부사절에서는 현재시제로 미래를 나타낸다. nice 가 형용사이므로 be동사 is를 써서 If the weather is nice tomorrow가 된다. 2 먼저 있었던 다소 긴 시간 동안 진행되고 있었던 시제는 과거진행형을 쓴다. 의미상 접속사 는 when을 써서 When she was walking이 된다.

모범답안

1 but it was closed
2 and (he) watched a film[movie]
3 so she didn't eat dinner

모범답안

1 I don't think that computers will have emotions.
2 I think that it is difficult for some people to focus on work when they are at home.
3 I don't believe that people will be happy all the time.
4 I don't think that it is difficult for some people to learn languages.

모범답안

1 Unless Nancy stops eating sweets, she won't lose any weight.
2 If I see Kevin this afternoon, I'll tell him to phone you.
3 When the temperature reaches −15℃, the lake freezes.

모범답안

1 Jane has lost ten kilos since she joined a health club.
2 My dad hasn't had any accidents since he bought a new car.
3 I haven't seen Kelly since she moved to Scotland.

모범답안

1 I cooked dinner / our guests arrived
2 he ate lunch / he played soccer with his friends
3 They had lunch / they sat on the beach
4 I'm going to play tennis / I finish my homework

Chapter 05 관계사   p. 133~160

1-1 주격, 목적격으로 쓰이는 who   p. 135

Challenge 1

01 I have a boyfriend who(m) I can trust.
02 I met the couples who have just got married.
03 The woman who lives next door is a doctor. 또는 The woman is a doctor who lives next door.
04 Do you know the people who live in Singapore?
05 I know a boy who plays online games every night.
06 I met friends who(m) I've known since elementary school.
07 This is the man who saved her life.
08 The girl who was injured in the accident is now in the hospital.
09 She is the teacher who(m) I really wanted to meet.
10 I like the girl who(m) I met at the party.

1-2 주격, 목적격으로 쓰이는 which, that   p. 137

Challenge 1

01 This is the iPhone which I bought yesterday.
02 These are the problems which I can't solve on my own.
03 The woman who lives next door is a dancer.
04 Look at the house which is covered with snow.
05 I saw the children who were playing soccer at the park.

Challenge 2

01 Kathy has some photos. / I took them.
02 Sunny is my friend. / She lives near the school.
03 I gave her the book. / She wanted it.
04 I saw an old castle. / It stood on the hill.

1-3 소유격 관계대명사 p. 139

Challenge 1

01 who   02 whose   03 which
04 who   05 whose

Challenge 2

01 I saw a girl whose hair is blonde.
02 There is a man whose car was stolen.
03 There is a woman whose cat died.
04 We have a puppy whose name is Happy.
05 There are many words whose meanings I don't know.

1-4 목적격 관계대명사의 생략 p. 141

Challenge 1

01 which   02 없음   03 없음
04 that   05 whom

Challenge 2

01 She is the woman who(m) I want to marry. / She is the woman that I want to marry. / She is the woman I want to marry.
02 I never found the book for which I was looking.
/ I never found the book which I was looking for.
/ I never found the book that I was looking for.
/ I never found the book I was looking for.
03 The woman to whom I was talking was interesting. / The woman who(m) I was talking to was interesting. / The woman that I was talking to was interesting. / The woman I was talking to was interesting.

1-5 what과 that / 관계사절의 수일치 p. 143

Challenge 1

01 This is what I wanted.
02 She showed me the thing which she bought yesterday.

03 I can't believe the thing which Scott said.
04 This is what I want to draw.
05 What I really want to be is a nurse.
06 I don't believe the thing which Julia told me.

Challenge 2

01 is   02 were   03 that
04 that   05 that   06 that

2-1 when, where, why, how p. 145

Challenge 1

01 where   02 how   03 where
04 why   05 when

Challenge 2

01 for / which   02 where   03 how

Challenge 3

01 I went back to the village where I was born.
02 Tell me the reason why you didn't call me.
03 That is how I solve the problem. 또는 That is the way I solve the problem.

2-2 관계부사절의 독특한 특징 p. 147

Challenge 1

01 when   02 who(m)   03 why   04 which
05 which   06 when   07 who(m)   08 where

Challenge 2

01 where / the room / the room that
02 when / the time / the time that

이것이 시험에 출제되는 영문법이다! p. 148

Ex1 (c)   Ex2 (c)   Ex3 (c)   Ex4 (d)
Ex5 which[that] you bought yesterday
Ex6 ① This is what I wanted.
     ② This is the thing which I wanted.
Ex7 is → are   Ex8 (b)

| 해설 |

Ex1 선행사가 사람이고 동사 is가 있으므로 주격 관계사 who 를 쓴다.
Ex2 the dress는 wear의 목적어이다. 따라서 목적격 관계사

로 쓰인 ③이 정답이다.

Ex3 전치사 about에 대한 목적어가 없으므로 선행사가 사람이면서 목적격 역할을 하는 관계사 who(m)이 온다.

Ex4 선행사가 사람이고 관계사절 내에 온전한 문장이 놓여 있다. 따라서 빈칸은 소유격 관계대명사가 들어갈 자리이다.

Ex5 the iPhone과 대명사 it은 같은 대상이다. 목적어 역할을 하는 관계대명사 which나 that을 이용하여 두 문장을 연결할 수 있다.

Ex6 the thing과 it이 같다. it을 which로 대명사 처리하여 the thing which로 쓰거나 한 단어로 what을 쓸 수 있다.

Ex7 관계대명사절을 제거해 보면 주어는 the people, 동사는 is이다. 주어가 복수이므로 동사 is를 are로 바꿔야 한다.

Ex8 the way와 how는 함께 쓰지 않고 둘 중에 하나만 사용한다.

기출 응용문제　　　　　　　　　　　p. 150

1　is my friend whose hair is black
2　This is the house where I lived.
3　where there is a lot of fresh air
4　whose color is red
5　which I really like to play
6　whose job is a journalist
7　why she cried　　　　8　③　　　　9　③
10　the / place / where　　11　①

| 해설 |

1 her를 소유격 관계사 whose로 바꿔 문장을 연결한다.

2 in the house를 관계부사 where로 바꾼다.

8 사람(girls)과 사물(chairs)을 모두 선행사로 쓸 수 있는 관계사는 that이다.

9 선행사가 사람(daughter)이므로 관계대명사 which는 쓸 수 없고, 주격 관계사절 뒤의 문장에는 주어가 없어야 한다.

10 선행사가 장소이므로 관계부사 where를 쓴다.

11 ①에서 관계사절(which grow in my garden)을 제거하면 주어는 the apples, 동사는 is이다. 주어가 복수이므로 동사 is를 are로 써야 한다.

중간·기말고사 100점 100승　　　　p. 152

1　who 또는 that　　　　2　whose　　3　that
4　③　　　5　①　　　6　in / which
7　at / which　8　for / which　　　　9　①
10　③　　　11　what I told him　　　12　①
13　③　　　14　what
15　Is this the book which you were looking for the other day?
16　that　　17　which 또는 that
18　whose　19　⑤　　　20　in which / when

21　for which / why
22　who was late for school today was Susie
23　an actress who(m) many people like　24　②
25　The children loved the beach where[to which] they went last summer.
26　①　　　　　　27　the house where I grew up

| 해설 |

1 선행사가 사람(person)이므로 who 또는 that을 쓴다.

2 빈칸 뒤에 명사와 be동사가 따라오므로 소유격 whose를 쓴다.

3 사람과 사물(동물)이 함께 선행사로 나오므로 that을 쓴다.

4 ③은 관계사 that 바로 뒤에 동사(lives)가 나오므로 주격 관계사이고 주격 관계사는 생략할 수 없다. 나머지는 모두 목적격 관계사로 생략 가능하다.

5 선행사가 장소에 속하고 뒤에 「주어＋자동사」로 완벽한 문장을 이루므로 관계부사 where를 쓰고 두 번째 문장에는 이유를 나타내는 관계부사 why가 적절하다.

6-8 관계부사는 「전치사＋which」로 바꿔 쓸 수 있다.

9 ① 주격 관계사 who 뒤에는 동사가 바로 와야 한다. 그런데 뒤에 명사 wife가 있고 「be동사＋보어」의 완벽한 문장이므로 소유격 whose를 써야 한다.

10 소유격 his를 대신하는 관계사는 whose이다.

11 '내가 그에게 말한 것'은 what I told him의 어순으로 쓴다.

12 선행사가 사람이고 주격 관계사이므로 who로 바꿔 쓸 수 있다.

13 ③의 which는 wrote 뒤에 목적어가 없으므로 목적격 관계대명사이다. 따라서 생략 가능하다.

14 선행사 없이 쓸 수 있는 관계사는 what이고 「what+to부정사」는 '무엇을 해야 할지'의 의미이다.

15 it이 the book과 같은 사물이므로 전치사 for의 목적어 it을 목적격 관계대명사 which로 바꿔 쓴다.

16 첫 번째 문장은 명사절 that, 두 번째 문장은 서수(the first)가 붙은 선행사가 있으므로 관계대명사 that이 온다.

17 호텔을 무조건 장소로 보고 관계부사 where를 쓰면 안 된다. stayed at에서 전치사 at의 목적어가 바로 the hotel이다. 따라서 목적격 관계대명사인 which 또는 that을 써야 한다.

18 빈칸 뒤에 명사 mother가 나오고 완전한 문장이므로 소유격 관계사 whose를 쓴다.

19 in that은 함께 쓰지 않는다. in which만 가능하다.

20-21 when은 in which로, why는 for which로 바꿔 쓸 수 있다.

22 주격 관계대명사로 만든다.

23 목적격 관계대명사로 만든다.

24 whose＝of which

25 to the beach를 장소를 나타내는 관계부사 where 또는 the beach를 which로 관계대명사 처리하여 to which로 쓴다.

26 ①은 의문사이고 나머지는 관계대명사이다.

27 선행사 the house를 쓰고 관계부사 where 다음에 「주어＋동사」를 쓴다.

A   1   who takes care of your teeth
    2   who acts in a play
    3   who looks after the flight's safety procedures and passenger comfort
    4   which you eat with
    5   which tells the time

B   1   how you sold your car at a good price
    2   why Kathy left him three days ago
    3   when we were all excited about the World Cup
    4   where we first met

C   1   Edison invented machines which do wonderful things.
    2   This is the room whose wall is white.
    3   I met a woman whose daughter is a movie star.
    4   There is a river which flows in front of my house.

D   1   I bought recently has already crashed several times
    2   we planted last year have doubled in size
    3   I took to Korea arrived on time
    4   I'm interested in is the study of people and society

실전 서술형 평가문제 A   ·   p. 158

모범답안

1   who draws pictures
2   which helps you find your way
3   who saves people's lives
4   which shows what time it is

실전 서술형 평가문제 B   p. 159

모범답안

1   which is in Africa
2   whose most famous painting is the Mona Lisa
3   who wrote *Hamlet*
4   whose capital is Buenos Aires
5   who helped the poor and ill in India

실전 서술형 평가문제 C   p. 160

모범답안

1   when the Korea-Japan World Cup was held
2   where they are getting married
3   why I dislike her[him]

| 해설 |

A **1-3** 선행사가 사람이므로 who를 쓴다. **4-5** 선행사가 사물(sticks / a thing)이므로 which를 쓴다.

B **1** 선행사가 방법이므로 how를 쓴다. the way와 how는 함께 쓰지 않는다. **2** 선행사가 이유(reason)이므로 why를 쓴다. **3** 선행사가 시간이므로 when을 쓴다. **4** 선행사가 장소(cafe)이므로 where를 쓴다.

C **1** They를 관계대명사 which로 써서 문장을 연결한다. **2** Its를 whose로 바꿔 문장을 연결한다. **3** Her을 whose로 바꿔 문장을 연결한다. **4** It을 관계대명사 which로 써서 문장을 연결한다.

D **1** it을 관계대명사 which로 바꾼 후 생략하고 I bought recently를 선행사 The computer 뒤에 붙여 완성한다. **2** them을 관계대명사 which로 바꾼 후 생략하고 we planted last year를 선행사 The trees 뒤에 붙여 연결한다. **3** it을 관계대명사 which로 바꾼 후 생략하고 I took to Korea를 선행사 The plane 뒤에 붙여 연결한다. **4** it을 관계대명사 which로 바꾼 후 생략하고 I'm interested in을 선행사 Anthropology(인류학) 뒤에 붙여 연결한다.

Chapter 06 문장의 형식과 종류 p. 161~188

1-1 1형식 / 2형식 동사 p. 163

Challenge 1

01 is
02 are
03 a cat
04 three balls
05 sugar
06 snow

Challenge 2

01 이다
02 있다
03 이다
04 있다

Challenge 3

01 strange
02 bad
03 happy
04 soft
05 beautiful
06 angry

1-2 3형식 / 4형식 동사 p. 165

Challenge 1

01 3형식
02 2형식
03 1형식
04 4형식
05 3형식

Challenge 2

01 for
02 of
03 to
04 for

Challenge 3

01 made us dinner
02 show a cheaper one to me

1-3 5형식 동사 p. 167

Challenge 1

01 to sing → singing 또는 sing
02 to clean → clean
03 gone → go
04 help → to help
05 calling → to call
06 eat → to eat
07 repair → repaired

Challenge 2

01 keep you healthy
02 asked my little sister to turn off
03 had my house built

Challenge 3

01 playing the piano
02 ringing loudly
03 burning in the oven

2-1 의문사가 있는 의문문 p. 169

Challenge 1

01 Why did you write a letter to Bob?
02 Where does Tom play soccer after school?
03 When can you make a cake?
04 When does the airplane leave for New York?

Challenge 2

01 Who is
02 Where do
03 Who is
04 When did
05 How was
06 Why do
07 Where did

2-2 부가의문문 / 선택의문문 p. 171

Challenge 1

01 isn't it
02 can't you
03 does she
04 does she
05 wasn't it
06 does he
07 will you
08 shall we
09 are they
10 wasn't it

Challenge 2

01 Steve likes the soccer player, doesn't he?
02 Would you like coffee or green tea?
03 Will you go to Lotteria or McDonald's?
04 You were late for school again, weren't you?

2-3 감탄문 / 제안문 p. 173

Challenge 1

01 How beautifully she sings!
02 What interesting books they are!
03 How delicious this cake is!
04 What a boring film it was!
05 What beautiful eyes she has!

Challenge 2

01 He is a (very) good singer.
02 The movie is (very) sad.
03 Those are (very) fresh fruits.
04 This ring is (very) expensive.

Challenge 3

01 Let's go to the movie theater.
02 Let's not go to the library.
03 Let's not have fish for dinner tonight.
04 Let's paint the door.

2-4 간접의문문 p. 175

Challenge 1

01 who Tom is
02 if[whether] she is married
03 If[whether] she likes Paul
04 where Susan works
05 if[whether] your mother is at home
06 why he left here

Challenge 2

01 How do you think he solved the problem?
02 Where do you think he went yesterday?
03 Who do you believe did it?
04 Who do you think will win the game?

이것이 시험에 출제되는 영문법이다! p. 176

Ex1 (b)   Ex2 (a)   Ex3 apples / him
Ex4 (c)   Ex5 (d)
Ex6 What nice people they are!   Ex7 (b)
Ex8 How do you think he can solve the problem?

| 해설 |

Ex1 주어가 셀 수 없는 명사(snow)이므로 be동사는 is를 써야 한다.
Ex2 2형식 감각동사(look)는 형용사를 보어로 가진다.
Ex3 give는 3형식으로 고칠 때 전치사 to를 사용한다.
Ex4 「have+목적어(the computer)+과거분사(repaired)」의 구문이다.
Ex5 have는 일반동사이므로 don't you?로 부가의문을 만든다.
Ex6 동사 뒤에 people이 있으므로 What으로 시작하는 감탄문을 만든다.
Ex7 「의문사+주어+동사」의 어순으로 간접의문문을 만든다. 의문문에 did를 쓰지 않고 대신 동사 run을 과거형 ran으로 고쳐야 한다.
Ex8 생각의 동사 think가 있으므로 의문사를 문장 맨 앞으로 보내고 「주어+동사」의 어순으로 쓴다.

기출 응용문제 p. 178

| 1 ⑤ | 2 There / are | 3 ③ |
| 4 ①, ⑤ | 5 ① | 6 ② | 7 ③ |
| 8 playing soccer with her friends |

| 해설 |

1 4형식을 3형식으로 바꿀 때 teach는 전치사 to, cook은 for, ask는 of를 쓴다.
2 '~가 있다'를 나타낼 때 there be 구문을 쓴다. 여기서는 주어가 복수(many members)이므로 There are를 쓴다.
3 나머지는 모두 5형식 문장, ③은 '나에게 연을 만들어 주었다'는 뜻의 4형식 문장이다. make 동사는 3 / 4 / 5형식 문장을 모두 만들 수 있다.
4 목적격 보어에 to부정사가 있으므로 사역동사인 make와 let을 쓸 수 없다. make와 let은 목적격 보어에 동사원형을 쓴다.
5 Yes / No로 답하지 않았으므로 의문사로 물었다는 것을 알 수 있다. 비교의 대상이 사람이므로 Who가 알맞다.
6 명령문의 부가의문문은 will you?를 쓴다.
7 선택의문문에서 비교의 대상이 사람이면 Who, 사물이면 Which를 쓴다. 여기서는 basketball과 baseball이 비교되고 있으므로 Which가 맞다.
8 「지각동사+목적어+동사원형 / 현재분사」를 쓴다. 여기서는 진행 중인 동작이므로 현재분사를 이용하여 I saw Jane playing~ 으로 쓴다.

중간·기말고사 100점 100승 p. 180

1 ①	2 ①	3 ③	4 ④
5 ③	6 ①	7 ④	8 ④
9 ④	10 What / a / boring
11 How / expensive
12 What / beautiful / eyes
13 ③	14 Which / or	15 ②	16 ③
17 ④	18 He looks[seems] happy.
19 to	20 made	21 why / she / is
22 if 또는 whether	23 Which / want / or
24 ①	25 ④	26 ③
27 to have breakfast
28 take the school bus

| 해설 |

1 ① 사역동사 have의 목적격 보어로 동사원형(clean)을 쓴다.
2 ① 사역동사 have의 목적격 보어로 동사원형(clean)을 쓴다.
3 had는 명령(~하라고 시키다)이지만, encourage는 명령의 뜻이 아닌 격려 또는 부탁의 의미이다.
4 전에 어디서 만났기(met you somewhere before) 때문에 look familiar (낯익어 보이다)가 되어야 자연스럽다.

5 간접의문문은 「의문사＋주어＋동사」의 어순으로 쓴다.

6 look은 부사를 보어로 쓰지 않는다.

7 have, make, help, let은 모두 목적격 보어에 동사원형을 쓸 수 있지만, order는 to부정사를 목적격 보어로 쓴다.

8 want는 목적격 보어로 to부정사를 쓰고, let은 동사원형을 쓴다.

9 4형식 동사 give는 3형식으로 바꿀 때 전치사 to를 쓴다.

10 명사 movie가 있으므로 What으로 시작하는 감탄문을 만든다.

11 형용사 expensive가 있으므로 How로 시작하는 감탄문을 만든다.

12 명사 eyes가 있으므로 What으로 시작하는 감탄문을 만든다.

13 의문사가 있는 의문문은 Yes나 No로 대답할 수 없다. 둘 중에 하나를 선택해야 하므로 Busan is warmer.가 알맞다.

14 선택의문문 비교의 대상이 사물이면 Which를 쓰고, 둘 중에 하나를 고르게 할 때 접속사 or을 쓴다.

15 「감각동사＋목적어＋동사원형 / 현재분사」의 어순에서 현재 흔들리고 있는 순간을 표현하므로 목적격 보어에 현재분사를 쓴다.

16 「have＋목적어(her purse)＋과거분사(stolen)」는 '(목적어)가 동작이나 행위를 당하다'의 의미이다.

17 Because ～는 이유에 대한 대답이므로 Why로 시작하는 의문문이 필요하다는 것을 알 수 있다.

18 「look[seem]＋형용사」의 형태로 쓴다.

19 4형식 동사 give를 3형식으로 고칠 때, 전치사는 to를 쓴다.

20 「make＋목적어＋형용사」 (5형식)
「make＋간접목적어＋직접목적어」 (4형식)
「make＋목적어＋동사원형」 (5형식)

21 이유를 묻는 의문사 why를 써서 why she is로 문장을 완성한다. 간접의문문이므로 「주어＋동사」의 어순에 주의한다.

22 의문사가 없는 의문문을 간접의문문으로 만들 때는 if 또는 whether를 써서 「주어＋동사」의 어순으로 만든다.

23 선택의문문에서 사물을 비교할 때 Which를 쓴다. 동사 want를 쓰고 두 개의 대상 사이에 or을 쓴다. and를 쓰지 않도록 주의한다.

24 look은 보어로 형용사만을 가진다. tired만 형용사이고 beauty는 명사, 나머지는 모두 부사이다.

25 「give＋간접목적어(us)＋직접목적어(some useful advice)」의 4형식에서 목적어 앞에 전치사 to를 쓰면 안 된다.

26 ① don't you? ② didn't he? ④ are they? ⑤ does she?가 되어야 한다.

27 5형식 동사(tell)이므로 목적격 보어에 to부정사를 써서 to have breakfast로 문장을 완성한다.

28 사역동사(have)이므로 동사원형 take를 써서 take the school bus로 문장을 완성한다.

중간·기말고사 평가대비 단답형 주관식　　p. 184

A 1 if Kathy is in her office
　2 how old the building is
　3 when Paul will be here
　4 why she was angry
　5 how long Mary has lived here

B 1 made me laugh
　2 saw you dancing[dance] with her
　3 me not to touch

C 1 They play tennis
　2 He can't swim
　3 She was sleeping at 12:00
　4 It is snowing in the mountain

D 1 What tall buildings they are!
　2 What sweet watermelons they are!
　3 How long her hair is!

| 해설 |

A 1 Is Kathy ～?를 Kathy is로 써서 if Kathy is in her office로 쓴다. 2 how old를 한 덩어리의 의문사로 처리하여 「how old＋주어＋동사」로 쓴다. 3 「의문사＋주어＋조동사＋동사원형」으로 쓴다. 4 「why＋주어(she)＋동사(was)」로 쓴다. 5 how long을 한 덩어리의 의문사로 처리하여 「how long＋주어(Mary)＋동사(has lived)」로 쓴다.

B 1 「made＋목적어(me)＋동사원형(laugh)」로 쓴다.
2 「saw＋목적어(you)＋목적격 보어(dancing / dance)」로 쓴다. 3 「동사(warned)＋목적어(me)＋목적격 보어(not to touch)」로 쓴다. 부정어로 만들 때 to부정사 바로 앞에 not을 붙인다.

C 1 부가의문문이 부정이므로 긍정인 They play tennis로 쓴다. 2 부가의문문이 긍정이므로 부정인 He can't swim으로 쓴다. 대답문의 주어인 he를 주어로 사용한다. 3 부가의문문이 부정이므로 긍정인 She was sleeping at 12:00으로 쓴다. 4 부가의문문이 부정이므로 긍정인 It is snowing in the mountain으로 쓴다.

D 1 「What＋(a / an)＋형용사＋명사＋주어＋동사」 2 「What＋(a / an)＋형용사＋명사＋주어＋동사」 3 「How＋형용사/부사＋주어＋동사」

실전 서술형 평가문제 A　　p. 186

모범답안

1 The doctor[He] advised me to go on a diet.
2 He had[made] me wash the[his] car.
3 She[Miranda's friend] told her not to drive so fast.

Chapter **07** 전치사 p. 189~212

3-3 동사와 함께 잘나가는 표현들   p. 203

Challenge 1

01 of	02 on	03 at
04 to	05 to	06 of
07 of	08 to	09 for
10 for	11 for	12 after
13 of		

이것이 시험에 출제되는 영문법이다!   p. 204

Ex1 (d)	Ex2 (a)	Ex3 (d)	Ex4 (d)
Ex5 (b)	Ex6 (c)		

| 해설 |

Ex1 night은 전치사 in이 아니라 at을 쓴다. at lunchtime, at Christmas, at present, at sunset 등이 전치사 at과 함께 쓰인다.

Ex2 특정 기간을 나타내는 명사(구)이므로 전치사 during을 쓴다.

Ex3 '~까지'를 나타내는 전치사는 by이다.

Ex4 'A와 B사이'는 「between A and B」를 쓴다.

Ex5 look for, wait for는 숙어처럼 굳어진 표현들이다.

Ex6 be interested in을 쓴다.

기출 응용문제   p. 206

1 ④	2 ①	3 ④	4 ②
5 ③	6 through	7 ⑤	8 ②

| 해설 |

1 be surprised at, 그리고 구체적인 시간 앞에 at을 쓴다. 따라서 공통으로 들어갈 전치사는 at이다.

2 구체적인 시간의 길이를 나타낼 때는 for, 요일이나 날짜 앞에는 on, '~옆에'라는 뜻의 전치사 by가 차례대로 들어간다.

3 현재까지 우승을 못했으므로 현재를 포함한 완료시제(has not won)를 쓰고 '1950년 이래로'는 시작점을 나타내는 since를 쓴다.

4 기차가 떠난 후에 역에 도착했으므로 after를 쓴다.

5 around는 시간 앞에서는 '약, (몇 시)쯤'의 뜻으로 쓰이고, 명사 앞에서는 '~주위에'의 뜻으로 쓰인다.

6 '~을 통과[관통]하여'의 뜻인 전치사 through를 쓴다.

7 '(질병, 부상 등)으로 죽다'는 주로 die of를 쓴다.

8 ②의 like는 가장 좋아하는 음악이 무엇인지를 묻는 동사이다. 나머지는 전치사로 쓰였다.

중간 · 기말고사 100점 100승   p. 208

1 by	2 during	3 from	4 ①
5 ⑤	6 On / her[the] / way / home		
7 ④	8 ③	9 for	10 ④

11 A monkey is climbing up the tree.
12 She is reading in front of the door.
13 Let's meet at the bus stop.   14 ①
15 ③

| 해설 |

1 교통수단을 나타낼 때 by를 쓴다.

2 정확한 시간의 길이를 언급하지 않은 기간이므로 during을 쓴다.

3 '언제부터 언제까지(어디부터 어디까지)'의 의미인 from A to B를 쓴다.

4 정확한 시간의 길이를 언급하므로 ①의 during을 for로 써야 한다.

5 ⑤의 by는 '늦지 않게 ~까지'의 의미로, 어떤 행위나 일이 그때까지 완료되어야 하는 것을 나타낸다. 따라서 전치사 by보다는 12시까지 계속해서 공부를 하는 상황을 나타내는 전치사 until이 적절하다.

6 「on the[one's] way+장소 부사(home)」는 '(집으)로 가는 길에'의 뜻이다. '장소 부사' 대신 「to+장소 명사」를 쓸 수 있다.

7 '~타고(교통수단), ~로(방법)'를 나타낼 때 전치사 by를 쓴다.

8 월 앞에 in, 방향을 나타내는 전치사 to, 그리고 비교적 넓은 장소를 나타낼 때 전치사 in을 쓴다.

9 정확한 시간의 길이를 언급하므로 전치사 for를 쓴다.

10 '~안으로'의 전치사는 out of가 아니고 into를 쓴다.

11 climb up the tree(나무 위를 오르다)를 써서 문장을 완성한다.

12 in front of the door(문 앞에서)를 써서 문장을 완성한다.

13 구체적인 장소에는 at을 써서 at the bus stop으로 문장을 완성한다.

14 날짜나 요일 앞에 on, 연도 앞에 in을 쓴다.

15 take pride in=be proud of(~을 자랑스러워하다)

실전 서술형 평가문제 A   p. 210

모범답안

1 Helen's toy is under the table.
2 Helen's shoes are under the bed.
3 The cat's basket is on the floor.
4 Helen's cat is in front of the armchair.
5 Helen's painting is on the wall.
6 Helen's books are by[beside, next to] the cat's basket.

실전 서술형 평가문제 B

p. 211

모범답안

1 She is behind the door.
2 They are at a[the] (birthday) party.
3 He is under the tree.
4 She is sitting on the table.
5 They are at the bus stop.

실전 서술형 평가문제 C

p. 212

모범답안

1 lived in Korea from 2002 to 2010 /
lived in Korea for eight years /
lived in Korea until 2010 /
has lived in Australia since 2010 /
2 worked in a hotel from 1999 to 2005 /
worked in a hotel for six years /
worked in a hotel until 2005 /
has worked in a restaurant since 2005

Chapter 08 가정법

p. 213~235

1-1 현재와 미래를 나타내는 1차 가정문

p. 215

Challenge 1

01 helps / will finish
02 eat / will put on
03 sneeze / close
04 go / will see
05 die / don't get
06 go / will catch
07 break / grows

Challenge 2

01 When[If] the temperature reaches −15℃, the lake freezes.
02 Unless Jane stops eating sweets, she won't lose any weight.
03 When babies are hungry, they cry.
04 If I see Tom this afternoon, I'll tell him to phone you.

1-2 가능성이 거의 없는 2차 가정문 I

p. 217

Challenge 1

01 were 또는 was
02 didn't have
03 had
04 were 또는 was

Challenge 2

01 If we stayed in a hotel, it would cost too much money.
02 If we told them the truth, they wouldn't believe us.

1-3 가능성이 거의 없는 2차 가정문 II

p. 219

Challenge 1

01 If he had a car
02 If I were a millionaire
03 If she studied hard
04 If I were tall
05 If I knew her phone number

Challenge 2

01 If Michael weren't sick, he might come to see us.
02 As we don't have a car, we can't go on a vacation.
03 If I knew her well, I could invite her to the party.
04 As my brother isn't hungry, he won't go out for dinner.

1-4 가능성이 0%인 3차 가정문

p. 221

Challenge 1

01 have been
02 had worked
03 would have baked
04 would have been

Challenge 2

01 would have gone
02 hadn't been
03 would have taken

Challenge 3

01 had / been / would / have / eaten
02 had / not / been / could / have / joined
03 had / gotten / could / have / gone

2-1 현재 또는 미래에 대한 소망 (wish+과거시제)

p. 223

Challenge 1

01 I wish that he were[was] a pilot.
02 I wish that I had a puppy.
03 I wish I were[was] a university student.
04 I wish Jessica knew my phone number.
05 I wish I could speak Chinese.

Challenge 2

01 I wish (that) I had a job.
02 I wish (that) I could speak English.
03 I wish (that) I knew how to drive.

Challenge 3

01 I wish you wouldn't smoke anymore.
02 I wish you wouldn't make the same mistake.
03 I wish you would buy me a new car.

2-2 과거에 대한 소망(wish+과거완료)

p. 225

Challenge 1

01 had finished   02 hadn't eaten
03 had studied

Challenge 2

01 I wish I hadn't eaten so much.
02 Bob wishes he had learned to play a musical instrument.
03 Brian wishes he had finished high school.
04 Jennifer wishes she had brought her digital camera.

이것이 시험에 출제되는 영문법이다!

p. 226

Ex1 (b)   Ex2 (c)   Ex3 (b)   Ex4 (a)
Ex5 I had checked the e-mail, I would have attended the meeting
Ex6 had been saved

| 해설 |

Ex1 주절이 could have bought이므로 if절에는 과거완료 (had had)를 쓴다.
Ex2 주절이 미래(be going to go)이므로 if절은 현재(finishes) 를 써야 한다.
Ex3 주절의 시제가 조동사 과거(would)이므로 if절의 시제도

과거인 weren't를 쓴다.
Ex4 가정법 과거를 직설법으로 고칠 때, 과거는 현재로 고치 고 긍정은 부정으로 고친다.
Ex5 직설법 시제가 과거이므로 가능성이 없는 3차 가정문으로 바꾼다. 즉, didn't check는 긍정인 과거완료(had checked)로 바꾸고, didn't attend는 「조동사+현재완 료」를 써서 would have attended로 바꾼다.
Ex6 과거에 대한 소망이므로 「wish+과거완료」를 쓴다.

기출 응용문제

p. 228

1 loved	2 ③	3 ⑤	4 ①
5 don't listen		6 ②	
7 could finish it		8 ⑤	

| 해설 |

1 현재에 대한 소망이므로 「wish+과거시제」를 쓴다.
2 ③의 could have bought를 could buy로 고쳐야 한다. 2차 가정문은 if절도 과거시제, 주절에도 「조동사 과거+동 사원형」을 쓴다.
3 주어가 3인칭 단수(it)라 하더라도 2차 가정문에는 weren't 를 쓴다. 주절에 있는 조동사 과거(could)를 보고 if절에 과 거시제를 써야 한다는 것을 알 수 있다.
4 현재와 미래에 대한 소망이므로 「wish+과거시제」를 쓴다.
5 「명령문+or」은 '그렇지 않으면'의 부정의 의미를 담고 있으 므로 if~not으로 문장을 완성한다.
6 직설법을 가정법으로 바꿀 때 현재는 과거로, 부정은 긍정으 로 바꾼다.
7 가정법 과거완료를 직설법으로 바꿀 때 주절의 「조동사 과 거+have+p.p.」는 「조동사 과거+동사원형」으로 하되 부정 은 긍정으로 바꿔 준다.
8 직설법 시제가 과거이므로 3차 가정문인 가정법 과거완료로 바꾼다. if절에는 「had+p.p.」, 주절에는 「조동사 과거+have +p.p.」를 쓴다.

중간·기말고사 100점 100승

p. 230

1 ①	2 ③	3 ④	4 ②
5 knew	6 had / attended		
7 weren't / help		8 ③	
9 If I had million dollars, I could buy you a car.			
10 If we had gotten free time, we could have gone to the movies.			
11 ②	12 had		

| 해설 |

1 주절에 조동사 과거(would)와 동사원형이 있으므로 if절에도 과거시제를 쓴다.
2 주절에 조동사 과거(could)와 동사원형이 있으므로 if절에도

과거시제를 쓴다.

3 주절에 조동사 과거와 현재완료가 있으므로 if절에는 과거완료(had taken)를 쓴다.

4 직설법 과거시제(fastened)는 가정법 과거완료로 고치고 긍정은 부정으로 고친다.

5 현재와 미래에 대한 소망이므로 wish 다음의 절은 과거시제를 쓴다.

6 돌아갈 수 없는 가능성 0%인 과거시제(didn't attend)이므로 wish절에는 과거완료(had attended)를 쓴다.

7 If절은 be동사의 과거시제인 weren't를 쓰고 주절에는 조동사 과거(would) 뒤에 동사원형 help를 쓴다. 주어가 3인칭 단수라도 가정법에서는 were를 쓴다. (wasn't를 써도 틀린 것은 아니다.)

8 어렸을 때(when I was young)라는 과거의 돌이킬 수 없는 상황이므로 wish절에는 과거완료를 써야 한다. 따라서 learned를 had learned로 바꿔야 한다.

9 직설법 현재는 가정법 과거시제로 바꾸고 부정은 긍정으로 바꾼다. 따라서 don't have를 had로, can't buy를 could buy로 바꿔 문장을 완성한다.

10 직설법 과거시제는 3차 가정문인 가정법 과거완료를 쓰고, 부정은 긍정으로 바꾼다. 따라서 didn't get을 had gotten으로, couldn't go는 could have gone으로 바꾼다.

11 「wish+과거시제」는 현재나 미래에 대한 소망이므로 직설법 시제는 현재시제를 써야 한다. 부정은 긍정으로 바꿔 I'm sorry I live in a big city.로 써야 의미가 같아진다.

12 직설법 시제가 현재이므로 현재나 미래를 소망하는 「wish+과거시제」를 쓴다. 따라서 have의 과거 had가 두 문장에 공통으로 들어간다.

중간·기말고사 평가대비 단답형 주관식　　p. 232

A　1 had / been 　　2 have / visited
　　3 knew / would / do 　4 had / kept

B　1 If I were rich, I could buy a digital camera.
　　2 If I had time, I could help you.
　　3 If she didn't work at a restaurant, she would have time to relax.
　　4 If the weather were fine, we could go on a picnic.

C　1 If you had asked for help, I would have helped you.
　　2 If Scott had fallen off his bike, he might have hurt himself.
　　3 If Sunny had introduced me to Lisa, I would have talked to her.

D　1 If you write on the desk, you'll be in trouble.
　　2 If the T-shirt is expensive, Lucy might not buy it. 또는 If the T-shirt isn't expensive, Lucy might buy it.

| 해설 |

A 1 주절의 시제가 「조동사 과거+현재완료(have+p.p.)」이므로 if절에는 과거완료(had been)를 쓴다. be동사의 p.p.형은 been이다. 2 if절의 시제가 과거완료이므로 주절의 시제는 「조동사 과거(might)+현재완료(have visited)」를 쓴다. 3 if절 안에는 과거시제인 knew를 쓰고, 주절에는 조동사 과거를 써서 what would you do～?로 2차 가정문을 만든다. 4 yesterday가 지난 과거를 나타내므로 가능성이 전혀 없는 과거의 소망인 「wish+과거완료(had kept)」를 쓴다.

B 1-4 시제가 현재이므로 모두 2차 가정문(가정법 과거)을 만들어야 한다. 시제는 모두 과거시제(조동사도 과거)로 만들고 긍정은 부정으로, 부정은 긍정으로 바꿔 문장을 완성하면 된다.

C 1-3 가능성이 없는 3차 가정문(가정법 과거완료)이므로 if절에는 과거완료(had+p.p.), 주절에는 「조동사 과거+현재완료(have+p.p.)」를 쓴다. 부정은 모두 긍정으로 바꿔 문장을 완성하면 된다.

D 1-2 1차 가정문은 if절의 동사를 현재, 주절의 조동사도 현재로 짝을 맞춰 써주면 된다. if절 안에는 조동사를 쓰지 않으므로 2의 경우 If the T-shirt is expensive, 또는 If the T-shirt isn't expensive로 문장을 완성한다.

실전 서술형 평가문제 A　　p. 234

모범답안

1 If I were you, I would wake up earlier in the morning.
2 If I were you, I would go shopping with her.
3 If I were you, I would go to a department store.

실전 서술형 평가문제 B　　p. 235

모범답안

1 If Lisa had liked him more, she might[would] have married him.
2 If Jane didn't really like her job, she wouldn't work very hard.
3 If Kathy had heard the phone ring, she would have answered it.

실전 서술형 평가문제 C　　p. 235

모범답안

1 I wish I were in Lotte World now.
2 I wish I had learned how to ride a bicycle.
3 I wish I hadn't told a lie to my teacher.

ice.

중학영문법 2-B

한국에서 유일한 중학영문법 알짜 3000제

 정답 및 해설